Very Private and Public Relations

Jim Dunn

THOROGOOD

Thorogood Publishing Ltd
10-12 Rivington Street
London EC2A 3DU
Telephone: 020 7749 4748
Fax: 020 7729 6110
Email: info@thorogoodpublishing.co.uk
Web: www.thorogoodpublishing.co.uk

© Jim Dunn 2008

A CIP catalogue record for this book is available from the British Library.

ISBN 1 85418 392 3
     978-185418392-7

Book designed and typeset by Driftdesign

Printed in the UK by Ashford Colour Press

CONTENTS

*To Arthur, of whom much more later, and to
Bronwyn Gold Blyth who died much too soon.
Always creative, enthusiastic and ready to put something
back into tourism, she was a good friend in the
shark-infested waters of PR.*

ACKNOWLEDGEMENTS

I HAVE ONLY A FEW REGRETS in my life and one, near the top of the list, is that I never kept a diary. Therefore, what follows is sometimes sketchily remembered. So I thank all those who prodded my memory and helped fill in the blanks. Some names and situations have been changed – to protect the innocent and me...

Thank you to Hilary Kingsley who listened and put it all down on paper, accepted or re-wrote my efforts (mainly re-wrote, after trying to fathom out my writing) and took kindly to my corrections – which were few. I really must get computer trained.

I'd also like to thank travel and transport journalist Roger Bray for his early, terrifying lessons in how to deal with the media and for the background information provided by his excellent book, written with Vladimir Raitz, *Flight To the Sun – the Story of the Holiday Revolution* (Continuum.)

Thank you also to Cheryl Thomas, my editor, and to the four friends who read early efforts. Particularly I'd like to thank Stephen Dunk who readily agreed to read the final draft while we all cruised the Turkish coast on holiday. He took the task seriously and his comments were helpful and important.

Finally, thank you to the travel industry for giving me a great and rewarding life, mostly for free, and to everyone who worked at TPS over the years... even the snakes.

1

OOR HOOSE

I WAS CONCEIVED ON ISLAY, the whisky island, off the west coast of Scotland and I was a mistake. It's a desolate place even now at times, dramatically beautiful at others. Then, I imagine, its bleak landscape matched the mood of my mother Mary Halbert, née Gray who, even in shopping lists, would sign herself thus. Sometimes she'd even add 'and oblige', for some mysterious reason known only to her. It was the year after the war ended, a time when she was almost certainly still grieving for her first husband George, killed while serving in the army at the battle of Monte Cassino, near Rome, in the closing days of the war. Mary was pregnant with me and in no hurry to return, as she must, to her cool and disapproving mother, brothers and sister and the hospital on the mainland.

My father James – but always 'Jimmy' – Dunn from Glasgow had also been married before and his wife had died in childbirth (the child too had died) on New Year's Eve a few years earlier. Maybe he was still emotionally attached to her. At any rate he was not eager, by all accounts, to rush into a second marriage just to stop me from becoming a bastard.

Eventually my mother travelled back to Clydeside, arrived at the hospital in Johnstone, near Glasgow and gave birth on the 11th of February 1946. She might have raised me as a single parent, she told my sister many years on, had she not felt angry and indignant. As a result, a few weeks later, she presented herself at her lover's door with a newborn baby, me, in her arms, and announced to Dad, "Right, here you are!" I can just see her doing that...

The sight of me quickly concentrated my father's mind or "brought him to his senses" as Mary was to put it years later. Jimmy had been so angry at the news of the pregnancy that he had not spoken to my mother for months. So my mother had to plan her after-the-birth strategy. She would never have just dumped her baby and walked away, she told my sister, but the reality of me, pink, alive and his, together with her blunt announcement, was intended to make him do the decent thing. And it worked.

The pair soon married and began to make a go of family life in their 'hoose', a newly-built council house on the Midton estate built on farm land above Gourock, population then about 5,000, on Scotland's west coast, 25 miles 'doon the watter' from Glasgow. The move to the 'new hoose' was after a spell renting a room in Kempock Street in the centre of Gourock from my Granny Gray – Mum's mother – who had a sprawling flat on a first floor where she rented out rooms.

My earliest memory of the new Midton house is of there being no furniture whatsoever. We used the boxes in which oranges were delivered to the town's shops in those sparse post-war years, to sit on and eat off. Presumably they also formed the bases of our beds. These boxes were treasured by people like us at that time, not just because they were handy in the home but they were also useful on the fire when there was no money for coal. Which in our case was often.

We didn't stay long in this post-war 'scheme' house, almost certainly because we couldn't afford the rent. We soon moved to another 'hoose', actually a run-down upper flat of three rooms and a kitchen, with a big 'back green' – garden –

in which to hang washing and grow vegetables, up a 'close' in Cove Road, Gourock. Again we were council tenants but the rent was far lower. We were probably also much happier as this was a bit of a 'real hoose' – a flat – not a new-build in the middle of a field in the hills behind the town.

As an address, 47 Cove Road didn't have a lot going for it except that it was right on the promenade with the most spectacular views over the Clyde. Nowadays weekenders from Glasgow would fight each other to buy it as a "bijou" weekend retreat.

Look in a guidebook to Scotland today and you'll see Gourock described as a "shabby old seaside resort" or in other disparaging terms and the polluted state of the Clyde is roundly deplored. But, back then, my 'hoose' was part of Scotland's 'Riviera', a pretty coastal town, built to one side, or 'awe tae wan side', close to industrial Greenock with its declining shipyards and about a half hour drive to Glasgow. As soon as I could, I learnt to swim in the crystal clear and icy cold waters of the River Clyde. Mum took off her shoes on the promenade, tucked her skirt into her knickers and paddled out to a depth where I could swim. She then said, "Right, I'll hold your chin James to keep you afloat; now move your arms like this." She demonstrated the swimming movement and, in a couple of minutes, Mum's hand left my chin and she made for the shore, wet knickers and all. Well, I probably sank a few times, but I could swim!

Gourock was a spot for city dwellers to escape to for holidays and look out on a usually calm, mirror-flat River Clyde towards the beautiful scenery of the seaside village of Kilcreggan and the Holy Loch on the opposite side of the Clyde. The town came alive for "The Fair", two weeks in July when most of Glasgow took its annual holiday and people headed 'doon the watter', usually by steamer, to Gourock or Largs, further south, or Dunoon on the opposite side of the river. These were thriving holiday spots in an innocent, less sophisticated age, before the onslaught of the package holiday to Spain, which virtually killed them off. There were nine busy shipyards in the Clyde area around Gourock, Port Glasgow and Greenock in the 1950s. Very little remains today of the shipyards, cranes, freighters and liners, but then anything from small boats to super tankers were built there. Greenock, the next town up the Clyde from Gourock, was the first Scottish port to import sugar in bulk from the West Indies and a great refinery industry grew up there creating many thousands of jobs. In the same century, the 18th, Greenock was the birthplace of the great inventor James Watt whose improved steam technology changed the face of the world. Greenock's most recent invention, it is rumoured, is the deep-fried Mars Bar.

Cove Road, Gourock, is cut in two by Tarbet Street. Houses on one side were grand, comfortable villas, some split into two, many then owned by men in middle management at the shipyards at Greenock such as Scotts, where so many famous ocean-going liners including the QE2 were built, or the then newly-opened offices of the American computer company IBM, still among the biggest employers in the area. Many of the people who lived on that side owned cars, some of them snazzy models. Others like the Tough family, whose sons Frank and George went to my school, Gourock High, had an old open-topped car – a bit of a bone-shaker but a car none the less – which would now qualify as a classic. I don't remember the make but, being the early 1950s, it was probably an Austin Seven or Eight. If I waited around long enough some Sundays, they'd take me for a ride down the coast but, often as not, they'd set off without me. They also had a motorcycle and sidecar on which Mr and Mrs Tough in full leathers would take themselves off in a flurry of exhaust.

We didn't live on that side. We lived on the council side; a row of terraced dwellings, each two homes, one on the ground floor the other on the first floor, both equally damp, with outside stairs and toilets. Today all these humble houses have been torn down and the whole character of the place is changed. Then these 'hooses' or flats were distinctive and to live in one of them marked you out. Despite my father's earnings from the pubs – firstly in Glasgow and then in Greenock – and I never knew how much those were, and my mother's from cleaning other people's houses and offices at a rate of about two shillings and six pence an hour (12½p), we were poor, very poor.

Number 47 had no bathroom but a toilet at the top of the back outside stairs. It had running cold water in the kitchen and a great deal of running green mould inside the bedrooms. My little bedroom was at the back of the house, overlooking the outside stairs and the garden, or the small jungle where potato plants, roses and weeds vied for space, that passed for one. The travelling knife sharpener would visit the area every month. We'd know he had arrived because he'd play the spoons to tell us he was in the back green. A scintillating tour de force of tinkling spoons would bring out the neighbours with their blunt knives.

As a small boy I would often play on the sandy beach just below the house. I didn't build sandcastles. I'd build little houses with driveways and roads on which to park my second- or third- hand Dinky toy cars. Later on I enjoyed sprucing myself up to be taken across the quiet road to sit on a seat on the promenade, watching the world go by. In my memory, these always seemed to be cloudless, sunny days but they couldn't have been. Scotland's west coast has some of the worst weather in Great Britain.

When I wasn't happily on my own, amusing myself with the sand, I was playing with the daughters of our neighbours, the McDowalls; Rena, Bunty, Helen and Margaret. More precisely, they were 'playing' with me: bullying, teasing and generally beating me up. These four tomboys, with their brother Stephen and their parents, lived up the same close. They were a very rough, wild family indeed. Mr McDowall seemed permanently out of work and on the dole. Mrs McDowall and my mother had a strange love-hate relationship. It was love when Mary was carrying my sister and Mrs McDowall was also pregnant. As soon as they each gave birth, hostilities recommenced. What had started this war of neighbours I don't know. But almost any issue, from the positioning of the 'middens' – rubbish bins – to washing-line territory, seemed to provoke a fierce exchange of insults, threats and tussles between the adults and, sooner or later, unfortunately, secondary skirmishes between the girls and me. Needless to say I never won and I retain a small battle scar under my right eye, where Rena whacked me during one incident.

On the rare occasions when we were all on friendly terms, I would enjoy playing 'shops' with the girls and, even more fun, join them in dressing up in our mothers' clothes and high-heeled shoes. Rena and her sisters didn't know it, but I enjoyed swishing a skirt and clip-clopping grandly around the close far more than they did.

Indoors I fought a losing battle to retain any sort of dignity. But alas we couldn't afford dignity. While I was small enough to be picked up, my mother would stand me in a basin in the kitchen every morning to wash me, a process watched by the whole family and by any passing neighbour. My sister, born six years after me, got similar treatment. What a day it was when we progressed from heating water in kettles, pouring it into basins and rushing to use it before it got cold, to getting it from a gas geyser over the sink!

For most of the year our home was cold, damp and bleak. Central heating was light years away from Gourock, never mind number 47. In the winter, which seemed to be most of the year, I'd wake up in the morning and scrape ice off the *inside* of the window. When it was very cold, my parents; Sinclair, my half brother, ten years older than me – my mother's son from her first marriage; my sister and I huddled together at night in one bed for warmth. My regular sleeping arrangement, though, until I progressed to my own little damp room and single bed at the back, was to share the set-in bed off what we grandly called the sitting room – nothing more than a bedroom with a sofa, in fact – with Sinclair. So the first erect penis I experienced, apart from my own, that is, was my half-brother's, as we experimented as boys can do.

Luckily I got on well with him, and my sister and I rarely fought. I was her babysitter when Mum and Dad would pop out for a social evening to one or other of the pubs in Shore Street: The Darroch or The Wherry. Later, she would go to work as a print assistant at the same place I landed up, Simpsons. She went on to create her own life happily married to a welder, with whom she had three sons, John, Paul and Mark. A sweet-natured child, my sister was always number one with Dad, definitely a daddy's girl. But even when my father and I were cool towards each other, I never begrudged her his affection.

During the winter days we would gather together in one room around a coal fire and 'coorie doon', snuggle up as Mary would put it. When there was no money for coal, as was frequently the case, my mother and I would comb the shingle shore of the Clyde near our home (we wouldn't have called it a beach – that sounded far too upmarket) where we would trundle around collecting wood to dry and burn. The shore would also provide for us in another way, as Mum had found the favourite corner where the small McLean's Shipyard and Boat Repairers next door to us dumped miscellaneous waste. My ever-resourceful Mum somehow discovered there were clippings of copper and brass among this waste and she and I would rummage each day and collect them, then take them to the scrap dealers at the nearby Gourock Quarry where they were weighed and sold. The money, usually a few shillings, would help put food on the table.

Our food was bought at Colquhouns, a little general store on the corner of Cove Road and Tarbet Street, where Mum had a running weekly 'tick' account. Many were the weeks when she hadn't the funds to clear this account but old Mr Colquhoun was usually understanding and patient as he was with many of the other families. We weren't the only locals with regular cash shortages. No matter how much Mary owed though, Mr Colquhoun always had a big penny caramel sweetie ready for me – provided I had the penny. The tiny shop was full of goodies from gobstoppers to pear drops, lemonade, the ubiquitous Irn Bru, fresh bread and, of course, Mum's all-important Woodbine fags – she was always a heavy smoker, latterly up to sixty a day.

Apart from money worries, ours was a life free of the sorts of stresses many families seem to suffer today. We didn't worry about our 'status' – we were too busy just staying alive – and we certainly didn't worry about security. Perhaps I was too young to be aware of it, but crimes such as burglaries and street violence were almost unheard of then. Anyway, we never locked the door up the close at the top of the stairs for the simple reason that there was nothing in our house anyone would want to steal. Almost everything we owned was what other people discarded or came from jumble sales. My mother was a serial jumble sale attender. I would certainly know where to find her every Saturday at two in the afternoon, an hour before the opening: at the front of the jumble queue at the local church hall, whether it be St John's, Old Gourock or the Bethany Hall.

Probably a lot of the things she brought home from these sales were useful and welcome. A selection of oddly coloured woolly jumpers for me, suits for my father, shirts and shoes for all of us, for example. But I remember other items Mum brought home, the useless ones, so much more vividly. These would include women's clothes to wear at a cocktail reception – rabbit fur stoles and hats, elbow-length evening gloves, cocktail dresses far too long or tight for her. Mum never received an invitation for such a function, of course, nor probably would she have recognised one if she had, but it didn't blunt her enthusiasm for her 'party' wardrobe. Discarded wedding hats were another of her specialities and she would parade around the kitchen amid great laughter in her new finds. They would never be worn outside and never returned to another jumble sale but merely left in numerous piles around the house until she eventually found someone to give them to.

Thinking of those piles of clothes reminds me of Mary's way with words. She had a whole stream of sayings which would come into play at various times of the day. When I was getting up in the morning, knocking into bundles of jumble in every room, looking for my shirt or pants, I'd ask her if she'd seen them. She'd be sure to say, "They're up the wife's arse in the brewery". Now, I've thought about this for years and I still cannot work out where the saying comes from. Whose wife? Whose brewery? She would only ever say, "It means I don't bloody well know where your pants are!" as she made the tea and toasted the bread on a long fork at the fire for breakfast while getting ready herself to clean other people's houses.

If she tuned into the Third Programme (now Radio Three) by mistake, she'd snap, "Turn that stuff off – that's the music that killed the cat!" or "That music would tear the shirt aff yae!" On days when the weather was good, she'd observe, "The coos (cows) are doon – it's going to be a lovely day." I'd say, "But Mum, the coos are sitting down because it *is* a lovely day." If your palm was itchy, she'd urge, "Quick, rub it – that means money!", so I went around wishing for itchy palms. She also read the future in tea leaves in the neighbours' cups, predicting sudden fortunes, wonderful romances or mysterious woes, so building up their hopes or plunging them into despair. Many a day I'd come home from school to find the house in complete silence. As I opened the kitchen door I'd see Mary looking quizzically at a tea cup and its leaves. Looking on would be a few neighbours, hanging on her every prediction.

Then there was Griff the gas salesman. His main claim to fame was selling a gas fridge to the Dunn household in Cove Road. On the face of it this was good news for the family. But Mum's inability to remember, or indeed afford, to put a shilling in the meter to ensure the gas pilot light did not go out meant that the fridge – and consequently the food – regularly went off. I suppose it was lucky that there was rarely much food in the fridge.

Mary was absent-minded in other ways too: when trying to light the living room fire she regularly set the chimney alight and filled the house with sooty smoke. And she was so engrossed in the television coverage of the funeral of Pope

John XXIII in 1963 she forgot she was filling our funny little washing machine. The water overflowed and flooded the kitchen of Mrs Lyons, our inoffensive neighbour downstairs, who was also quietly watching this funeral on her TV set. I came home from school at least twice to find the house full of firemen when Mum had set fire to the chimney.

Shopping trips also brought out colourful and unfathomable Mary-isms. We'd be walking along Kempock Street on a Saturday morning doing the weekly 'messages', heading for McKechnies the butchers (she always called meat 'butcher's meat', as though there were another kind). In the queue she'd invariably begin talking to someone. When they'd been served and had left, she'd say to me, in hushed tones, "Lovely wummen there. Always remember, James, the best Christians are no' always in the Church!" Aye.

Mary had no dress sense at all – she couldn't afford it. If anything, her style was Jumble Chic. She'd wear anything as long as it was warm and kept out the west of Scotland weather and it fitted her reasonably well. She'd go through a stage of wearing wide-brim sun hats in winter, all from jumble sales, and I remember her "tammy" period when she bought a selection of these brightly coloured caps and wore them around Gourock to great acclaim. She would wear flower-patterned pinnies around the home and for her work in other people's houses, a packet of fags never far away. She always smelt of fresh soap with a touch of nicotine as I'd snuggle up to her as a child.

2

GRANNY MOLLY AND OTHER FAMILY

SATURDAY MORNINGS OFTEN MEANT The Bakery Visit. Granny Gray, Molly, had found a source at Mackay's Bakery at Gourock Pierhead, a kind soul who gave her all the previous few days' leftovers of bread, fruitcake – or flies' graveyard as we called it, shortbread and broken biscuits. Mum and I would meet Granny and Mum's younger sister, my Aunt Betty, in the bus shelter next to the Pierhead Post Office, opposite Mackay's, to divide the spoils. What I always noted (though never dared comment upon) was that Aunt Betty, the favourite daughter, was usually given the better bits of cake. We always ended up with the broken biscuits and crumbling lumps of cake and I knew for certain that Aunt Betty's bits tasted sweeter.

Granny Molly had led a colourful life. She married three times and her third husband, 'Grandpa' Jock was a seaman who sailed the high seas, visiting many Asian countries. He had a collection of Chinese ivory ornaments, probably worth a fortune today, which fascinated me as a boy of about five but he wouldn't tell me anything about them. I don't remember him uttering a word to me. He simply sat in silence, occasionally strumming a mandolin he'd brought home from some faraway place. They too lived in the large, cluttered and fusty apartment on the first floor of a Victorian terrace in Gourock's main street, Kempock Street, where we had first rented. Compared with our home it was spacious with at least four rooms, which were usually let to young newly-married couples, a large kitchen and a bathroom and toilet. Despite this luxury, Granny would regularly lift her skirts in full view of my mother and me as we drank our morning tea and pee in the small kitchen sink in a cupboard off their sitting room. Oddly I don't recall being shocked by this. It was just something Granny did.

Granny had a skincare routine which few were tempted to copy. Creams and lotions from the 1950s chemists were not for her. She preferred a toning liquid which she felt was more natural. It came from babies' nappies, wet ones. The day's first soggy nappy would be her chosen face flannel. It helped to have a new baby in the family. I believe I obliged for some time as did my cousins. But a neighbour's baby would do just as well. She insisted the infant urine gave her a good complexion, which I seem to recall she indeed had.

Mum would not criticise Granny Molly, though she had every reason to do so by all accounts. Family folklore has it that Molly put my mother and her brother, my uncle Alec, into a children's home in Bridge of Weir, near Glasgow, for two years; only reclaiming them briefly when their father returned to Clydeside. The favourite, my Aunt Betty, stayed with her mother. Alec moved to Islay as a teenager and worked in the fields and on smallholdings and my mother joined him with half-brother Sinclair during the war to work as a Land Girl on farms where help was needed and sometimes in the big houses as a maid. Reconciliation with Granny Molly came only when the two children were earning money. Despite Molly's detachment from her daughter Mary, it was Mum who helped care for Molly when she was terminally ill, nursing her to the end.

Following Alec was how Mum came to be on Islay where my father was a barman at the local RAF station, now the site of the island's airport. One evening, Dad told me that he'd once served Douglas Bader, the World War Two hero who'd lost both legs in an air crash but continued to fly with artificial limbs. I was so impressed that I couldn't wait to announce at school the next day that my Dad had served with Douglas Bader. When I related my friends' astonishment to Dad the next night, he had to explain that he served the fighter pilot with drinks across the RAF mess bar and had never taken to the skies himself.

Mary and Jimmy's 'winching' – that's Scottish for courting – took place among the heather on the hills of this brooding but beautiful west coast island when they could get away together. They went to local dances – or ceilidhs – and Mum's carriage for the evening was always the local funeral hearse, which Dad borrowed from his pal, the undertaker. It was after one of these ceilidhs that I was conceived, according to my mother, on a moonlit hillside while a great white stallion, on the other side of a fence near where the hearse was parked, looked on. Well, I believe it!

Mum and Uncle Alec were living in the loft of a small Islay farmhouse with the chickens and other animals on the ground floor. It was undoubtedly a primitive existence. The toilet was outside, Mary told me, "Chilly – but with great views". They had next to no money and when she was getting ready to go out in the evenings, Mum did what most women in wartime who couldn't afford nylon stockings resorted to: she 'tinted' her legs with diluted gravy browning and pencilled a line on the skin from the heel up to the back of her knee.

As a wider family, we were not close. My father's relations in Glasgow thought he had married beneath his station, although his and their station was a good way down the line in any case. Dad's brothers and sisters would come to see us at Cove Road from time to time and those visits always felt to my parents and to me like curiosity calls on the Poor Relations. I, on the other hand, looked forward to these occasions, as it happened, and was intrigued by my uncles and aunts. I'd lean against my mother as she sat by the fire and I'd watch these smart Glasgow people with wonderment. I liked Aunt Edie and Uncle Sam, she with the gin-soaked voice and long cigarette holder, he dapper as could be, in his beautifully-cut lounge suits. Even more interesting were Aunt May, a spinster and Uncle Peter, a bachelor who wore suits of Prince of Wales check with great panache. When the visitors got up from their chairs to leave, I'd swiftly position myself near the front door in the hope of a pat on the head and a parting gift of a shilling or, if I was really lucky, a half crown from Uncle Peter. If I was successful, which I usually was, the money was quickly transferred to Mary's purse. She told me later it often paid "the insurance", not on the valueless house contents, of course, but a policy costing two shillings and sixpence a week for life "to pay for her funeral". I believed all this at the time and was happy to contribute the money to the house – it never occurred to me to complain about the money being taken from me.

Aunt May and Uncle Peter shared a smart flat but on a council housing scheme built on the outskirts of Glasgow to house people bombed out of the city centre during the war. Glasgow suffered badly from bombing raids by the German Luftwaffe as they attacked the Clyde shipyards. Aunt May ran a small tobacconist's shop in the Shawlands district of Glasgow and Uncle Peter worked for McTears, the Glasgow auctioneers. Their flat was full of shining and possibly valuable ornaments and antique furniture. On the few occasions we visited him, Uncle Peter would be dressed in a silk dressing gown, lounging on the sofa with a cigarette in a holder, very much a languid Noel Coward figure. Was he, I often wondered as I grew up, homosexual – gay – like Noel Coward? Sadly he was killed in a car accident in the 1960s so I was never able to broach the subject with him. I would overhear talk of his holidays on the Isle of Man – alone – but my father would always add, perhaps a little defensively even to my young ear, that there was 'a woman' but no more details were ever forthcoming. Aunt May lived on to a grand old age and would stay with me later in the 1970s when we had a weekend cottage in Suffolk. Her habit, on each first day of May, her birthday, was to run her bare feet, hands and face on the grass so that, as she insisted, the morning dew would improve her complexion. When she did this in Suffolk, I had a terrible fear that she would choose a patch of the lawn on which our large Labrador dogs had peed copiously the previous night. Dad's other sister, Aunt Annie, blossomed into a favourite of mine. She was full of life and laughter even in her eighties and enjoyed regular trips to Benidorm in Spain for winter sun. There she would dance the night away in the cafés on the promenade, the life and soul of any party.

My other grandmother, Granny Dunn, Dad's mother, was completely different from Granny Molly. She was an older, gentler soul who always wore black when I knew her, presumably in mourning for her late husband, whom I never knew. At the Cove Road street party for the Queen's Coronation in 1953, when she was in her late eighties, she sat quietly wearing a small black hat and black costume amid a sea of Union Jacks. She died soon after that event. One afternoon we all rushed to Uncle Peter's flat in Glasgow where she lay in bed, surrounded by her sons and daughters. I watched in childhood bewilderment as Uncle Peter patted brandy on her lips. Even to a seven-year-old, it was clear that brandy was not required: her life which had begun in Victorian Britain was ebbing away.

When I was about ten, my mother got the job of cleaner at the offices of James Adam and Son, the other small Clydeside shipyard at the far end of Cove Road. The offices were a three-bedroomed bungalow conversion. It was hard work for less money – about twelve shillings a week for an hour every weeknight but two on Fridays. It could only be cleaned after six at night when the office closed or before nine in the morning when they re-opened. I went along willingly to help her. My job was to wash all the dishes used for coffees, teas and lunches that day – this was before the age of the dish-washer – then help Mum polish the boss's office, boardroom and main office. We were a good team and it was here that I learned the art of housekeeping from Mum which I've never forgotten. In years to come, when I told a cleaner how I wanted my home maintained, I knew what I was talking about. I'd done it myself. Windows, woodwork, brasswork, carpets, curtain rails, picture frames, dust traps of all descriptions – I've blitzed them all and I like to think I know what 'clean' looks like.

As with the cobbler who lets his own children go barefoot, my exhausted cleaning-lady mother was too tired from char-ring in other people's homes to be a stickler for hygiene and order in her own. She would let things go. While it irked me from time to time, it didn't seem to frustrate her but occasion-ally she and my father would have a row over the untidy state of the house. He never lifted a finger to help – that would not have been his idea of a man's job. He'd come home in the evenings or a lunchtime and expect a meal or his 'tea' on the table, no matter how hard my mother was working. From cleaning houses she would rush to do the 'messages' for food to provide meals for her hungry and demanding household. Meanwhile he would read his Daily Record and consider the racing schedule.

3

PARENTAL WARS

MY PARENTS' RELATIONSHIP WAS, for many of the early years, a rocky sort of compromise. They had rows. Some I'd join in, always to defend my mother; others I'd just sit and quietly observe. I was the cause of some disagreements when my father came home from the pub, usually the worse for drink, for his dinner. It annoyed him that I was there, not outside playing boisterously with the other boys. I'd sit still by the fire, often quite frightened, beside my Mum, clutching one of my much-loved Enid Blyton story books she'd found for me in a jumble sale – adventures of The Famous Five or The Secret Seven. Dad would bait me. I remember one evening as he raged, Mum said, "Stop it Jimmy, he likes to read," while at the same time slipping her hand down gently to turn my book up the right way. I did love Enid Blyton's Famous Five. There was Julian, Dick, Anne, George and Timmy the dog. I can't remember how many of the twenty-one Famous Five adventures I read, but as soon as Mum brought them home from a jumble sale, I devoured them.

One particularly unhappy period for Mum came when she discovered lipstick on my father's shirt collar. At that time, Dad was working as a barman on the busy Clyde steamers which ferried passengers around the holiday resorts of Dunoon, Innellen and Rothesay. One day she was washing his shirts – he was always immaculately dressed and well-known in the neighbourhood for his smartness, thanks to my mother's efforts – when she noticed a lipstick mark on one shirt collar. To this day I don't know if Dad had relationships with other women while he was married to Mum. There was certainly a rumour back then that he and a young waitress on the steamer were "carrying on". I think it's more than likely he just flirted with female staff and customers and enjoyed the odd kiss and cuddle. He was an attractive man, with a muscular build, who never lacked the attention of women, despite being completely bald from his early twenties at a time when this was not fashionable. He had a shiny pate surrounded by a small rim of hair about which he was sensitive and fussy. He would pat it into submission with chip – or was it bacon – fat from the frying pan. He later progressed to Brylcreem under protest from Mary at the mess – and presumably the smell – that his kitchen tonic left on the pillow cases.

Whatever the truth of the lipstick smudge, it wasn't something Mum was going to overlook. When Dad came home that night there was a confrontation in true "tenement symphony" style, at top volume and in full view and hearing of most of the neighbours. A couple of slaps, a lot of tears and a shouting match ended in both parties storming off in different directions. I joined in feebly at one point, pleading "Leave her alone!" as he shouted at Mum. Eventually they resumed talking and the matter wasn't referred to again. Mercifully, major rows like this weren't frequent but they did argue a great deal in those early days about money, me and my increasingly "different" and solitary life. In later years, however, my parents settled into a contented and loving time together.

Both were eventually to die of heart attacks, my mother aged 74, my father aged 83. Their health was not helped by their living conditions in Cove Road, although those improved when I was able to buy a council house for them in another part of the town in the 1980s and install central heating. But the fact that they each lit up more than sixty cigarettes a day affected them more. Undoubtedly Mum enjoyed smoking. I can picture her now puffing away in front of a roaring coal fire and our small, flickering black and white television, relishing every drag as she watched re-runs of all the great Hollywood movies of the 1940s. She loved all the musical films starring Fred Astaire and Ginger Rogers and knew every word of every song in *High Society* with Bing Crosby and Grace Kelly. A James Cagney film would find her sitting in rapt silence with an inch of fag ash poised to be deposited only at the end of a tense scene. Her heavy smoking probably shortened her life but if it did one positive thing, it persuaded me never to become addicted myself to nicotine and to avoid the company of smokers if I possibly could.

Mum's ashes were scattered on the Clyde at Cardwell Bay across from her last home in Gourock. It wasn't a serene occasion – but Mary would have seen the funny side. The undertakers from Greenock arrived with the urn for the solemn business of releasing the ashes across the water. But we'd forgotten that the shore would be occupied; half a dozen families with noisy children were playing, picnicking and generally enjoying the brief spell of sunshine. We had to wait for them to leave and for the coast to be clear. When it was, the wind worked against us. Just as we opened the urn, its direction changed and blew the ashes all over the three of us.

Still, it gave us a chance to assess Mary's life. We decided that even if it had not been easy, she'd had many enduring pleasures. Apart from smoking, and yes, gossiping, tea-cup reading, watching films and attending jumble sales she'd enjoyed looking after animals. From her young days, mostly on the smallholdings of Islay, to her life on the mainland when number 47 always seemed to be teeming with cats and dogs, she took to them and they to her. I have a memory of her regularly escorting a family of ducks across the road, holding up traffic until they'd safely arrived on the opposite pavement, often with the help of the local police, whom she called out for the job. The ducks would sometimes follow her for protection up the close and try to get into the house. Then she'd need help to round them up to evict them.

She had sometimes to be cruel to be kind, though. One day I came home from school to find her squatting over a large basin, covered by a lid at the top of our outside stairs. "What are you doing?" I asked. Her answer amazed me. "Drowning kittens, James," (I was always 'James' to her) she said. When I protested, she quietly explained that we couldn't afford to keep them nor to have the mother cat doctored. If she didn't drown them, the kittens would grow up wild and would probably suffer and starve.

In her last years she looked after a family of swans on the shore in Gourock's Cardwell Bay, in front of the ground floor flat which they had by then moved to. You'd find her down there, surrounded by swans as she fed them bread gathered daily from neighbours and, when replete, they'd settle down, feet tucked under, contented, beside where she stood or knelt. I will always remember her there, looking out at that magnificent view of the Clyde with the swans and often the cygnets around her.

Everyone in the area had known Mary Dunn and she them. She was immensely warm-hearted, forever doing 'obliges' as she called them, minding children or dogs, doing 'messages' – shopping – or simply creating laughter, for neighbours, friends and especially for me. She was 'camp' as the gay parlance goes, eccentric and at times outrageous. Happiest if she was making other people laugh. But then there are a lot of mums like her.

After Mum died, Dad wandered around like a lost soul; depressed, unhappy and lonely. My sister and I tried everything we could think of to help. But nothing could replace his Mary, the woman he had been reluctant to wed, had occasionally clashed with, but grew to love deeply. She had been the centre of his life.

How many of their many early collisions were caused by me, I don't know. My father probably felt generally trapped in a family situation he hadn't bargained for with a stepson and a "surprise" son of his own and then a daughter. He was very much a man's man. He enjoyed his friends, though there weren't many of them and none was close; he enjoyed his drink and his visits to the local pubs; his own interests. He was essentially a shy man yet he was definitely master of the house. I'm fairly certain my mother never knew how much he collected in tips at the pub or how much was in his weekly wage packet, that small brown envelope I remember hearing being rustled as he opened it under the table in the kitchen every Friday night. He would then surreptitiously sort out 'our' – Mum's – share, pocket the rest and keep all his tips. With 'our' share, Mum was left to get on with paying the rent, the bills, putting food on the table, taking care of the home and raising us three children. He was no New Man.

For all the struggles it was a good childhood and I recall blissfully carefree times. My half-brother was a kind-hearted lad who often took me around with him – to the local fair when it visited town, with its dodgems and ghost train, and to my first, and last, Punch and Judy show. We couldn't afford holidays away to the emerging Pontins and Butlins holiday camps of the new "leisure" market, whatever that was. Nor could we even consider a caravan for holidays. This mobile "box" was becoming de rigeur among the more posh Gourockians. Sinclair grew up to become a merchant seaman, working on the ships and tugs on the Clyde, then switching to the RAF and dying on Christmas Island in 1960. Alas he didn't die in heroic circumstances but after a drinking binge in this remote posting. But the grief was as sharp for my poor mother, who lost two dear ones to the armed forces. The news came by telegram, arriving as we watched the grand Royal Wedding of Princess Margaret and Anthony Armstrong Jones on television in Cove Road. As the trumpets sounded and the little screen was filled with pictures of the great and good in all their finery, sights she'd normally love, tears flowed down Mum's cheeks.

4

A SON TO BE ASHAMED OF

MY FATHER GREW TO LOVE ME, I'm sure of that, and later he would be quietly proud of what I achieved. But in the fifties and early sixties it became clear to both of us that I wasn't the boy he would have chosen. I would never be a man's man. I would be a man who wanted men. I didn't want to become big and tough, to win fights and become a hero on the football field. I wanted to read books, hear stories, to write and draw, dance with my mother in the kitchen to old jumble sale Victor Silvester '78' records, sing and act. In gym class at school I was not a star. Once I turned up in hard walking shoes and was bawled at by the gym master. "It's all I've got sir. We can't afford sand shoes," I stuttered feebly as the other boys sniggered. In games' periods, I was the kid who was always left to the very end when the team captains picked their players, the one no one wanted in their team because I was dreamy, uncoordinated, useless. I couldn't kick a ball to save my life.

One day my father insisted on coming to watch me in a school football match. I begged him not to and I know he was bitterly disappointed at what he saw – a gangly, uncoordinated, effeminate son hiding from the ball. He was very silent at the end of the match. I was embarrassed and angry that I had to take part in it in the first place. He so much wanted a son as butch and hearty as he was. I baffled him. He just didn't know what the hell he had in front of him, though I think my mother guessed fairly early on – mums tend to know.

I believe I was homosexual in the womb. I came out that way then and I've not felt the need to 'come out' in any other sense since. Maybe there was some genetic inheritance – if my suspicions about Uncle Peter were correct, it could be the case – but the fact is I'm neither proud of it nor sorry about it. To be gay seemed completely natural to me then as now. Although I've always liked and got on with women, I can recall being fascinated by a number of men I thought of as handsome from an early age, well before I was ten. When I noticed the handsome Italian who owned and ran Gerry's, our local ice cream shop at the top of Tarbet Street, I must have been about five. He had the most delicate hands with a light dusting of silky dark hair on them and, I swear, it was watching those hands that made the three penny cornets I saved up to buy taste even more delicious.

Unwittingly, brother Sinclair also nurtured my growing interest in men as a child. I was about seven when he used to take me to watch Gourock's football team play in Darroch Park. What happened on the field was always less engrossing than the after-game visits to the dressing room in a large Nissen hut at the end of the field. Some of Sinclair's friends also took an interest in me, this young boy increasingly keen on sex, in the outside lavatories at the back of the houses in Cove Road. I was passed around. All good, innocent(!), growing up, fumbling fun behind locked doors.

From the age of five, I attended the 'wee school', the Eastern Primary, minutes from our house. These days it's a block of flats. Then it was a standard local authority low, grey-bricked Victorian building with high beamed ceilings and classroom walls painted in bilious shades of pink and beige, battered desks and small, wobbly chairs. And I loved it.

On the first day I sat in the front row absolutely petrified as our teacher, Miss Webster, began the uphill task of civilising her new charges. I soon began to relax and now I look back with much affection on Miss Webster, a small, young woman who could be fearsomely firm, and the other teachers, all of whom I remember clearly to this day.

They included Miss Johnson, a large woman who taught 'first years'; Miss Rose who cut her hair short as a man's, wore a wide, tartan skirt, big brown brogues and went on hearty walks; there was Miss Bell, gentle and self-contained; Miss Orr, of the swishing skirts and a striding walk who came to school on her moped; Miss Campbell who taught geography, and glamorous Miss MacMillan – Jess – in her tight skirts and jumpers and high stiletto heels. She certainly fuelled the fantasies of many small boys in her class. We gossiped endlessly about her after she was seen sitting on a park bench one lunchtime with our headmaster Mr Thomson. It led to a delicious rumour that they were 'going out'. What the real story was, I never knew. When in my teens I joined the Gourock Drama Group, she and I would meet again – she too was a member – and I grew to like her enormously. Jess was the Group's star player, considered a fine actress, always word perfect and usually winning rave reviews for her performances at the Greenock Arts' Guild.

I wasn't a bright spark at school. At least I never felt bright. I was quiet and obedient. But I learned to read, write, do sums easily enough and I enjoyed geography sessions. As an adult I learned to appreciate Robert Burns but as a boy I hated those moments when it was my turn to recite his poems to the class at the school's annual Burns Recitation competition. I couldn't bear the spotlight. Now I can't get enough of it.

I was around ten years old when, at Mum's instigation, I discovered the delights of 'the wee Gooks', our local Gourock cinema at the Pierhead. The programme changed three times a week, on Mondays, Wednesdays and Fridays, and we would sit in the seven penny seats, the cheapest ones, right at the front where you had to tilt your head up at about 70 degrees to see the screen. It was a small cinema, known locally as the flea-pit, with about 200 lumpy seats and a black and white chequered linoleum floor, washed regularly with strong-smelling disinfectant. A new world opened up for me as I passed through the green and black art deco doors and looked at the black and white photographs of film stars lining the walls inside. It was here I was first introduced on the screen to a host of Hollywood and Pinewood stars of the day: Kirk Douglas, Victor Mature (that torso!) and Jack Hawkins, and marvelled at the first widescreen films in Cinemascope and Todd AO, still on the small cinema screen of course.

Here I saw *Calamity Jane* and my heart soared for the first time as Doris Day sang *Once I Had a Secret Love* to Howard Keel. Even now I'll sing it to anyone unlucky enough to give me the chance. It was here also that James Cagney and his gang of tough guy characters became firm favourites with my mother. We saw all today's classics, such as *Seven Brides For Seven Brothers*, *The Wizard Of Oz* and the Sinbad pirate films. My mother and I got full value from our nights at 'the wee Gooks'. Not only did we see all the latest films, the Pathé news-reels, the B movies and the shorter second film, we'd also benefit from the cinema's efficient heating before braving the winter storms on our journeys home to the cold house at number 47.

These journeys were always broken by a visit to Dom's fish and chip shop on Shore Street for a 'poke' of hot chips in yesterday's newspaper. Bliss!

5

SEX EDUCATION

SUMMER NIGHTS IN GOUROCK WERE also often blissful for me as a child. I would swim in the Clyde during the day and, in the evenings, I'd sit on the promenade in front of our house with my mother and all the other housewives, among them Mrs Middleton and Mrs Balfour and her daughter Margaret. I'd lap up the gossip and revel in the titbits about the reputations and sex lives of neighbours and acquaintances. The women didn't think I was listening or perhaps didn't care, assuming that I wouldn't understand what was being said. But I did understand. I still chuckle recalling how one of the clan regaled the group with the news that her husband never asked for sex. She always woke up in the middle of the night, however, to find him 'doing it'. My mother retorted, "Girls, once you give a man a taste of it, he'll *never* be satisfied."

This was the time when the Polaris submarine base was established in the Holy Loch in Argyllshire across from Gourock and near Dunoon and both towns were inundated with young American sailors and servicemen. The tenders from the base would unload sailors at the Cardwell Bay Jetty, right opposite number 47, and the young men would then head for the nightlife in Greenock and Glasgow. There was always plenty of activity for a young boy to survey from our front room window. Local girls would meet their American boyfriends off the jetty and canoodle in the local cafés with them. 'Ladies of the Night' would ply their trade from the back of a nearby Daimler owned by the town's funeral and wedding car hire company. From my window I'd see it rocking slightly, the driver outside, leaning against the railings, presumably with a worthwhile tip in his pocket, enjoying a cigarette. The next day this car, surprisingly none the worse for wear, would ferry a blushing bride or two to the church.

One night when all the family were tucked up in bed, there was an almighty rumpus under my bedroom window at the back of the house over the 'close', the alleyway which ran from front to back of the house. A young American sailor and a girl had been getting to know each other very well under my window. Then came a scuffle and the sound of someone running up the stairs, on to the green and through the washing to clamber over the stone wall into the neighbour's garden. It turned out that the girl had stolen the sailor's wallet containing his money, shore pass and identification. He'd chased her but she'd disappeared. "Keep the cash," I heard him shout plaintively, "just give me back my passes!" To me, this and other couples' behaviour was fascinating.

Many of the liaisons between the sailors and the local girls resulted in happy marriages and a large American community sprang up in and around Dunoon. It exists today although the base has been largely disbanded. Similarly many of the local girls married and moved to America.

On a few occasions, because I looked older than my years, when Mum and Dad were out at the pub I too would entice a sailor up the close to my room for slightly different entertainment. What, apart from an erection, compelled me to do this so young, is something I can't explain. No one "taught" me or "interfered" with me to start me on this path, it just came naturally. I would lean out of the window or I'd be sitting on the bench on the promenade and along would come a young sailor and occasionally, when I'd smile, we'd get talking.

Sex had already reared its head inside number 47, though I didn't identify it as such when I was small. Mostly it was a case of my being in the wrong place at the wrong time. I remember being put to bed in the set-in bed in the front living room. Very soon I was sitting up, crying and observing my father doing something very odd to my mother. A few years later, after the birth of my sister, I was regularly sent to Gilmours, the chemist at Cardwell Bay, with a note to hand over the counter. After a few trips I opened the note and read, "Three in a packet, please". I imagine my parents thought I wouldn't find out what I was buying for them or, if I did, I wouldn't know what condoms were for.

I once walked in on Mary and Jimmy making love on the kitchen floor in front of a roaring fire on a wet Scottish Sunday afternoon. It might have been romantic – but for my intrusion. It's true that we had no locks but it was possible to wedge the door shut. The older I got, the more surprising their behaviour seemed. And when I myself became sexually active, it seemed positively weird that they were still 'at it'.

Late one Sunday evening when I must have been 13 or 14, I arrived home from trolling around either Gourock or Greenock. By now I had become well and truly sexually active and leading a heavily closeted and promiscuous gay life. I didn't understand all this terminology then of course. I just got erections and liked to be with men to satisfy my need. How did I learn to "troll", "cruise" or whatever the term is? I don't know. Something attracted me to gents' toilets to watch and look for men. I can't remember whether I thought this seedy and depressing – it was just something I had to do. As was my habit on returning home, I first made myself a cup of tea and then made my way to my parents' bedroom at the front of the flat, overlooking the Bay, to sit at the end of the bed and tell them about my evening. Not the truth, obviously, but a fictional account about seeing friends or walking, or answering "nothing" when I was asked what I had been up to – anything that would prevent further, more detailed questioning. Then I would finish my tea and go to bed. My parents never pressured me nor made me feel uncomfortable – they just seemed to accept what I said. On this occasion, however, I soon heard moaning from their room. There were also banging noises from their bed which backed on to the wall of my room.

So I crept down the hallway, past the kitchen and front sitting room, and peered through the slightly opened door of my parents' room. What I saw reflected in the wardrobe mirror which faced their bed was – horror of horrors! – Mary and Jimmy engaged in intercourse. I crept back to my room and soon there was peace. But I couldn't help noticing that Sunday night was "the night" for my parents.

Sinclair continued to add to my sex education. When he left home to join the RAF he would often come home on leave bringing girls with him to meet the parents. The flat wasn't big enough for five of us, let alone for a girlfriend, but somehow we made room. And I tended to find my half-brother and his girlfriends in all sorts of situations and positions...

Then came what comedians would now call my "Suits You, Sir!" experience. I was taken by Mum to Burton's, the men's outfitters in West Blackhall Street in Greenock, to be measured for my first suit, a very important occasion for a young man and, for me, also very interesting. I noticed the salesman take more than a passing interest in me. Let's say he did more than just measure my inside leg inside the changing room cubicle while my mother waited outside, having a cigarette and, I could hear, chatting to the other assistants. This is an additional service available in tailors' shops around the world, though not something they actually promote.

There's a distinct possibility that the salesman was encouraged by me as I was going through a make-up wearing phase. I'd buy a small tube of foundation from Woolworths and dab it on to cover my increasing beard growth. The problem with make-up, I found, was that once you start, it's hard to break the habit. Mine lasted a few years before I settled for a "butch" five o' clock shadow.

I hesitate to say I was Gourock's first cross-dresser but what my family made of the make-up has never been discussed. I was just a gay boy growing up in 1960's Scotland. When I got home of an evening, I do believe Mary and Jimmy must have been very patient with me. I was leading a very lonely life cruising toilets in the area. I had no friends – at least none they knew about – and it must have worried them what I was up to.

Mine was about the last generation in Renfrewshire to sit the 11+ and I passed. Just. I moved up to Gourock High School, a mixed secondary school. It had a 'technical' – 'T' – class for pupils deemed less academically able. It was into this category that I landed, to my horror, with a school timetable that included woodwork, metalwork and lots of sport, everything I hated and was useless at. Mr Charles, the technical teacher, was long-suffering with other pupils but soon abandoned me to a seat at the back of the room. I can recall only a few occasions in three years when he spoke to me and then he probably did so only to see if I was still alive.

I did, however, suddenly begin to enjoy PE classes (when a jumble sale had produced the right shoes) – especially in the changing rooms beforehand when I'd furtively watch the other

boys undress. And I loved the time we spent with our diminutive music teacher Miss Scrimgeor. She somehow managed
to train our class of rough and ready Scottish boys to give a
not-bad rendition of (curiously) the rousing Welsh anthem, *Men
Of Harlech*. She also managed to silence us when she brought
in her record of Wagner's *Ride of the Valkyries* to play on the
school gramophone. We did enjoy that one.

I did very well at the music classes – so well that Miss
Scrimgeor gave me regular work digging her garden for 2/6
an hour. The other pupils at school generally ignored me. No
one noticed that I alone hadn't gone on the first ever school
cruise on the *SS Uganda*. The reason was it would have cost
fifteen pounds and I knew Mary and Jimmy simply could not
afford that amount. I didn't cause a fuss. There was no money
for it and that was that.

Boys seemed unsure of me, possibly sensing that I was
different from them and I was not much more popular with
girls. One girl however was very keen on me and I was embarrassed that everyone at school was talking about it. She would
wait for me at the gate at four o'clock and I remember going
to her house for tea because I thought it would be rude to refuse
the invitation. I seem to remember a quick kiss but nothing
more except huge embarrassment and a rush for the exit and
home.

There were more kisses with two neighbours, sisters, of
about my age. We spent a great deal of time in the loft of a
barn over the back green wall from Cove Road. We rolled
around all three of us and there was the almost compulsory
fumbling but no more. There was also the daughter of a family
from Glasgow to whom my mother would rent out one of our
rooms for their holiday every summer. We needed the money
so we squeezed in together to cope with them. I enjoyed

walking around with her hand in hand – I just thought that was the right thing to do – but, by that time, I was confident of my preference for men.

6

POOFTER

THEN THE BULLYING AND NAME-CALLING started. 'Poofter', 'pansy' and 'diddy' (never understood that one, perhaps 'Diddy Dunn' sounded satisfyingly mocking) were favourites. They were hissed at me as I passed on my way to school or on my way home. I was embarrassed and hurt but did nothing. What could I do? I wasn't the fighting type. I just went on my way. A boy called Tom was a bully at school, at least to me. When I was around 13, his family moved into Cove Road. He quickly got my measure and the name-calling and baiting began. The railway from Glasgow runs along one side of Cove Road into Gourock station. The longest walk on earth was from our house to his just at the railway bridge, a walk I had to take every day to and from school. Tom and his friends would line up against the promenade railings and begin the litany of insults and sniggers.

Luckily my mother was prone to leaning out of a window and making her presence felt. In Scotland this process is known as a 'hing', as in 'hinging oot the windae', and it was prevalent before the age of television. Outside was the TV of the day – the soap opera. Anyway when she appeared there was instant silence from Tom and Co. It sometimes paid to be a mummy's boy.

Some of the boys who bullied me were the ones who liked to be masturbated in the school toilet cubicles during the break.

I'm not sure what that says about them except that there's nowt so queer as folk. For me it became a low period. I knew I was effeminate but I could do little about that. I felt odd and lonely, knowing that I didn't fit in with regular school activities such as sport or metalwork. At one point I even joined the Boy's Brigade, urged by Mum and Dad but much against my better judgement. I hated every second of those Friday night meetings at the Old Gourock Church. Marching and signalling were not for me. And the sight of me in a beret and kilt must have brought many a true Scotsman to tears.

I was always timid and shy, a description of myself I find hard to believe these days. In class I'd always do what I was told, keep quiet and never put my hand up to say I didn't understand. So it was a complete shock to everyone, especially me, when I became a victim of Brown Bess, without deserving it. Brown Bess was the huge, dreaded leather strap used by 'Pappa' McPhail, our irascible elderly algebra teacher. Why 'Pappa', I never knew. A less fatherly figure you couldn't imagine.

The boy who did deserve the treatment on this occasion was actually a friend, a farmer's son called George. Now, all boys of 13 have near permanent erections and George was no exception. George was remarkable in that he was a big, lively boy and his erection huge, so huge that it earned me six painful strokes on the hands and arms. And I didn't go anywhere near it!

The class was in the middle of a particularly convoluted lecture by Pappa that few of us could follow. The perfect moment, George must have decided, to take his impressive member out of his trousers to show it off. When a sufficient number of boys sitting near him had spotted what he was doing, he grinned with delight and began knocking the engorged member against the underside of his desk, making low thudding noises which were somehow more hilarious than any sound we'd ever heard in any class. Thud. Thud. Thud. Several of us began giggling but only I was noticed. "Dunn!" shouted Pappa. "Get out here and roll up your sleeve!" Shock! Shame! Ouch! George's erection disappeared immediately and I returned to my seat, humiliated and extremely sore, to a chorus of giggles.

This was the only time I was punished at school by teachers. I was appointed a prefect at one stage, which helped me overcome my shyness a little. But to this day I have little understanding of algebra or geometry.

While I became reasonably good at exercises in gym classes I continued to be nelly on the sports field and I proved equally inept in the craft classes. The teachers, as I said, seemed to abandon me. I was left to get on with making a stool in wood-work for about three years and even then I doubt it was safe to be sat on.

Whether there were parent-teacher evenings at Gourock High in those days, I don't know. If there were, I suspect my parents would have had neither the confidence nor the time to attend them. All teachers must have been available to parents for discussions on their offspring but to the best of my knowl-edge my parents just let things go on as they were. This isn't a criticism of them. They probably didn't pay too much atten-tion to their "rights" and were far too busy trying to scrape together enough money to keep house and home together to worry whether James' education was on course.

It was my English teacher, Mr McGlashan, who took me under his wing and tried to rescue me from the hell and the boredom of the technical class. He failed. The powers that be decided there was no reason to move me to a higher grade where I could study more English, geography and history, as I wanted. The Dunn family didn't put up much of a fight either. So in tech class I stayed but, when I was with Mr McGlashan, I was in my element – writing essays, reading and learning not just about great writers and the history of the British Empire but also about jazz and ballroom dancing. Mr McGlashan, a dance and jazz fan, brought drumsticks into school and taught us rhythm on the desk and he gave ballroom dancing lessons in the gym after school had finished.

So the first man I ever danced with was my English teacher as he took me through the steps of the foxtrot and the cha-cha to the latest EPs of Victor Sylvester and his Orchestra on the school record player. On the dance floor, unlike on the sports field, I was completely co-ordinated and have loved all sorts of dancing, especially ballroom, ever since. In this, I took after my father. He was a marvellous ballroom dancer as was my mother. Those were the days of the great seaside ballrooms at Cragburn Pavilion in Gourock (now a block of flats) or 'doon the watter' at the big ballrooms in Rothesay and the other resorts. In Cragburn I would happily while away the summer afternoons and evenings sitting on the sidelines, as Mary and Jimmy would glide past so elegantly to the strains of the local Henri Morrison Orchestra.

I was a flop at almost everything at secondary school. There was only one year during my time at Gourock High when my average exam mark soared. The reason was that I cheated. I wrote out the answers to what I thought would be our history paper questions on a few sheets of blank paper. I got lucky. Those questions came up and I sneaked out the paper and copied out the answers. I think I got 93% that year for history. My schoolmates – some of my tormentors – knowing what I'd done, looked on with disbelief at the audacity of it. It gave me great pleasure to cock a snook at them but it earned me no pats on the back from teachers or my parents. Perhaps they suspected. It is a complete mystery to me, even now, as to why I did it. I wasn't *interested* in my examination results and I was under no pressure from my parents. I can only conclude that the necessary devious nature of my 'other' life, my intensifying secret preference for sex with men, had spilled over to my schooling.

I couldn't wait for the 8-week school holiday each summer. I would laze around, help Mary clean her houses, forget all about school and bullying. I was never bored or miserable and the highlight of the holidays always came the night before we returned to the drudgery of school life. The local ferry boat owner, Roy Ritchie, who ran a daily service between Gourock and surrounding seaside villages such as Kilcreggan, Dunoon and Millport, would take kids of all ages from the Cove Road area on an evening sail or 'run' as we called it.

My generation was the first in Scotland to sit O-Levels, like pupils in England and Wales. I failed all of mine spectacularly and left school at 16, officially a loser with no qualifications. Now what would become of me?

7

SECRETS AND LIES

TECHNICAL CLASSES WERE NOT ENTIRELY the cause of my scholastic failure. I made no effort to study in the evenings because from 11 years of age I was not just sexually active, I was sexually hyperactive and that took time.

Almost every day I looked forward to 'adventures' from my 'troll'. I didn't use that word, I learnt it many years later and, for the uninitiated, although it now seems to be in the general language, trolling or cruising is the gay man's quest for sex. Back then I had a regular routine, trolling between the five gents' toilets on my target list around Gourock. I'd meet all sorts of characters, mostly older men looking for sex. One man of about 30 I approached was baffled. I'd interrupted him watching through a hole in the wall separating the men's loos from the women's. He looked extremely bemused and it wasn't long before we were meeting regularly. I think I may have awakened his bisexuality.

Before my evening excursions, I'd come home from school, change and report for my nightly paper round for Johnson's paper shop at Cardwell Bay. On weekdays this would usually take about an hour and I would be at the shop at eight on Sunday mornings to deliver the Sunday papers. I would deliver the evening paper The Greenock Telegraph and on Thursdays, the local paper, The Gourock Times, a four-page broadsheet. My interest in print media must have started

47

here as I delivered other publications of the day such as The Radio Times, She, Woman's Realm, Weekend, Reveille and Titbits. I'd then come home and help tidy the house.

Our 'hoose' was always in a mess and in need of a good clean-up. No one ever had time to do it. I could understand that Mum had no heart for housework after spending the day cleaning up other people's mess. Dad worked long hours and came home exhausted and frequently inebriated. Sinclair was working on the Clyde boats and my sister and I were at school.

But there was that gap after school and after my paper round when I could be the housewife. We didn't have a vacuum cleaner and certainly no polish because our furniture wasn't worth polishing. I can remember cheap, post-war, second-hand oak bits and pieces and plenty of Formica, the equivalent in the 1950s of, say, stripped pine in the 1970s. Cleaning of the threadbare carpets was done simply with a brush and shovel and the linoleum I washed on my hands and knees. Perhaps it's because I looked at dirt so closely and sighed so regularly at the stream of jumble sale junk coming through the door that I'm now fastidious and tidy to the point of obsession.

Once the cleaning, by my standards, was finished, I'd have something to eat before getting ready for the night. I say 'something to eat' and that about sums up Mary's cooking. She was, alas, no Delia Smith and I doubt she'd ever set eyes on a recipe book. She boiled vegetables until they were grey and tasted so unpleasant that for many years after leaving home, the memory lingered so that I couldn't bring myself to so much as try a green bean or a morsel of cabbage. When we had meat, which wasn't often, she'd bake it until it was rock solid. Only chicken seemed to survive her 'overkill', though quite how was a mystery. Her baked scones – rocks, more like – were so indigestible they would stay with you for what felt like about a year. We never had 'starters' – those didn't feature in my life until well into the 1970s.

Looking back we seemed to get by on mountains of bread and potatoes with small helpings of mainly fried eggs, bacon, bought pies and sausages, very little fruit and lots of strong tea. We didn't often get ill, so she must have been doing something right. I suspect that something was her vegetable soup. Most of what went into the pot which gurgled away on the stove, being regularly topped up, was freshly grown in the garden. It didn't look great but it usually tasted wonderful.

After the meal I'd boil a kettle of water, push everyone out of the kitchen, strip and wash at the sink by standing in a basin of hot water, shampooing my hair and grooming myself in the best way an adolescent with next to no money or privacy could manage. Then I went out into the Gourock night, progressing later to haunts in Greenock.

Once out in the places where gay men and boys met other men and boys, mainly those five public lavatories, I had a very good time. I'm no oil-painting now but back then I was tall and slim with good teeth, good legs and slim hips. In my much-patched white jeans (I could not afford to replace them) with my longish brown hair shining, I was hardly a match for Sean Connery or the sort of caber-tossing Scottish hero you'd see pictured on a packet of porridge but I considered myself passably handsome. I was certainly in demand.

Homosexuality between consenting adults under the age of 21 was illegal then and any man found with me could have been arrested and sentenced to several years in prison. But the illegality of what I was doing – the fact that I was instant jailbait to many of my partners – never entered my head, nor did it seem to enter theirs. It was just too exciting.

49

It's generally assumed that men who go 'cottaging' are older men looking for young flesh. That's not a true picture. As a young teenager I went out looking for sex with men I fleetingly fancied and, although I drew the line at many, it didn't matter if they were five, ten or twenty years older. Many's the cold, wet wintry night that I went from public loo to public loo, wrapped up in my long, black, hooded duffle coat, looking for partners for company and sex. Looking back, they always seemed to be wet, wintry nights but my nocturnal perambulations were certainly not confined to winter.

When the special looks or the quick flashing signals worked and I picked someone up or was picked up, we would have sex in a cubicle or, if he had a car, we'd drive off somewhere remote in the hills above the Clyde. I was taken to shipyards, offices, hillsides and houses – derelict and occupied – and experienced the act in the front and backseats of probably every make of car then on the market – from Triumphs, Rovers, Austins and Morrises to Wolseleys, Renaults and Jaguars.

In none of these rough and ready liaisons was I ever brutally treated. In fact, the opposite was true. But the first time I was penetrated it was in a rough, quick, crude way and it was an excruciatingly painful experience. I hadn't objected to it but let's say I don't miss it. I'd been attracted not by the man but by his car. Expensive cars were 'pullers' then as now. His was a smart but old Jaguar. I'd not been in one of those before. In I got excitedly, luxuriating in the leather seats. We drove to his lock-up in the centre of Gourock and I was deflowered in the most matter-of-fact way, bending over the front passenger seat. Romantic? Not remotely.

There was never a question of money in these transactions despite the fact that this was Clydeside in the 1960s when unemployment and poverty were rife and any money on top of the tips I earned delivering papers would have been useful. It never entered my mind to charge and the men I went with couldn't have afforded it anyway. I did, however, on one occasion inadvertently find myself playing the rent boy and I was not as successful in my scale of fees as I was to become later.

It occurred during my first holiday away on my own when I must have been about 12. I was staying with my Aunt Nancy, Mum's sister-in-law, who lived in Milton Street, Edinburgh, just behind Holyrood Palace. And I was having a marvellous time with the men of this glamorous city as a new face on the block. In no time I was cruising Princes Street Gardens and the local railway stations. I found myself in a loo in the main railway station, Waverley, where an older man was standing nearby at a urinal. He flashed me and also flashed a one pound note, a lot of money to me in the early sixties, especially as I had none of my own. I needed pocket money so I readily followed him outside.

Before anything happened, he took me to lunch – well, I would have called it "dinner" then – at a smart restaurant on the Royal Mile. I had never eaten out other than a 'fish tea' at the Pierhead in Gourock on the rare occasions when my parents had a little spare cash and we'd get there at about five on a Saturday afternoon. This Edinburgh restaurant was more than posh by my standards then. I was overwhelmed. I can't remember what I ate but every time I attend the Edinburgh Festival now and I walk down the Royal Mile I remember the occasion with affection and smile.

After the meal, my patron took me to one of the stairways on the Royal Mile. Those circular stone stairways run down to near Princes Street Gardens. And it was on these stairs that we had sex, stopping just before some passers-by would have seen us. Before he left he gave me a ten shilling note! I should have insisted on the promised pound but he must have assumed I had eaten the other ten shillings' worth at lunch.

It's possible, as you read this, that you are shocked and even disgusted not only by my candour but by the fact that gay men behave in this way, driven by our baser instincts. Perhaps you think it totally against nature, uncivilised, debauched. I can only say that I have never felt, for one moment, that frequent casual sexual encounters between homosexuals are unnatural or anything to be ashamed of. No one "taught" me my sexual behaviour. I felt it was something I wanted and needed to do and I was never ashamed of doing it. Of course I know many people disapprove but I'm afraid I can't apologise to them. No doubt almost everyone in that small town on Clydeside all those years ago would have disapproved of my nocturnal antics and I still wonder how I kept the secret and got away with it. My parents would ask where I was going and I'd say 'out!' I some-times invented fictitious names of friends and Mum and Dad – bless them – would never probe. I suspect they knew nothing of what went on. They probably never had a clue. I sensed that my mother made extra efforts to preserve the peace. Maybe she countered my father's anxieties by pointing out that I wasn't running wild, I wasn't a hooligan. But my father always behaved rather coolly towards me then – and no wonder. Yet however reluctant he'd been to accept me orig-inally, I was his child and he must have known I was up to something. But what?

Discussing my sexual preferences either with him or my mother was never an option. People just didn't talk about those of us who were 'different'. We wouldn't have known where or how to begin. It still pains me to think how I would have disappointed Dad if he'd known how I spent my time back then. Yet I take comfort from the fact that in his eyes, somehow I turned out all right and later on he was able both to like me and to feel proud of me.

I don't want to give the impression that my parents were negligent. They may have seemed disinterested in my comings and goings but I have always been good at white lies and they were both preoccupied with earning a living and keeping the family afloat. This strain showed in many ways, one being that my handsome, bald father was hitting the booze. He would come home from 'the shop' as he called it when the pub closed at around two in the afternoon and in the summer would 'hing oot the windae' as my mother liked to do. The difference was that he would fall asleep in this position and his bald head would roast in the sunshine. Neighbours would call out to him but by then it was often too late. For most of the summer, he had a sore, peeling, sun-burned head.

Dad was, as I've said, essentially quiet and retiring, never an argumentative man, except with my mother, and then usually when he was drunk. And to my knowledge he was never violent towards her. He did however hit me once and it came as a great shock. I came home one night after eleven and the door that was never locked had the latch down. The reason was that I was supposed to be in by 10.30pm. I knocked and Dad opened the door and, to my total surprise, instantly slapped me hard across the head. "Where have you been?" he shouted, as though releasing pent-up fury. "Look at him, his eyes are all red!" I wasn't aware of sore eyes but minutes before I had been having alfresco sex up in the hills above the town with a gorgeous airman whom I'd first met in a public loo in Glasgow. He told me he always wore his RAF uniform to 'troll' as it brought him more success.

There was a second confrontation when the whole family were present. Sinclair, who had by then joined the RAF and was stationed at Finningley near Doncaster, was visiting home with Phyllis, his girlfriend and soon-to-be wife. An argument started, I can't remember how. All I recall was Dad turning to me and calling me a poof. I said "Yes, I am. What of it?" It seemed to shut everybody up. A silence returned to number 47 and I had the impression that my father was washing his hands of me. My sexuality was never mentioned again.

Incidents like this probably happen up and down the country every day in families where there are gay teenagers. There is a lot of pain but often they help young people to grow the extra skin they need. You have to be strong – some would say hard – to survive because it's you alone against the world. Or, at least, that's how you feel.

Dad seemed to me to be very unhappy at the time and maybe my admission of what I was added to his unhappiness. There were issues between him and Sinclair, who was not his flesh and blood, as well as his issues with me – a gay son whose emerging lifestyle he couldn't begin to understand. In the late sixties, homosexuals in small communities were almost never "out". We didn't officially exist. I certainly wasn't "the only gay in the village" but it was never discussed.

My parents dealt with 'the situation' in entirely different ways. When nosy neighbours would say something like, "No girlfriends yet, James?", Mary would almost always jump to the rescue with, "He's got no time for girlfriends. He's too busy with his own life." She knew I was different but she certainly wouldn't have known what being gay was about. But she had chosen to support her son without the subject ever being discussed. My father could not do the same. His heavy drinking was part of the answer. And this drinking was to lead to our family's great public shaming and to my own most intense humiliation.

8

THE EMBEZZLEMENT

DAD HAD MOVED FROM RUNNING a pub in Greenock to running the bar in the clubhouse of the Greenock Morton Football Team, a very important job in this west coast community where religious differences were sharply noticeable. Catholics supported the Celtic football team, Protestants supported Rangers, there was no question about that. But next in the priority of citizens of the Greenock area was support for their beloved Morton Football Club.

I always thought of Dad as a barman who occasionally liked a drink himself. The truth was I didn't know how much he drank because there was rarely any sign of his doing so at home, except when he fell into a deep sleep 'hingin' oot the windae', that is. The only times when the best glasses and the whisky would be produced on the kitchen table were towards midnight on New Year's Eve or if relatives from Glasgow or Edinburgh honoured us with a visit. On those occasions, we learnt to watch Dad like hawks because his measures of the golden stuff or "Scottish water" could be lethal. On one afternoon, Aunt Nancy dropped in and suffered so much from Dad's hospitality that she left the house, smart hat askew, singing her heart out and staggering. Not quite the behaviour expected of a genteel lady who lived just over the wall from Holyrood Palace in Edinburgh! Mum on the other hand never drank straight spirits but chose, when asked, an Advocaat, that sweet egg and brandy concoction fashionable then. She maintained, authoritatively, "Table wine is basically vinegar, James," continuing with "but always remember a drunk man always tells the truth".

Dad had been working in his new job on West Blackhall Street at the Supporters' Club for some months when I became aware from hushed conversations between my parents that local Customs and Excise officers were investigating him. He had been putting half crown coins in the bottom of each optic so that when people ordered a shot of a spirit – whisky, gin or rum – they actually received less than the standard measure. It may have been an old dodge but when I heard about it I couldn't help but feel a certain degree of amazement at his ingenuity. Anyway, Dad was arrested, charged with embezzlement and there was a brief court appearance at which he was found guilty and fined £500, a huge sum in those days. It was always assumed that we as a family benefited from this fiddle but Dad almost certainly drank the difference.

The consequences for the family were painful. Stealing from the local football club was tantamount to treason and the Dunns were notorious for a long time. I felt particularly victimised because it was I who had to deliver The Greenock Telegraph all around the town with Dad's guilt sensationally splashed as headline news – "Morton Barman Fined £500 For Theft". With every newspaper I folded and pushed through a letterbox my embarrassment deepened. I dreaded that someone would open the paper, read out the court report and quiz me about it before I could disappear to the next customer on my round. I got over it, of course. But I don't think Dad ever did. He might as well have been given a long prison sentence. Not only had we to pay the fine in weekly instalments, he also lost his job and his prized pub licence, so he was never allowed to be a publican again. With that, my Saturday morning job at the Morton

Supporters' Club of sorting the beer bottles into their proper crates also went.

Dad had never dirtied his hands with manual work before all this – in fact publicans used to take pride in the hands that offer glasses – but he was reduced for the rest of his working life to finding labouring work on building sites all over the west coast of Scotland, getting up at dawn to pick up transport. It was a crushing blow and he was desperately ashamed for many years.

It was left to Mum to raise the money for the fine. She went literally cap in hand to the good-hearted Mr and Mrs Gilmour, who owned and ran the chemists at Cardwell Bay and for whom she cleaned daily. She borrowed the money each week and paid it back by working extra hours.

I can't recall the court case being discussed at home in front of us children, though presumably my parents talked about it together. It was cloaked in silence. There was even less money for food and I recall many visits to a pawn shop in Greenock with Mum. We'd climb the stairs to this dreary place, wait our turn with other poor and shame-ridden people in silence, then enter a cubicle. I'd squeeze in with my mother and we'd present my father's 'good' suit – I can't recall that we ever had anything else of value to pawn – accept the money offered and leave as quietly as we'd come.

The consequences for my mother, who as a two-and-six-an-hour cleaner held the keys to some of the houses of the town's most respectable people – bank managers, chemists, solicitors and traders – might have been devastating but they weren't. No one questioned *her* honesty and she didn't lose a single cleaning job as a result. Undoubtedly the whole case was a strain for her but she was always her usual loving self to us.

Everyone who knew my mother warmed to her. She had no side, wasn't self-pitying or pessimistic. There wasn't a day when I didn't adore her. And there wasn't a day when we didn't roar with laughter about something or other.

9

TELEVISION TIME

MARY WAS SMALL, SLIM BUT grew a little rounder with age so that I began calling her my 'wee bundle of fluff' – not a flattering nickname but such was the humour we shared. While my father never lifted a finger at home – he never moved other than to get up from his bed or chair and go to work – she was very practical and active. Somehow she had the energy after hours of cleaning other people's houses and offices to look after the small garden and vegetable plot at the back of number 47. This was a garden that certainly needed a makeover had Charlie Dimmock been around then. In truth it was an unruly mess with a small Nissen hut in the corner and weeds a-plenty. But Mum tended it carefully and with a practical eye. With her green fingers she grew beautiful roses as well as vegetables such as potatoes, cabbage and cauliflower; all of which we tried to eat – after she had cooked them to oblivion.

Mum always watched the sixties' gardening icon Percy Thrower on his Friday evening show *Gardening Club*, in front of the fire in the front room (in these pre-central heating days a fire was essential in Scotland – even in August). Before we acquired our own television set, we used to trudge up from Cove Road, rain, hail or snow, to Aunt Betty's house on the Midton council estate.

It was worth the effort for television taught me a lot. From watching Percy Thrower, tending his TV garden on the roof of London's Lime Grove studios (a far tidier and more lush pasture than ours at Cove Road, it goes without saying), I learned how to sow seeds, pot plants and generally take an interest in growing things. It's an interest which became highly satisfying later in my life.

At Aunt Betty's each Saturday evening we'd avidly follow *Dixon Of Dock Green*, the granddaddy of television cop shows, followed by variety with *Billy Cotton's Band Show*. It was during his appearances on this show that I fell 'in love' with the handsome pianist Russ Conway across a crowded and stuffy front room. And with longing in my heart, we'd trudge back down to the cold, damp 'hoose' in Cove Road.

There was a great celebration that Saturday in 1959 when our own first telly arrived from McMorlands Electricians in Kempock Street and *The Lone Ranger* burst out into Cove Road. From then on, we started Saturday evening viewing earlier, at five, with The Lone Ranger and Tonto, the masked champion of Western justice and his Indian sidekick, and we became telly addicts. The highlight of Sunday evening's television was *What's My Line?* with Eamonn Andrews and his panel of David Nixon, Gilbert Harding, Lady Isobel Barnett and Barbara Kelly who attempted to guess the occupations of members of the public as they "signed in" with a clue.

Years later I replaced Mary and Jimmy's old black and white television set with a new, large colour version with a remote control. The technician who installed it said to Mum as he was leaving, "Just point the remote control gadget at the signal and it'll change channel or switch it off and on for you. You don't have to touch the knobs on the set." My sister visited soon after this to inspect the shiny new telly but couldn't find Mum in the house. Then she heard her in the back green and found her, in a very bad mood, with the TV's remote control in her outstretched hand aimed in the direction of the aerial on the roof. "What a bloody carry on just to change over to the BBC!" she shouted.

When my mother died in 1990, I put a note on my wreath which said: "With much love and thanks for the laughter." The fun we had together was what I remember most about my childhood and teenage life until I moved away from Gourock. Mary and I would squirt water at each other as we chased around the house in games of extreme silliness, one with a jug, one with a cup, often soaking a room. We would dance around the small living room when there was music from The Victor Silvester Orchestra or the Ted Heath Big Band on the Light Programme. If there was none to be found, we would get out her collection of precious '78' records, collected from jumble sales, of course, and play them on our wonky wind-up gramophone, also from a Church Hall sale. Later I would progress to my own record player, a Dansette, also bought from McMorlands in Gourock for the vast sum of £18, which I'd saved from my paper rounds. The deal on the paper round was very Scottish. I'd deliver for free at no cost to Johnstone's the newsagent but was told to ring the bell of each customer every Friday evening. The majority would tip me – some never answered.

Mary liked to make an event out of the smallest occasion. When we all went together to see the film *South Pacific* with Rozanno Brazzi and Mitzi Gaynor at the Gaumont Cinema, Greenock, Mum turned up not with sweets, as she always tried to bring, money permitting, but with a bagful of fruit – loads of it – pears, bananas, grapes and oranges. She said :"That's what they eat in the South Pacific, so let's get in the mood" as we made our way to the seats.

She also introduced me to the delights of BBC radio, encouraging me to listen to the Home Service (now Radio Four) and the Light Programme (now Radio Two), a lifelong treat. I was with my mother in the Cove Road kitchen in 1956 when we heard sombre reports of the Hungarian uprising and its aftermath and, on a lighter note, we were devoted fans of the Scottish radio soap series *The McFlannells*, an everyday story of Glaswegian folk with, among other well known voices, Rikki Fulton's as the Reverend McCrepe. We also followed the national comedies such as *Whacko* starring Jimmy Edwards, and *Life With the Lyons* with Bebe Daniels, not to mention *Hancock's Half Hour* and *The Goons*. *Round The Horne* on the Light Programme every Sunday lunchtime was my special passion. The show was revolutionary in its relentless use of innuendo and its running sketches of the exploits of an outrageously camp duo, Julian and Sandy, played by Kenneth Williams and Hugh Paddick. Like most of the nation, I suspect, Mum and I never quite understood many of the jokes, but we both found the series hilarious.

Years later I was to meet Kenneth Williams in London and was bitterly disappointed by the actor. He struck me as an embittered old queen, churned up in his own selfish world to the exclusion of everyone else. But 40 years earlier with Hugh Paddick as Sandy to his Julian, 'resting' gay chorus boys who, among other occupations, ran a domestic help agency, Rentachaps, he spoke to me of a big camp world out there waiting to welcome me, one of its own. I think I always knew I would sample that world for myself one day – but I didn't know when that day would come.

10

FIRST LOVE

WHEN I MET MY FIRST LOVE, the wonderfully handsome man I'll call Tony, my 'after-dinner' excursions became nightly, whatever the weather. I was at Gourock High School and the chances of my working for my O-Levels dwindled to nothing. I didn't care. I paid attention to Tony and nothing else. We met in a toilet in Clyde Square in Greenock and we found not only that we enjoyed sex together, we also clicked. I was 14, he was 25, though he didn't know until much later that I was so much younger. For nearly three years I was completely besotted with him to the exclusion of almost everything else. After my mother, he was the first major influence in my life. Looking back, I'm certain I loved him and he me. He certainly taught me a great deal about sex. Ours was both a romantic relationship and a sexually highly-charged one.

I spent every waking moment thinking about him or being with him and I would go into a deep decline and depression when I had to wait more than a day to see him. Then I'd count every second until his car would appear.

Tony had the face and body of a film star. He was confident in his work as a police constable and I felt extremely lucky to be his boyfriend. There were very few days in those three years when he wasn't on duty that we didn't make love. And it was a relationship completely hidden from everyone else. It had to be.

Tony's job was such that he would have been ostracised, if not sacked and possibly jailed, had his colleagues sniffed a hint of his orientation. So secrecy was vital for him. He also knew how the police worked in patrolling public toilets, so we never had sex in a toilet. Luckily we didn't need to.

Tony lived in Greenock with his mother who, conveniently, used to visit her sister most evenings to watch television together. Once Tony had ferried her to the sister he would drive to Gourock, wait a few streets away for me, then we'd drive back to Greenock and sneak into his mother's tenement flat where we'd make love in comfort in his small bedroom and single bed. We knew we would not be disturbed because his mother relied on him to collect her in the car to return home. He would then drive me back home then pick her up. I loved the fact that Tony had his own car but I also enjoyed the Lambretta scooter he owned before buying the car. Not only were scooters very fashionable in the early sixties, they offered the passenger sitting snugly behind the driver the opportunity to slip their hands into the driver's trousers. Not recommended for road safety but good for sex.

Tony was terrified of being seen with me because I was so young, and we certainly couldn't go around like straight couples or dream of openly setting up home as people can today. Acceptance of openly gay relationships was decades away and it has yet to arrive in some areas of the United Kingdom even now.

Yet, despite these difficulties, he opened up a new world for me, for which I will always be grateful. He introduced me to the thrill of listening to live music. He took me to concerts at the Glasgow Odeon when the MJQ – The Modern Jazz Quartet – or the wonderful Ella Fitzgerald were appearing or when The Scottish National Orchestra were performing in concert in the city. I remember a very long evening listening to Britten's *War Requiem*. When *West Side Story* was on tour from the West End at the King's Theatre, Glasgow we were there as we were for all the West End plays and musicals that visited Glasgow. Being among a large crowd Tony felt 'safe' about being spotted with me, a teenager.

Sometimes we'd drive out to a café in the back streets of Greenock where we could be fairly sure to be the only people there. We'd sit and talk and listen to 'our' song from that time, *Love Letters* sung by Kitty Lester. What the café owner, a tough-looking guy, thought of two young men repeatedly playing such a slushy song on his jukebox, I don't know.

On Sunday nights, when Tony wasn't on duty, we'd snuggle up together in his single bed and, after sex, watch TV for an hour or so until it was time for him to collect his mother. It's these times I associate with that legendary programme, *Sunday Night At The London Palladium*. With Tony I watched a young Bruce Forsyth compering in his camp way and introducing international stars of the day such as Maurice Chevalier, Judy Garland, Frank Sinatra and Edith Piaf. He held me in his arms as Piaf sang *Je ne regrette rien* and asked, "Have you any regrets, Jim?" Regrets? Me? With this stunning, romantic man? Come on!

I also associate these stars and the television series, perhaps oddly, with Robertson's jam and its now politically incorrect golliwog labels and wrappings. We may not have lived in the King's Road but it was still the so-called "Swinging Sixties" and Tony was an imaginative lover. It was his idea to coat my toes and my genitals with jam, usually strawberry or raspberry flavour. As Bruce flounced, Tony licked. It worked well.

Other times Tony would take me down the coast road to another resort, Largs, about 15 miles away, and we'd stop off on the way, tuck the car behind bushes and find a convenient hidden spot on which to put down blankets. Tony would always be prepared with an under blanket and a top blanket. After this alfresco sex, we'd go for coffee and perhaps ice cream. By ice cream, I mean something special, certainly better ice cream than most we would then have found south of the border.

The reason was that Scotland has, for decades, had a secret ingredient: Italian immigrants. From the second half of the 19th century, it's said that thousands of Italian immigrants struggled to get north of the border after fleeing poverty. Most walked to the French coasts, took a boat to Britain and then walked up to Scotland where relatives who'd arrived earlier would accommodate them, particularly in the coastal towns – so the story goes. They began selling ice cream either from a barrow or from the new sort of cafés their longer-established compatriots were opening up. After all that effort, the least we natives could do was to eat their delicious ice cream and drink their aromatic strong coffee. Tony and I often went to Nardinis, the great art deco café and ice-cream parlour on the promenade at Largs, far enough away from our homes, he felt, for us to escape being noticed and recognised.

In Gourock, the Ashton and Continental cafés in Kempock Street became our local community centres where all my teenage schoolmates would hang out sipping unfamiliar real coffee and listening to the latest hits on the jukebox. I never dared go there with Tony. I went there only occasionally and then with Mum while doing the 'messages' on Saturday mornings. As a gay teenager, I missed the classic 1950s and 1960s rite of passage, the endless hours of idle chatter, jokes and joshing in coffee bars, youth clubs and the like. My 'real' teenage life was secret and based on sex.

Tony and I only rarely risked being seen there in public. We could hardly make contact. Even if we'd had a telephone in Cove Road, which we never did, he could never ever have called me. To the world at large Tony was a regular, straight guy and he had to play a regular, straight game; pretending to be interested in girls and taking them to police dinner dances so as not to arouse any suspicion among colleagues. And he was in great demand from women because of his clean-cut good looks, charm and, not least, his steady job. And after he'd spent an evening with a girl, suffering the strain of playing the role of interested boyfriend, he knew a further strain awaited him: he had to cope with a jealous teenager – me. Those early days of our relationship were madness. I was 14 going on 15 – grown up, becoming independent, but having to hide my true feelings and life. I was not easy to be with. Tony wanted a lover, not a growing teenager.

He wanted to be open about our relationship, though, I'm sure of that. He could be as softly romantic as any man could be with a woman. He even wrote me a poem on St Valentine's Day, on paper covered in coloured hearts, which I've kept to this day.

My Valentine to the one I love

So many times I think of you,

I wonder really what to do.

I don't suppose it is so very bad,

But you are such a little lad.

So young and gay to be tied this way,

So young to say I'm here to stay.

Your life should be full of laughter and fun,

Don't you ever wonder what you've done.

A life of eternal hide and seek,

Sometimes we'll meet, but dare not speak.

A casual glance, then turn away,

A longing heart broke for yet another day.

I feel so happy when I think of you.

I'll tell you what I want to do.

I want to stand on the highest steeple

And shout of my love for you to all the people.

For you my love grows more and more

Of that I have an endless store

Month after month, year after year,

With only perhaps an occasional tear.

Okay, not Rabbie Burns but not bad for a copper.

Although I never denied my sexuality, I too was living a lie. With Tony. I was ashamed of my poor home and my family, this to my eternal regret. To Tony I pretended I was older than I was and that I lived on the posh side of Cove Road in one of the better houses. Most incredibly perhaps, I said my father was a producer for BBC TV Scotland, producing, of all things, *The White Heather Club* with singer Andy Stewart! The mind of a teenager works in mysterious ways. This was a weekly 'hoochter choochter' programme, meaning that it was 30 minutes devoted to the music and dance of Scotland, appreciated by a minority of licence payers and tolerated by the majority. In fact, we suffered *The White Heather Club* only while waiting to watch the *Tonight* current affairs programme which followed it.

The regular stars of *Tonight* included Cliff Michelmore, Geoffrey Johnson Smith, Fyfe Robertson and Alan Whicker, who is now a good friend. Like most viewers then, I held these people in awe. The idea of Jimmy Dunn, my father, mixing with them as a TV producer was bizarre but something compelled me to tell those lies, thinking that embellishing my background would strengthen Tony's feelings for me. It was madness. I see now that Tony wasn't interested in my family. He was interested in me. And whether he ever believed my fantasy, I don't know. But he did eventually find it out.

After we'd been together for about a year, I went on holiday to Belgium with him. Don't ask me how a 15-year-old explained to his parents a trip abroad with a person they'd never met or knew anything about. I just announced I was going and they accepted it. I think it was a measure of my increasing independence and tenacious secrecy.

I must have saved money from my newspaper delivery tips. My mother obtained a passport for me. It was at this time I learned I was 'born out of wedlock' as it used to be so grandly termed – my birth certificate was printed in red, as was the custom in those days if you were a bastard. She even decided to wave me off from the railway bridge along Cove Road. I can see her there now, in her headscarf, her little coat, carrying a shopping bag on the way to the next cleaning job. And there was I, going off on my first ever holiday with an older man she had never met and waving back to her from the train.

I find it surprising but my first trip out of Scotland made little impact. I can recall good sea swimming and the wide sandy beaches of De Panne and other resorts along the coast near Ostend. I vividly remember sex in the tent with Tony. That was good. The next year we went on a camping holiday together again. This time we toured Scotland. Again, I remember the sex, little else.

My secret life continued to eclipse everything else. But one problem was looming large and I could not duck it. At 16 I needed work. I had given the subject no serious thought. I had thought only about Tony. I had no clue about how my future should or would pan out. As far as Tony was concerned, I was already employed as a reporter on Scottish TV News. Very untrue. But very glamorous.

11

MR JAMES

WHAT I FOUND MYSELF DOING after leaving school was, in fact, sweeping floors, making tea, cleaning lavatories and boiling down hot metal to skim off the ink, all this in a basement which housed the offices of the local Gourock newspaper and print shop. It was to become my first job and a wonderful one to boot.

It came about through Mr McGlasham's efforts to get me moved out of the technical class at Gourock High into his English and History classes. One of the projects he asked me to undertake was produce a little news-sheet, cutting out pieces from magazines and making it look busy, appealing and readable. It was my first publishing effort. It hadn't impressed the senior teachers of Gourock High but it impressed Mary, my mother. She knew absolutely nothing about publishing but she knew I liked writing and newspapers so, one Saturday morning, she took me and the publishing effort along to a somewhat surprised Jimmy Simpson, the proprietor and editor of the now defunct Gourock Times. This was a four-page weekly broadsheet with a healthy circulation of about 5,000. There were no other journalists employed apart from Jimmy, who each week wrote all the editorial and rewrote reports submitted by different organisations such as the local Women's Guilds, the Rotary and drama clubs. He also found the time to run the print shop which undertook all the general print work for the town such as council minutes, cinema posters, restaurant menus, dance tickets and business cards. The newspaper was set on a linotype hot metal machine but all the headlines were hand set in metal or wooden letters. You find the letter trap and wooden letters on sale in antique shops today.

In addition, Mr James was a stalwart of the community, a pillar of local society. He would attend council meetings, advise on local issues, attend numerous functions and sit on the magistrates' bench as a Justice Of The Peace. He also found time to be an enthusiastic member of the Scottish curling scene.

The Simpsons, a wealthy old Clydeside family, had once been one of Mary's employers – she had been their cleaner – and Jimmy or 'Mr James' as everyone called him, had known me since I was a small boy and my mother since she was a young girl. He agreed to take me on as an apprentice compositor for £12 a week, which was pretty good, plus overtime, if I wanted it, on Saturday mornings. I agreed with some trepidation. I didn't know it then but this was my first step in a career in the world of media and Mr James would become my first hero in life. At the interview Mary did all the talking and Mr James probably had little say in the matter.

The print shop was in a dark, dank basement down stairs off Kempock Street. There was a wooden floor and, on benches, dozens of shallow trays of typefaces in "hot" metal. In one corner were dusty files of back copies of the paper – they seemed to go back about 100 years – and there was an outside lavatory from whose grimy window could still be gleaned another stunning view across the Clyde. Upstairs was Simpson's Stationers and Newsagents selling all the daily and evening papers, envelopes, cards, notebooks and hardbacks. The shop, like the print room, was very successful and at morning and evening paper time, it was a hive of activity. Everyone would meet up at Simpson's.

I started almost immediately and it was fortunate that work engaged me in a way school never did because I really loved the job and found Mr James an inspiration. My life now had a new routine. I would get up at about 7.45am and would have toast and tea while listening to the Light Programme which, in the pre-Wogan days, had continuous orchestral music interrupted every ten minutes by an announcer reading the clock twice as in, "The time is seven fifty, seven fifty." By 8.20am I was at work with one hour for 'dinner' and a leaving time of five prompt, six on a Thursday when The Gourock Times was being printed and we'd hand fold the 5,000 copies of the broadsheet straight off the press. We'd then bunch them into delivery numbers for each newsagent in the town.

About the same time my relationship with Tony was in decline. He got tired of me. Maybe he asked himself where the relationship was going. Perhaps I was only good for bed. Partly, I'm sure, it was because of my stories about myself and my family, stories which he must have realised were fiction. He was after all a policeman. One day I spotted him sitting on a seat on the promenade in front of what I'd told him was my house on the posh side of Cove Road. I came out of my close, in a different part of the street. For three years he had dropped me off right outside my actual home believing I lived much further along. Now he realised the person he thought I was just didn't exist. I was entirely to blame. I had been rumbled.

Finally, after I'd been working for a few months, came the day Tony said simply: "I don't want to see you any more." He had met somebody younger.

I went into a deep decline. I had no friends, I'd had no teenage life. I had concentrated on this relationship, this sex-feast, over the past three years. I was tearful and depressed for many months. Weekends I'd often just spend my days in bed. What my parents thought I never knew – it was never discussed.

Tony was all I could think about. I would wait in the shadows late at night by his garage in Greenock, waiting to see him as he drove in from his nights out with his new boyfriend. We had arguments, he'd drive me home. I told him I'd commit suicide by jumping into the local quarry but it didn't move him. I was just behaving like a silly teenager. I remember telling him I'd wait for him in Clyde Square in Greenock between seven and eight under the arches of the town hall every night until he arrived. I was there for weeks and weeks. I know Tony was asked by mutual gay contacts to meet me to stop me wasting my time and wailing incessantly. Yet he never turned up. It was finished.

Now this fuss seems juvenile and my broken heart hardly unusual. I had not divulged my secret affair to a soul and now I had no one to talk to about it. There was no one to understand my shock and pain, no one to comfort me or tell me to turn the page. Consequently it took me many years to get over the break-up.

I didn't see Tony again until years later when I had moved to London and came home to Scotland regularly to see Mary and Jimmy. I traced him through the local police offices in Greenock and invited him to meet for coffee, which we did. And it was only coffee. We arranged to meet where we had first met, Clyde Square in Greenock, but not in the toilets this time. He arrived looking as handsome as ever and we drove to a coffee bar. I still had feelings for him – he was, after all, my first love at 14 – but he had moved on and had a new man in his life – and so had I.

12

THE LOVE TRAIN

MY APPRENTICESHIP WITH SIMPSON'S involved attending
a printers' college twice a week in Glasgow, travelling the half-
hour journey by train from Gourock station at the Pierhead.
I dreaded college and, after one visit, I decided it was far too
rough and butch a place for me and never went again. I
continued to draw travel expenses, however, and told Mr James
that I was attending, enjoying myself and, most importantly
to him, learning.

In reality I used the time either seeing the sights of the big
city of Glasgow, such as they were in the 1960s, and, well, basically trolling the city's gay haunts. I was, after all, now a free
agent. In those days there were a few gay bars but they were
not gay bars as we know them today. They were rough places
in dubious areas and customers would invariably cause
trouble at closing time. I tried to stay away from them. There
was also the Gay Gordon bar in Buchanan Street which was,
funnily enough, gay; the Duke of Wellington in Renfield Street,
and the appropriately named Guys in Hope Street where I'd
meet other young men over what had become my favourite
drink – Bacardi and Coke. One bar friend went from humble
beginnings as a pop record pusher in the early days of pop
radio to become a wealthy pop impresario. There was also
a series of toilets frequented by gays. Needless to say I included
these in my regular night-time itinerary. So my boss and my

parents thought I was attending college and learning a trade. But all I was doing was seeking "trade" – sex – around the gay and often dangerous meeting places of the city.

I'd end my 'big nights out' in Glasgow by catching the last train to Gourock. Now, if a reporter from a tabloid had ever spotted what took place on that late service from Glasgow Central station, the shock-horror headline would have been something like 'West Coast Love Train'. All human life with all its proclivities could be found on board.

The train left at 11.15pm pulled by a big, black, panting steam engine, driver hanging out of the window, and carrying a good few soon-to-be panting humans. It arrived at Gourock about 45 minutes later. Today's open compartments may be better for security but they're a lot worse for late-night sex. These trains usually had about eight or ten coaches, each divided into individual compartments with two long banquettes upholstered in a velvety material. The carriages were being taken back to the Gourock base ready for the morning's rush hour. This being the 1960s it has to be said, however, that there wasn't much rush in the rush hour. Gourock hadn't yet been discovered by Glasgow commuters.

I'd arrive at the station at about 11pm and walk the entire length of the train looking to see if there was anyone on board I fancied. If there seemed no one worth bothering about, I'd take a compartment by myself and wait to be joined. If a man came in and I didn't like the look of him, I'd simply jump out and move along the platform until I spotted someone with whom I'd like to share my journey and rush into his compartment. How cruel youth can be! This platform dance went on right up to the 'off' and the activity would start between stations. You soon learned how long you had between stops – usually about 10 minutes. So you soon knew how much fun you could have during the Glasgow to Paisley stretch, how much between Paisley and Woodhall, then between Woodhall and Port Glasgow and so on and on through Greenock Central, Fort Matilda and Gourock.

Some people took amazing chances like encouraging mini-orgies in a compartment or slipping off and changing partners half-way through the journey. It wasn't only gay men who'd use the train for sex but winching couples returning from nights out in Glasgow at the 'pictures' or single people looking for that last bit of fun. One traveller who always made a beeline for me was adept at standing on the seat immediately the train pulled out of the station and removing the light bulbs. True gentleman that he was, he always put them back before he disembarked at Port Glasgow.

Let's not get too carried away. Glasgow might be a gay-friendly place now but in the early 1960s it was positively barren of gay entertainment and certainly an unsavoury place at pub closing time, especially for 17-year-olds like me who might be wandering around. I saw brawls, knife fights and all sorts of drunken behaviour most weeks. Again sex had to be conducted at great risk of being attacked, in the open air, in derelict tenements in the Gorbals district or in toilet cubicles. If I was lucky there was a car back seat for the purpose.

It may seem extraordinary now that I wasn't beaten up for being gay or just for being there. Queer bashing was very fashionable in those days so I was certainly vulnerable, going as I did into deserted buildings with strangers. I suppose I was streetwise and even after a few drinks at Guys, I was always aware of potential dangers. But back then, when the pubs closed, Glasgow was a vast sea of vomit from Buchanan Street to Sauchiehall Street with most people on the streets almost incapable of standing up, let alone having sex or landing punches on passing gay boys. It's more than likely that one reason there were so few gay haunts was that drink, while it makes a few men take more risks in their search for sex, usually suppresses the need in others. Drunk, most are simply not capable of it.

Back then, most young men lived at home until they married or at least until well into their twenties. A gay bar in mid-sixties Glasgow, when I was trolling or cruising that city, amounted to a smoke-filled room smelling of stale beer and smoke with sad young and not-so-young men solemnly sipping their drinks, heads down, furtively raising their eyes to look round every few minutes. When a new face appeared at the door, all heads would turn and, when you went to the loo, all eyes – and a few men, you hoped – would follow you.

You rarely hear of brawls in today's gay bars. People are too concerned with their hairstyles and their expensive clothes to risk damaging them. Then it was different. All bars in Glasgow were pretty rough and downright dangerous near closing time as people drank to the last possible minute before being thrown out at 10pm. Among my growing circle of acquaintances there were a number of muggings and one vicious murder of a young, gay man who picked up the wrong person to take home. Me? I had a few narrow escapes, the occasional knife flicked in my direction for what little money I had or after I had picked the wrong person up and gone into a cubicle in a notorious loo.

The most violent times in the city were the days when the two local football teams played each other. Rangers and Celtic fans usually expressed their loyalty to their teams with their fists as they sometimes do even today. I once travelled on the train from Glasgow to Gourock on one of those match days. The train stopped at a station just outside the city. I put my head out of the window and someone punched me. It was painful but unsurprising. I didn't have time to note whether my assailant was a Rangers or Celtic fan but his was the one and only act of actual physical violence I experienced in my entire time on the west coast of Scotland.

Elsewhere in Britain then, Peter Cook and Alan Bennett were bringing back satire at The Establishment Club; on television David Frost and his irreverent colleagues were emptying the pubs on Saturday nights with *That Was The Week That Was*; the sound of Procol Harum was in everyone's ears and the shops of Carnaby Street were dazzling the world with their "way-out" clothes and shoes. As I cruised around Glasgow, avoiding learning printing skills at college and dodging vomiting drunks after closing time, all this may as well have been happening on Mars.

At the back of my mind as I cruised, I knew I was in danger of failing again because of my secret life. I knew that Mr James would eventually receive reports from the college and know I'd been skiving. And that's exactly what happened.

13

COLUMNIST AND THESPIAN!

MR JAMES DID LEARN, OF COURSE, about my non-atten-
dance at college and I should have lost my job. He called me
into his office and very quietly told me of his conversation with
the college. He was his usual generous and understanding self.
He refused to take back the money I'd drawn as expenses and
said, "Well, Jim, what do you want to do?"

I said I'd always loved writing and suggested I put a weekly
column together covering the local "what's on" news. It could
be called "Stage and Screen", a really original title, I told him.
The problem was that there was very little going on in Gourock
and not much on the stage or screen either, so I'd have to look
further afield to Greenock, Port Glasgow and Glasgow if I
wanted to find any half-exciting news for a weekly show business column. But, as every cub journalist learns, local papers
thrive when they print local news about local people. So the
sources for my column would have to be the local cinemas
and drama groups. Then I'd see what I could write about the
professional theatres of Glasgow, like The Kings, The Alhambra
(alas, gone) and the Citizens'. I especially liked the Citizens',
not only because I knew it was a theatre where avant-garde
plays from all over the world were often performed, but also
because it was in the Gorbals area, then in the process of being
torn down and redeveloped. The shells of new flats and offices
were looming up beside ruined tenement buildings – excellent

places to take any "trade" I found of an evening. There were risks here too – but usually only of angering sleeping drunks or disturbing straight youths with their girlfriends.

Mr James considered my proposal and in the end, amazingly, said 'yes' to the column on condition I kept up my work as an apprentice compositor and continued to do the day-to-day cleaning jobs around the office. I think I'd have agreed on any terms. My head spun. My guilty days playing truant to have fun in Glasgow had earned me not the sack but my own weekly column! At a stroke I had entered the worlds of journalism and show business, quite suddenly my two favourite careers! And I was to be paid the princely sum of one pound and ten shillings extra a week for my efforts.

I had to write approximately five hundred words each Monday night. It took me about three hours! I would sit by the window in my parents' bedroom at number 47, looking out over the Clyde, and seek inspiration to create what I thought were witty paragraphs on entertainment gossip, local drama and films and end up tying myself in ungrammatical knots that Mr James would try to unravel.

There were four cinemas in the area, 'the wee Gooks', the local Gourock Cinema, which sadly closed down soon afterwards; and the Odeon, Gaumont and Regal cinemas in Greenock. As well as receiving all the press releases to do with upcoming films in these cinemas, I suddenly had free admission passes to all of them as well as to the local theatres like the Arts Guild in Greenock for plays; Cragburn Pavilion, Gourock for its summer variety shows, and the summer shows at Largs. My single social life took off.

Within weeks, I was even put on the press list for Pinewood Studios, near London, then the centre of the British film industry. That made me feel very important. I could also telephone London numbers and speak to the various film and theatre press officers, my first encounter with public relations. The world was beginning to open up for me!

Over the next few years, I was to meet most of the Scottish entertainment stars of the day and some from further afield and arrange short interviews either after contacting them directly or, more usually, by arranging a brief meeting through their agents or producers.

One of my first subjects was the glamorous singer Kathie Kay, then a household name from her appearances on *The Billy Cotton Band Show* on TV, (ratings often around 20 million). She was ironing her frock for the evening's performance in Gourock as I interviewed her.

Other interviewees included Clark and Murray, the comedy duo, who were very funny on stage but fought like cat and dog off it, and the Alexander Brothers, still going strong, who became world famous whenever a song and a kilt were called for. Donald "By A Babbling Brook" Peers, resurrecting his career in the sixties in the music halls of Scotland agreed to see me too. I met the singer Andy Stewart with his wife and asked her that awful showbiz question, "Tell me Mrs Stewart, what's it like to be married to someone as famous as Andy?" She gave me a long, pitying look and said, "Why don't we just discuss his singing?"

Jack Milroy and Rikki Fulton, two of the funniest men on the Scottish stage, had time for me. I also interviewed Jimmy Logan, then an international name, who had Gourock connections and I talked to him regularly for local angles. Kenny Ball and his Jazzmen, Acker Bilk and Moira Anderson all helped fill the columns with sundry quotes when they appeared locally.

My mother soon latched on to what I was up to and, of course, tried to help as usual. She got me an "exclusive" when the Scottish singer Kenneth McKellar was filming in Gourock. She simply "hijacked" him as only she could by walking straight up to him when he came off camera and introducing herself. Meanwhile she got a pal to run and fetch me. A bemused Mr McKellar was happy to chat. There was no chance, anyway, that my mother would have let him escape without a few choice "quotes."

Soon I had arranged a holiday, my first visit to London. This would include a trip to Pinewood in Iver, Buckinghamshire. This was 1964 and they were making *Wonderful Life* starring Cliff Richard, Susan Hampshire, Una Stubbs, Melvyn Hayes and others. I was introduced to some of them and I was, of course, completely bowled over by it. In the Pinewood restaurant were Carry On stars including Barbara Windsor, Hattie Jacques, Kenneth Williams, Sid James and Richard Wattis. My life as a star-struck fan had begun.

Naturally I saw as much of London as I could on this trip, especially a few gay haunts I'd heard about. One was a notorious sauna in Jermyn Street, off Piccadilly, which attracted gay customers. I saw for the first time couples openly caressing and even having sex in dark corners with next to no concern for who ever might see them. Clearly few of the customers felt threatened by visits from scandal-hunting press photographers because I spotted one of my heroes from my days of watching TV, pianist Russ Conway, looking almost unbearably handsome in a towel, close to a famous pop singer.

14

SHOW BUSINESS BECKONS

BACK HOME IN SCOTLAND, Scottish Television in Glasgow
– the ITV franchise said by the then franchise holder, Lord
Thomson, to be a 'licence to print money' – was advertising
for young people to take part in a new pop show compered
by Pete Murray, famous for presenting the *Six Five Special* pop
programme in the fifties and sixties, and I *had* to apply. They
were looking for young panellists to listen to records and review
them on air, just like the long-running *Juke Box Jury* on national
BBC TV, compered by a very young David Jacobs. I was
accepted for the Scottish version of the show. My appearances
were good publicity for The Gourock Times and my showbiz
column but I was, of course, excited at the prospect of being
discovered and becoming a TV star... I was after all only 18.

This was the second time I'd attempted to break into show
business. The first had been an application to audition as a
DJ for a pirate radio station, Scottish Radio. In the end I decided
not to follow it through and turned down the audition. The
idea of a life literally rocking and rolling off the west coast of
Scotland was not for me. But I did want to appear on TV with
Pete Murray so when we came to record the programmes, I
had a great time. The Scottish Television studios were based
in the old Theatre Royal at the top of Hope Street in the centre
of Glasgow – it has now been converted back to a theatre and
is the home of Scottish Opera. I was dazzled by Pete Murray,

tall and charming, and thrilled to meet Lulu, making her first ever TV appearance with The Luvvers, singing for the first time in public the song which was to be her big international hit, *Shout!*

Enthusiastic though I was, my skills as a judge of hits were non-existent. One of the records our panel reviewed was the newly released *I Can't Get No Satisfaction* sung by The Rolling Stones. I said the song was "appalling". That wasn't a word used much by young Scots then and it seemed to come as a surprise to Mr Murray. I was trying to sound sophisticated, of course. As the record became a worldwide hit almost the next day (and then a rock classic) I felt less and less sophisticated.

Back in Gourock, I began to dislike the day-to-day print shop work, the jobs which involved getting my hands dirty, but generally it was a good time as we were a happy bunch in our brown overalls. There was May Price, who printed the business cards and menus on the hand print machine; there was Tommy, who had the worst toupée in the world – it seemed permanently in danger of slipping off and getting mangled in the print machine; George Bruce and Angus Craig, the other compositors; Willie Stokes, the linotype operator, and Isobel – Issy – who worked in the shop upstairs until she left to work at Balmoral Castle for the Royal Family. She married a ghillie – and came back often to keep us up-to-date with all the royal gossip. A new arrival soon was Stewart Petersen, who later married my cousin Catherine and became editor of the daily Greenock Telegraph, a successful regional paper.

By now the pain of splitting from Tony was beginning to pass. I was getting my act together and starting to enjoy meeting lots of interesting men in Glasgow, all this still a secret from my family at number 47. As far as they were concerned, I had become a great fan of the theatre scene in the city. This gave me a cover for my other activities. One evening I took the train to Glasgow, met someone and spent the night with him. I rang Issy in the shop the next morning to say I'd be late for work and would she pass this on to Mr James. When I arrived mid-morning, Mr James asked: "Where were you?" I stuttered something about staying with friends in Glasgow. "As long as you weren't doing anything that would reflect badly on the newspaper," he replied sternly. I shook my head as if to say, "Oh, no, of course not." But of course I had been. Mr James, was, I suspect, another adult who wondered what I was up to but didn't know where to begin to ask.

The break-up with Tony meant that I was footloose and fancy-free. So I made a bee-line for Glasgow at every available moment. I was 18 and extremely promiscuous. Among a series of casual encounters and relationships which lasted a little longer (but not much), I recall one with a young actor living in a bed-sit in the smart West End of the city. It was a Sunday morning, I was still in bed and he padded across the room to put on a record. "Good morning. It's Sunday morning and this is Mahalia Jackson," came the voice on the record. I've liked that woman's singing ever since.

There was the tall, slim airman who I picked up in full uniform in Glasgow Central railway station – I saw him regularly. He was based at RAF Lossiemouth near Edinburgh but, efficiently, I thought, made the 40-odd mile trip to a hotel room in Glasgow for his private assignations.

There was also the good-looking salesman who I got to know well in the back seat of his car somewhere around Loch Lomond. When we met years later by chance in the travel business, we both found it highly amusing.

I discovered Carlisle through my friend Griff, the Gourock gasman who had introduced the gas fridge to our home in Cove Road. What a liberation! Griff would drive us down for long weekends and we'd stop off in every gay haunt or lay-by – we weren't fussy – on the way. We'd find gay parties without fail. In Carlisle I met Robert, nicknamed "the son of a preacher man". He gave me his father's religious ring, which I wore for a number of months while our "affair" lasted. Mary raised her eyes to heaven when she saw it but again she didn't ask any questions. There was another Carlisle guy whose mother was astonishingly tolerant. She put up with a creaking bed in the next room and cooked us a hearty breakfast in the morning.

Best of all in Carlisle then was Jack, queen of a household rather like the one in the film *Cage aux Folles*. Probably about 60, with dyed bouffant black hair, Jack was the campest creation I'd met to date and his neat, semi-detached house was a gay haven. He welcomed friends from all over the country – and probably the world for all I knew – and about 25 of us would be invited to his frequent parties. There was only one spare bedroom and we'd have to wait our turn to use it. We had to behave well – no unnecessary noise, no disturbing the neighbours – and guests would have to muck in during the day, sharing the chores of making meals, cleaning, dusting and hoovering.

I now had friends as well as lovers and I had great fun.

My weekdays were often enjoyable too. My social life in and around Gourock improved in leaps and bounds as a result of compiling the column. Evenings were spent at the Arts Guild in Greenock where several small amateur acting companies, including The Greenock Players, the George Square Players and our own Gourock Drama Group staged productions which I reviewed for the column.

My reviews were probably rather hackneyed but seemed to go down well. A few phrases certainly had an air of déjà vu: I'd steal them from reviews of other plays in the weekly national Stage newspaper, to which I subscribed. I'd compose my very limited comments then 'grand' it up with phrases pinched from reviews written by their professionals. The local productions were low-budget affairs, of course, by amateur groups but many were to receive national acclaim in Scotland and the Scottish drama community with fine acting coming to the fore.

It was here that I met Bill Bryden, who went on to produce at the National Theatre in London and actor-director Richard Wilson, famous as Victor Meldrew in TV's *One Foot In The Grave*. They were among several talented people who began their careers on my 'patch' and went on to be successful nationally.

My reviews of Gourock Drama Group's productions were the most difficult. If I was critical of anything or anyone on stage – I recall being unimpressed by their production of Terence Rattigan's *Separate Tables* for example, "very turgid" was my phrase – it became a major incident and the talk of the town. Complaining letters and 'phone calls would pour into the paper's office. The Group's members cleverly decided it was better to have me 'on side'. So they invited me to join them. I did not play hard to get. They were, as was every other drama group the length and breadth of the country, desperate to attract young male leads. I seemed to fit the bill.

This was how I met Murray Thompson, the talented local am-dram producer who was heading up the Gourock Drama Group at the time. He was a powerhouse of the amateur theatre in the west of Scotland. I liked and admired him. We had a friendship during my time at the drama group and I'm deeply grateful for all he did in opening up my young and unsophisticated mind to a whole new world of theatre, music, film and art.

He also introduced me to restaurants where I had my first taste of wine. I thought the then ubiquitous Mateus Rosé from Portugal, in the dark, squat bottles, was the cat's whiskers, almost as delicious as the other widely sold wine of the day, the German Liebfraumilch, Blue Nun! My first 'dinner' out, apart from those fish and chip teas with Mum and Dad at The Pierhead Chip Shop and with my 'ten shilling man' in Edinburgh, was in Greenock at the local 'tali' – Italian – café. I can't remember what I ate – probably spaghetti Bolognese – but I remember it seemed wildly exotic. Murray also took me to see many of the great productions at the Glasgow Citizens'. He knew his theatre and was a marvellous mentor. I felt I belonged in this world. I didn't truly belong yet, but one day I knew I would.

As an actor, I wasn't good. I was pretty but pretty awful. I was usually nervous, dreading that I'd forget my lines, a nightmare I still suffer from. But I was keen and I loved our rehearsals at the Old Mission Hall in Cardwell Bay, Gourock. When I was in a production, Jimmy Simpson wrote the reviews and, sometimes, he gave me a good notice. When he didn't mention me, I knew I'd been especially bad. I spent three glorious years in the drama group, playing mostly the juvenile leads badly but happily.

Among many roles, I was the male lead in George Feydeau's *Hotel Paradiso*, taking the outrageously camp Kenneth Williams part to much applause – it came naturally – and the young male lead in Thornton Wilder's *Pullman Car Hiawatha*. I was the policeman in *Midsummer Mink*, a production in which I managed to come in two scenes too early. This mistake happened because I'd been watching in the wings – enthralled as usual by the activity on stage. Now, standing in the wings is not allowed unless you are about to appear, as every true thespian knows. So when the young female lead came up from the dressing rooms, saw me and began walking on stage, pulling me in tow and speaking lines to me, I followed her, not knowing what else to do. Thus it turned out that I revealed the theft of the mink to the unsuspecting audience about an hour and a half too early. I managed to bumble off the other side of the stage but a sweating Murray rushed through the theatre to find out what the hell had happened. I wasn't the most popular actor in the group that evening.

A year or so after splitting with Tony I began seeing Andrew, whom I'd met – yes – in a Glasgow toilet. He came from Kirkintilloch, near Glasgow. This time I'd learnt my lesson and told him the truth about my background. I also told him I was in this amateur dramatics group and he wanted to come and see me perform, asking if he could bring a friend. I said, "Of course". My relationship with Andrew was short and sweet and very informal, with no commitment but, looking back, it was crucial to everything that has happened to me from then on.

15

LOVE AT FIRST SIGHT

THE PRODUCTION I INVITED ANDREW and his mysterious friend to attend was *Hotel Paradiso*. Andrew couldn't possibly have been as keen to see it as I was curious to see who he was bringing backstage. I cringe when I remember that I purposely kept my stage make-up on and stayed in my skimpy underpants – I don't know why. The vanity! But which actor doesn't want to impress his audience?

When I called "Come in" to the knock on the large communal dressing room door in the basement of the Greenock Arts Guild, I was totally unprepared for the person who walked in. Accompanying Andrew was Arthur Whieldon. He was tall, slim, with piercing blue eyes, a big smile and a soft, Northern Ireland accent.

We did little more than exchange 'hellos' and the two of them went off back to Glasgow. Yet it was long enough. I was smitten. The next day Andrew rang up to ask when we'd next meet and I remember saying something to the effect of: "Liked your friend. When you're finished with him, give him my number." He replied, "Yes, I think we are about to finish."

About a week later the 'phone rang in the Simpson's print shop and it was Arthur asking if we could meet some time. I was over the moon to be speaking to him but I couldn't see him for a few days due to work commitments. I always joke that I almost gave him the brush-off because I was due to review Billy Smart's Circus at the Battery Park, Greenock! Instead, I suggested we meet a few days later.

On our first date, Arthur arrived in his smart Morris Oxford, a car not often seen in Gourock in those days. It was so unusual, in fact, that people gathered round to inspect it. I'd told him to meet me at the spot in Cove Road near the good houses where I used to meet Tony. I slipped into the old pattern of lies about my family, almost out of habit, but it wouldn't be long before Arthur rumbled me. We went off to have coffee and drove out of town, parked and had sex. I found out he was 27, seven years older than I.

I knew straight away that I was in love with him; the strange thing was that I also knew it was real love. With Tony it had been, yes, sex and a juvenile infatuation. Love developed much later. With Arthur it was literally love at first sight.

I couldn't wait to see him again. As a trained accountant, Arthur worked for Bass Charrington, the brewers, as a computer systems analyst in their Tennant's Brewery just outside Glasgow city centre. His was mysterious work in the late 1960s, which I couldn't begin to understand. He lived in Queen's Gardens off Byres Road, now a fashionable district of Glasgow. This also impressed me when he told me about it. It was a flat in one of the imposing Victorian merchant's houses in the West End of the city. You entered a magnificent, tiled hall and then descended to the large basement flat he rented, the part of the house that was once the servants' quarters. And, even more exciting, he lived there on his own.

One summer evening, depressed at not being able to contact Arthur, let alone spend the evening with him – this was before the time when everyone had a telephone at home or a mobile – I hitched a lift to Glasgow with Griff, the man who sold Mary the gas appliance.

Griff had gone one better than me in filling his spare time. He'd joined a Glasgow musical society and needed to go back and forth to the city for rehearsals. Occasionally I would be his passenger. While he was learning to tap dance, I'd troll the bars. He was always much more sensible.

Although I hadn't been to his flat yet, I knew Arthur's address. So as soon as Griff dropped me off in the centre of the city, I got on the underground and came up blinking in the evening sun in Byres Road. Mum always said, "James, no matter where you are always use your good Scots tongue to ask directions", and that is exactly what I did. In a few moments, I had found Queen's Gardens and – bingo! – I saw him sitting on a corner ledge of his basement window, watching television alone. I ran to knock on the door. He was surprised and pleased and, from that evening, our relationship really took off. What was different and wonderful was that we became a couple, unafraid to be seen together.

From then on I spent most weekends in Glasgow, staying Friday and Saturday nights and returning late on Sunday to Gourock. We shopped together, walked around together, and occasionally went to restaurants together. The days of pretending to be strangers in public, of lurking in the shadows and only meeting out of town, were gone. I settled down to a life of relative domesticity, cleaning the flat on Saturday morning and washing Arthur's office shirts in the bath – we couldn't afford a washing machine. I'd soak them, rub the collars and cuffs with soap, hang them in the bathroom to dry and spend part of Sunday ironing them for the week ahead.

Within a few weeks, Arthur would drop me off at humble number 47, not the grand house I'd pretended was my home. And he walked up the outside staircase, past the outside lavatory and met Mary and Jimmy. It was probably something of a shock for him because he came from good, solid, middle-class Belfast stock, a family altogether higher up the social scale than mine. But if it was, he didn't show it.

It was clearly not too great a shock because he has supported me morally and emotionally until this day. He has never let me down though I have certainly let him down time and again.

Had I not, at 20, met him in my make-up and underpants in that dressing room at the Arts Guild in Greenock, I would not have had the life I've had, been the man I am. I would have stayed in Gourock and probably have risen to edit The Gourock Times for Jimmy Simpson and perhaps I would have become a grandee of the Gourock Drama Group – who knows...

It would not have been an unsatisfactory life. The life I've had with Arthur, however, has been varied, exciting, constantly challenging and it has made both of us rich in all sorts of ways.

16

ADULTHOOD

IN FEBRUARY 1967 I WAS 21. My parents gave me a one pound premium bond. I hardly expected more because I knew they couldn't have afforded an extravagant gesture and, anyway, I didn't feel I needed presents. I was happy with Arthur, with whom I spent the day in Queen's Gardens. He gave me several small presents and made more than enough fuss of me. In the evening, Murray called round with a bottle of champagne. Arthur prepared a meal – he understands food and has always been content to do the cooking – and we went to the theatre, though I don't remember what we saw. I do remember that I was floating on air: I'd drifted into a fantastic relationship and with it came an intriguing weekend life in a big, busy city – Glasgow, whatever else it was in the sixties, was certainly busy – and I was staying in a spacious and elegant flat, a different world from dear old Cove Road. I had effortlessly compartmentalised my life – with Glasgow came the gay life, with Gourock, the 'straight' life of work. And in both 'lives', I was learning a whole new way of thinking and behaving. I was growing up.

The theatre was still my passion and Arthur was more than willing to accompany me. On Saturdays I'd spend time learning to drive in his Morris Oxford. On Saturday nights we'd try to catch something at the King's Theatre, the Citizens' or the Alhambra where all the big stars of the day regularly appeared on their national tours. It was there at the Alhambra we saw Marlene Dietrich, Frankie Vaughan, Victor Borge, Ken Dodd and Cilla Black among many. Those were the days of the 'Five Past Eight' shows at the Alhambra or the 'Nightly At Seven Thirty' shows at the King's Theatre. Now I might find them cheesy. Then they were wildly glamorous.

If we didn't go to the theatre, we were equally content to stay home, reading or listening to music curled up on Arthur's huge orange, curved seven-seater sofa, a style very 'in' in those days. We'd chosen it together at John Lewis in Argyle Street, Glasgow, our first major purchase, and paid for it – a then breath-taking £140 – "on the drip", in monthly instalments. It was a good investment. When we didn't go out on Saturday nights, we'd snuggle up on it and watch *The Val Doonican Show* on the BBC. High culture indeed!

Arthur too remembers this as a good time. He'd been working in Glasgow for about two years by then, found the work boring and had made few friends in what seemed to be a very 'straight' office and so had little in the way of a social life. When I came along, I like to think I pulled him out of his shell. He stopped blaming Scotland for everything that was lacking in his life and began to enjoy it.

We even talked about buying a little house in one of the new developments outside Glasgow in Milngavie but I hesi-tated. I'd lived all my life as part of a family as council tenants. Anything more complicated than paying a weekly rent made me nervous. Years later, Arthur could tease me that this was the one and only time I hadn't jumped at the prospect of buying a new home and throwing myself into furnishings and fittings. But the mentality of the council house kid I'd always been had not yet worn off.

Soon I'd passed my driving test and had taken to using the Oxford to go back and forth to Gourock. I felt like a king at the wheel. My work was going well and I felt settled.

One Friday evening, however, when I let myself into the Glasgow flat, Arthur was looking grave. "I have some bad news," he said. He took a deep breath. "I'm being transferred to the Mile End offices of Bass Charrington in London."

Arthur remembers that there was only a nanosecond's pause before I said: "Fine, I'll come with you." His long, serious face broke into a smile. I'd meant it. I'd have agreed to go anywhere with him, if he'd wanted me. And luckily he did.

The next thing I knew, he'd been given a date to move and I knew I had to start telling people.

By this time Arthur had changed his car to a white Ford Capri, a fashionable, sporty model with its elongated bonnet and 'winged' back. They were rare in Scotland at the time and probably never seen in Gourock, and again, certainly not around 47 Cove Road. My parents were hugely impressed by the car, so I offered to take them out for a run in it which impressed them even more.

Technically I could make the car move but I wasn't too clear about such things as signals and brakes. Nevertheless, I decided to take them up the Lyle Hill, which overlooks Gourock and the Clyde and on which stands The Cross Of Lorraine, a monument commemorating the arrival of the Free French Forces in Clydeside, a major troop base during the Second World War.

At that time cows wandered freely from field to road and, as I approached one lumbering beast, I assumed – as any townie would – that it would move sharpish. It didn't. I experienced that intense panic as the possibility of a nasty dent in the brand new Capri flashed before me. I'm afraid I wasn't thinking of the pain and suffering of the cow. Mercifully, the car just brushed the animal without injury to either surface and I drove slowly back. My parents by then seemed slightly less impressed.

After the ride, I broke the news to Mary and Jimmy that I was leaving for London. They took it well, although Mum was clearly sad to be losing her "big son". Dad was silent as usual. At work Mr James was similarly sanguine. He said he was sad to see me go but realised I'd probably felt limited in Gourock. He wished me luck and wrote me the most glowing reference. I print it here (see opposite) not because I deserved his praise but because it shows the open and thoughtful person James Simpson, my first hero, was.

There were no leaving parties, no inquests. While Arthur arranged for what little furniture he possessed to go into storage, I simply gathered up my few clothes and books. I left my Dansette record player and records with my sister. I owned nothing else.

It was early summer 1969 and the big gamble was about to be taken. Arthur collected me and my bag of clothes from number 47 in his Ford Capri and drove slowly away from Cove Road; Mum standing waving at the end of the close, Dad 'hinging oot the windae', as always, waving goodbye.

It's only now that I think about what must have gone through my parents' minds as I sped off to London from Cove Road that day. Their son, just 23, off to faraway London, a city neither of them had ever visited, the equivalent of today's young people setting off 'travelling' to India or China. But I was departing with a man seven years older whom they'd met only a couple of times and of whom they knew little. They had no telephone for me to call and tell them how I was and where

THE GOUROCK TIMES

The Weekly Newspaper for Gourock and District and Lower Renfrewshire

Telephone: 31432   STD · 0GR-5-31432   ESTABLISHED 1915

Publishers: J & R. SIMPSON

Member of The
Scottish   Partners: Mary McK. Simpson
Newspaper   James C. Simpson, J.P.
Proprietors'   Printing and Publishing Office—
Association
                                                    60 Kempock Street,

                                                    Gourock, Renfrewshire.

Testimonial in favour of   24th June, 1969
JAMES DUNN, Gourock.

In the seven years that James Dunn has been employed in this
printing office he has grown in stature from schoolboy to man and in
the process has developed confidence, respect, courtesy, efficiency
ability to control and direct orders and staff.   He has completed
an apprenticeship in the caseroom as a hand compositor and his
standard of work has been commendable and always in good style
and taste.

Soon after assimilating the atmosphere of a small newspaper
office and all that goes on around, he ventured into print with
occasional short contributions.   In time his journalistic efforts
on films, folk, drama, pop scene--in fact anything topical--stretched
to a weekly column and in the past three years to a weekly double
column feature with illustrations and layout, all the make-up being
done personally.   Due to the rather conservative and in some cases
restricted outlook of this newspaper and the folk it serves, he may
not have been able to utilise his writing talents to the full extent.

His essay into the realms of amateur drama as critic and actor,
and his leading parts in the local Drama Group productions in past
years have earned for him much respect and praise.

He has always conducted himself at work in a manner beyond
reproach, and his attention to dress, punctuality, civility and loyalty
to the firm have not gone unnoticed.

While realising that the limitations of a small county
newspaper and commercial printing office such as this one cannot
continue indefinitely to hold the interest of an active young man
with a bright personality and ambition to succeed, we are very sorry
to lose his services.   We wish him every happiness and look forward
to hearing of his success in the future, whether it be with a composing
stick, typewriter, microphone and tape-recorder or in front of the
TV cameras.   We hope other employers will find as much pleasure
in working with him as we have had these past seven years.

                              Jas. C. Simpson
                                 (Partner)
                        Editor and Works Manager

I was staying. There was no e-mail. Yet they accepted my wishes, let go and wished us luck. They were simple people but very wise ones.

In the front passenger seat as we drove away, I quietly cried until we reached Scott's Shipyard in Greenock about 15 minutes' drive away – it's funny how you remember some instances with pin-sharp clarity – and then I tried to compose myself. Arthur was clearly worried about the effect on me of leaving my home, my Mum and Dad and, yes, Scotland. "What have you done?" he muttered, as we headed south.

17

ON THE FLOOR IN STREATHAM

I KNEW WHAT I HAD DONE. I had decided to leave all that I had in life, such as it was then, my family, my work, my little Scottish world and put my trust in Arthur's plans, such as they were. That was enough for me. Though I didn't know what was going to happen, something told me it was the right thing to do. I didn't know then that I would never yearn to return to Gourock. I forgot it almost as soon as my tears dried. I knew only that a bed on a floor in a south London flat awaited me.

I don't remember how long the drive took but, after a brief stop at Jack's place in Carlisle, I know I drove the final stretch of the M1 motorway into London in the Capri. I felt adult and excited. I'd been to London on a train before but driving, I was seeing it properly for the first time. As we made our way through the north London suburbs to the centre, I was amazed at the size of the city, so many people, so much activity, so many places to explore. The slums, the traffic, the ugly main roads didn't escape my notice. Nor did they put me off. I loved the contrasts, the variety, those unexpected patches of greenery. I took to London instantly and that feeling has never stopped. Since 1967 I've lived in many towns and villages but London is the only place where I really feel at home, feel I belong. I cannot do without a regular 'fix' of the place.

We were due to stay at the flat in Streatham, south London, of Ralph Rhodes, a friend Arthur had met in a bar in Manchester. He had generously offered his floor should Arthur ever need it. Thanks to Arthur's map reading we arrived at Ralph's address, a Victorian building (now a petrol station) on the south-west corner of Streatham Common. The rooms of his ground floor flat were large, the floor hard, but we were very grateful. Fearful of outstaying our welcome, we left after a couple of weeks when two other generous friends of Ralph's, Peter Stokes and David Braidley, offered us the spare room of their comfortable house in Bromley, south London.

While Arthur began his new job – it turned out he had to travel to Tottenham in north London each day – I set out to find work. It didn't occur to me to sign on for the dole and I don't know if I'd have been eligible. But luckily, in the 1960s, if you were enterprising enough to buy the London evening papers, the Evening Standard and the now defunct Evening News, and turn to the back pages, jobs weren't hard to find. Good jobs were perhaps as rare as they are now but straight-forward ones, which brought in that then much-needed commodity – money – were relatively plentiful.

I fixed three job interviews in those first few days. One was a book-selling job which turned out to be flogging sets of the Encyclopaedia Britannica door to door. I was naïve enough never to have heard of this soul-destroying work but merci-fully something inside me told me to get up and leave halfway through the group interviewing process. The second was with a firm called F.J. Parsons, printers and publishers, located in the Adelphi Buildings, once a top London hotel, in John Adam Street, just off The Strand. They published a number of steadily successful trade magazines; most notably Travel Trade Gazette, the weekly bible of the travel industry. When I went to see them I found they were looking for trainee journalists. Well, I was certainly a trainee but whether I was a journalist proper was yet to be established. I was interviewed by "Mr Derek", one of the Parsons family and head of the company. I was completely terrified during the interview but somehow I muddled my way through and, as I walked down the Strand afterwards, I thought I'd never hear from him again.

The third was a job in a theatrical agency in Curzon Street, Mayfair. As I was, by now, mad about show business, I had high hopes here. They asked me at the interview if I thought I could handle celebrities and I said, absurdly, I thought I could because of my experience in amateur dramatics! Even now I remember that long pitiful look and sad smile that they gave me. During the interview, three actors – whose faces I vaguely knew from television – wafted in and out of the offices. I imagined myself exchanging showbiz gossip with them, discussing roles, fixing press interviews, arguing with producers on their behalf. The possibilities were bewitching. My days of mingling with big stars had begun – or so I hoped.

By the time I got home, my hopes had begun to fade. What could I, a naïve boy from Scotland contribute to a sophisticated artists' agency in snooty Mayfair? A few days later I received a letter. Against all expectations I was offered the job. I couldn't wait for Arthur to make his way back from Tottenham to tell him! But he had his own views as to what my future career should be.

18

GEORGE – AND THE WORLD

WHEN I STARTED WORK FOR F.J. Parsons in the Adelphi Buildings in the autumn of 1969, I was completely overwhelmed. I had never worked in a large office, had no real administrative or journalistic experience, couldn't type, had no shorthand and knew nothing about the travel business in which Parsons specialised. I had no academic qualifications and didn't yet know my way around this huge city, although I was exploring a little more of it every day. At 23, I didn't have much of a clue about anything. All I knew, for certain, was that F. J. Parsons and I had each just made a massive mistake.

Strangely, I didn't blame Arthur although it was he who'd said: "Take the Parsons job." Mr James' glowing reference had doubtless helped me get it and the offer of it came in the post immediately after the one from the theatrical agents.

Arthur, who has always disliked (that's putting it mildly) what he sees as the falseness of show business and celebrities, told me when I asked him for advice that, in his view, it was possible I'd end up a successful impresario if I accepted the job for the theatrical agency. It was also possible I'd spend the next ten years as a glorified office boy and the nearest I'd get to the stars would be making their tea. He said the travel industry job sounded solid and reliable and actually more interesting. It was an industry that seemed, literally, to be taking off and I should get in on it. This is why I'd turned down

Mayfair and the stars. Instead, though I didn't realise it at the time, I'd headed for The World.

At F. J. Parsons, I had probably four bosses. After "Mr Derek" there was Stephen Roe, a devastatingly handsome young man and the editor of the then newly-launched Travel Trade Gazette International, sister paper of the successful UK version, which was taking the company into the emerging European travel trade market. He was one of their rising stars. The second was Mike Annetts, in charge of the successful UK Travel Trade Gazette or TTG as everyone in the industry called it. The third was group editor George Matthews, who oversaw other magazines including Recreation Manager, a monthly for managers of company sports clubs – also an emerging market, and Conferences and Exhibitions, for those involved in the fledgling meetings industry.

I liked George, who'd grown up in Folkestone, Kent, was then in his thirties and straight in every way. And he must have found something likeable in me as, over the following year, he and Stephen and the others were to have every reason to fire me but didn't. I'd sit for hours at my typewriter trying and failing to get my head around the travel business and the relationships between the different tour operators, trade bodies, commission rates and the complicated politics of the burgeoning industry that was the travel business in the early seventies. I was hopeless. Lost. Way out of my depth.

At lunchtimes I'd buy a sandwich in Villiers Street, down beside Charing Cross railway station, and walk across to the Embankment by the Thames, sit on a seat opposite the Royal Festival Hall, eat my snack and feel sorry for myself. I was dazzled by London and loved being with Arthur but I felt I just couldn't cut it as a trade journalist or any other kind of journalist, come to that. Occasionally I'd go to the nearby

Bulldog pub in John Adam Street with the other editorial boys but, easy going as they were, I felt I simply didn't fit in. I was gay for one thing – so I didn't talk about sex, unworldly and Scottish for another and the only things I could talk about with enthusiasm were current productions in West End theatres, which drew little or no response. But I listened, and I guess I didn't annoy them, and gradually I began to feel I was accepted. All I needed now was to get my feet under the table as far as the job was concerned, manage to get my fingers around the typewriter and my head around the new and rapidly expanding travel industry.

Those were the days when, it seemed, travel companies' budgets for entertaining, advertising and promotions were virtually unlimited. Journalists were courted by this young industry because they could deliver "free" editorial space as opposed to paid-for advertising space. People buy newspapers and magazines to read articles, not to study the adverts. That's what the PR industry tries to tell us anyway, but, ironically, without the money collected from advertising, of course, the publications wouldn't survive.

At any rate, journalists from TTG were wooed and fêted in pubs and restaurants all around The Strand in the seventies just as they are today. Editors were invited to lunch at The Savoy, a hop and skip from The Adelphi. Mere scribes were lured to lunch in the many other restaurants and pubs, many in what was soon to become the chic quarter of Covent Garden. For me, meantime, it was a sandwich by the Thames.

g pub in John Adam Street with the other editorial boys
sy going as they were, I felt I simply didn't fit in. I was
r one thing – so I didn't talk about sex, unworldly and
h for another and the only things I could talk about with
iasm were current productions in West End theatres,
drew little or no response. But I listened, and I guess
't annoy them, and gradually I began to feel I was
ed. All I needed now was to get my feet under the table
as the job was concerned, manage to get my fingers
d the typewriter and my head around the new and
y expanding travel industry.

ose were the days when, it seemed, travel companies'
ts for entertaining, advertising and promotions were
ly unlimited. Journalists were courted by this young
ry because they could deliver "free" editorial space as
ed to paid-for advertising space. People buy newspa-
nd magazines to read articles, not to study the adverts.
what the PR industry tries to tell us anyway, but, iron-
without the money collected from advertising, of
e, the publications wouldn't survive.

any rate, journalists from TTG were wooed and fêted
s and restaurants all around The Strand in the seven-
st as they are today. Editors were invited to lunch at The
, a hop and skip from The Adelphi. Mere scribes were
o lunch in the many other restaurants and pubs, many
t was soon to become the chic quarter of Covent Garden.
e, meantime, it was a sandwich by the Thames.

proper was yet to be established. I was interviewed by "Mr Derek", one of the Parsons family and head of the company. I was completely terrified during the interview but somehow I muddled my way through and, as I walked down the Strand afterwards, I thought I'd never hear from him again.

The third was a job in a theatrical agency in Curzon Street, Mayfair. As I was, by now, mad about show business, I had high hopes here. They asked me at the interview if I thought I could handle celebrities and I said, absurdly, I thought I could because of my experience in amateur dramatics! Even now I remember that long pitiful look and sad smile that they gave me. During the interview, three actors – whose faces I vaguely knew from television – wafted in and out of the offices. I imagined myself exchanging showbiz gossip with them, discussing roles, fixing press interviews, arguing with producers on their behalf. The possibilities were bewitching. My days of mingling with big stars had begun – or so I hoped.

By the time I got home, my hopes had begun to fade. What could I, a naïve boy from Scotland contribute to a sophisticated artists' agency in snooty Mayfair? A few days later I received a letter. Against all expectations I was offered the job. I couldn't wait for Arthur to make his way back from Tottenham to tell him! But he had his own views as to what my future career should be.

18

GEORGE – AND THE WORLD

WHEN I STARTED WORK FOR F.J. Parsons in the Adelphi Buildings in the autumn of 1969, I was completely over-whelmed. I had never worked in a large office, had no real administrative or journalistic experience, couldn't type, had no shorthand and knew nothing about the travel business in which Parsons specialised. I had no academic qualifications and didn't yet know my way around this huge city, although I was exploring a little more of it every day. At 23, I didn't have much of a clue about anything. All I knew, for certain, was that F. J. Parsons and I had each just made a massive mistake.

Strangely, I didn't blame Arthur although it was he who'd said: "Take the Parsons job." Mr James' glowing reference had doubtless helped me get it and the offer of it came in the post immediately after the one from the theatrical agents.

Arthur, who has always disliked (that's putting it mildly) what he sees as the falseness of show business and celebri-ties, told me when I asked him for advice that, in his view, it was possible I'd end up a successful impresario if I accepted the job for the theatrical agency. It was also possible I'd spend the next ten years as a glorified office boy and the nearest I'd get to the stars would be making their tea. He said the travel industry job sounded solid and reliable and actually more inter-esting. It was an industry that seemed, literally, to be taking off and I should get in on it. This is why I'd turned down

Mayfair and the stars. Instead, though I didn'[t] time, I'd headed for The World.

At F. J. Parsons, I had probably four bo[ ] Derek" there was Stephen Roe, a devastati[ ] young man and the editor of the then newly-[ ] Trade Gazette International, sister paper of t[he] version, which was taking the company in[ ] European travel trade market. He was one of[ ] The second was Mike Annetts, in charge of t[ ] Travel Trade Gazette or TTG as everyone in t[he] it. The third was group editor George Matthe[ ] other magazines including Recreation Mana[ ] managers of company sports clubs – also an[ ] and Conferences and Exhibitions, for thos[e] fledgling meetings industry.

I liked George, who'd grown up in Folk[ ] then in his thirties and straight in every [ ] have found something likeable in me as, [ ] year, he and Stephen and the others were t[o] to fire me but didn't. I'd sit for hours at m[y] and failing to get my head around the trav[ ] relationships between the different tou[ ] bodies, commission rates and the compli[ ] burgeoning industry that was the travel b[ ] seventies. I was hopeless. Lost. Way out [ ]

At lunchtimes I'd buy a sandwich in [ ] beside Charing Cross railway station, an[ ] Embankment by the Thames, sit on a sea[ ] Festival Hall, eat my snack and feel so[ ] dazzled by London and loved being wi[ ] just couldn't cut it as a trade journalist[ ] journalist, come to that. Occasionally [ ]

19

TRAVEL – FIRST STEPS

PRESS TRIPS WERE A MAJOR PART of this media-wooing process. I've always hated the word 'trip' – it smacks of the seaside. So let's call them press visits or (as some pompous PRs prefer) Media Familiarisation Visits. The events would be "hosted" in every detail. Every cost, of transfers, drinks, food, transport, airfares, hotel accommodation – you name it – was included and the system was, and still is, much abused. A group of specialist writers would be put together by invitation or tele-phone contact – in the seventies it was usually by a formal letter. In the TTG offices the mail was eagerly awaited as each morning in would flood a number of requests to the editor to send a journalist somewhere in the world.

Journalists were also learning that it wasn't necessary to wait to be invited. In those days, it was much easier than it is now to obtain, for example, free tickets to fly, well, anywhere. The fabulous "freebie" days of the travel industry in the seventies and eighties were just starting off and one call to an airline would usually result in tickets being sent round by hand almost before the telephone receiver was replaced. The same applied to hotel rooms and car hire.

And so it was that this stumbling and inexperienced would-be journalist was sent on his first press visit. No doubt my bosses were desperate for me to learn the ropes or perhaps just to get me out of the office. Anyway, I am forever grateful because, at the point where I felt I should quit, this first writing assignment had the effect of waking me up and slapping me in the face with the news that this was a fabulous industry to be in. Something in my head was saying, "Pay attention, Dunn. You're here. Don't muck it up. Get your act together and they'll let you stay."

I was sent, all expenses paid, naturally, to a travel agents' conference in Lake Lucerne, Switzerland. Wow! It seemed that it was only yesterday I'd been resting on my broom, squinting at the Clyde through a grimy window in Simpson's basement print room. Now I was sitting on the balcony of my suite – a suite! – in a five-star hotel overlooking this exquisite lake, writing a postcard to Arthur. I couldn't believe my luck, I told him. I could order drinks, meals, taxis. There was nothing to pay. I just signed a chitty. My job was simply to attend the conference and write a short report on the main issues raised when I got back. Even I could do that. Just.

Freeloading on this scale was a truly unreal world to me. But I made it my reality very quickly. Majorca with Thomson's Holidays, the big tour operator of the day, was my second group visit, again reporting on a travel agents' conference. Majorca was not the island it is today. In the early seventies, the now teeming resort of Magaluf was a tiny fishing village; Palma, the capital city, had no built-up suburbs and the motorway which runs in front of the imposing Gothic cathedral was just being built on land reclaimed from the beach.

With the other journalists, I participated in the regulation meetings with tourism ministers, did the compulsory tour of the island, sampled restaurants and bars and gathered enough material for a few newsy pieces and page leads in Travel Trade Gazette. I loved everything about Majorca and, on my return, wrote glowing pieces on the agents' event and the island – and they were published.

Me looking bemused – I never knew what to do with a football...

A room with a view. From my bedroom window in Cove Road, Gourock. I watched the American sailors from here...

With my sister and Dad and his 'bunnit' on the promenade at Gourock

Mum and Dad

With Mum and sister in Rothesay

Half-brother Sinclair soon after he joined the RAF in Doncaster

Granny Dunn with Uncle Peter – I had my suspicions about him...

(Below) Granny Gray – Molly – Mum called her 'an old bugger'!

Dad at the till

Gourock High School – I'm middle row left

Mum and me and the 'ootside' stairs... the toilet is on the right

With my Dansette record player

21 today!

*That's me, back right, with members of the Gourock Drama Group
circa 1968*

Mr James with the staff of The Gourock Times

With my weekly entertainment column in The Gourock Times

photo: George Young

PHEW! After five years, 400 columns, 300,000 words (strung together they'd measure several miles) how you poor people have suffered ... this is the last

jIm dunn

COLUMN

and who said "thank heavens"!

(K.O.) For "Kids Only" At The Regal In July

NLESS YOU'RE prepared to view once more the escapades of those tin-:lled screen heroes of way back—among them Laurel and Hardy, Sinbad, nd Tarzan—I'd advise you to stay clear of Ron Tannahill country, up he Regal way in July.

As next month is "Kids Only" ime. Well, adults just might be idmitted accompanied by a child, of course. And I'm not complaining. All too often cinema progammes today are aimed at the adult popu-lace, the result being that many children get an opportunity to view films not altogether suitable.

"The Belles of St. Trinians" ring out (once more) on the 7th with Alas-tair Sim and Joyce Grenfell on the ropes, Kerwin Mathews makes "The 7th Voyage of Sinbad"—it must at least be the eighth! soon after, "Tar-zan and Jungle Boy" also swing down from their tree-house next month and that funny pair, Laurel and Hardy, can be seen in two of their classics, "Pack Up Your Troubles" and "Jailbirds."

Says manager Ron, "July is essen-tially school holiday month, and if the weather were good, we would not be doing much business at all· if it's bad, however, the children will have somewhere to go, to keep them occupied."

Striking a note of freshness among those ancient reels are Mr Fred

Astaire and Miss Petula Clark in "Finian's Rainbow" on the 14th—a film worth seeing, as is "The Assassination Bureau" with Dianna Rigg and Oliver Reed in this spy-tale with a twist—as they say.

REVEALED AT LAST —THE CULPRIT!

— M E —

pic. George Young

BEING CHOKED! —The Price of Fame?

IT'S ALL so appropriate. One of the newest groups on the Gourock pop scene, "Shade," become from next Saturday the resident group at the newest pop placed for youngsters, Cragburn's Saturday afternoon Cafe session from 2 to 4.30 p.m.

The reason simply is that the boys, Roddy Brown (lead guitarist), Stuart Lees (rhythm guitar), "Hairy" Henry Steele (bass guitar) and vocalist John Lyons (sax) and Jim Stirling (drums) are all gaining a massive following, Because

THE POINT IS, I look so intelligent, don't I, to have been responsible for 60 months of irrelevancies! Anyway dear readers, I shall refrain from using that old cliche about "all four in my case it is so

My last column in The Gourock Times

122

With actress Judy Geeson at a film screening in the 1960s

Arthur and me on an early holiday to Hydra, Greece

20

THE CUP OF COFFEE THAT CHANGED IT ALL

MIRACULOUSLY, I SEEMED TO BE holding on to my job. I was even beginning to relax and enjoy going to work. But when George Matthews sidled up to my desk and suggested a coffee, a chill went through me. Surely I'd been mistaken in thinking I'd started to improve. Surely I'd been rumbled. Surely I was to be fired.

It turned out to be the most important cup of coffee I have ever drunk. In fact if George hadn't taken me off for a break at Lyons Corner House in the Strand next to Charing Cross station, "to discuss an idea", as he put it, I think, no, I'm convinced, I would soon have been unemployed.

George's brainwave, he explained, was to start a news agency specialising in the travel industry. I wore a listening face, nodded and smiled but I hadn't an inkling of what he was suggesting. The door to a future in a new world of spin and PR, in press liaison and public relations, was being opened for me with a flourish and I couldn't even recognise it. In fact, George's identification of a gap in the expanding world of tourism for media and press advice, which he was convinced we could fill, was a stroke of genius. New tour operators were springing up, airlines were expanding and hotels were opening and the people running them had little idea of how to get their message across to the media, how to distinguish their products from others, how to put together smart brochures and interact with the travel industry as a whole. George's new venture, to be called Travel Press Service – TPS – would know and it would make money from this knowledge. The journalists – George and I – me! – would advise companies in the travel business on the strange art of journalism and how to capitalise on the media to increase the awareness of their company.

Slowly it dawned on me that George was asking me to join him. It took so long because I couldn't stop thinking that George didn't need this and certainly didn't need me. He was brilliant at his job, wonderfully adept at dealing with chief executives, knew the ins and outs of the media world and he could have made a success in any part of the PR industry he chose. There were many other PR consultants operating at the time but few in the small-budget travel industry. Those who spring to mind were Jeff Rayner, Stuart Hulse and Stephen Danos – all well established in their own way in the travel PR business. So they would be our competition. George's plan was bold but he was determined to make a proper business out of it.

The deal as far as I was concerned was that I would be employed at TPS as a 'journalist-gofer' and I would also help produce the magazine Recreation Manager, which George was to take with him to this new TPS operation and edit under contract to F.J. Parsons. This specialist publication, subscribed to by managers of company leisure clubs, carried editorial on sports equipment, artificial sports surfaces, sports pavilion facilities and new leisure products of interest to companies – topics about which, of course, I knew a great deal......! I was being taken out of the frying pan into the fire. I knew next to nothing about journalism, the PR world or the travel industry but I was supposed to know a lot. And now I was supposed to know a lot about sports and social clubs! Me, the boy who no one ever wanted on his team, who couldn't kick a ball to save his life and who had never tried to join a social club because he doubted gay boys ever fitted in! Now I was being asked to edit an important monthly magazine for yet another baffling new industry!

George had even researched TPS's possible offices, he told me, and found three tiny rooms on the first floor above a sandwich shop at 131 Fleet Street where the aroma of toasted bacon sandwiches would be with us from now on. We were squashed nicely between The Daily Telegraph on one side and the glorious art deco building which then housed The Daily Express and The Sunday Express on the other so, from the start, we were going to be smack-bang in the middle of media-land. George had certainly thought it through.

He'd also sounded out Kay Miller to become part of the team. Kay worked with Robin Dewhurst, travel writer of the high circulation Sunday People newspaper who would go on to become a successful scriptwriter for Thames Television's long-running travel show, *Wish You Were Here*. George had fixed up a deal for him and Kay to answer the numerous holiday enquiry letters which The People received from readers, at 50 pence for every answer. Hardly high finance but this work became TPS's first contract.

Kay was to become a major part of our team. Petite and a lady of a certain age, she was to be George's secretary and assistant first and foremost. She was also to be 'office mother' and lastly she was to be in charge of everything from petty cash to pencils to supplying vitamin pills to us when she thought we looked peaky. She turned out to be immensely efficient and we couldn't have operated so smoothly in those early days without her.

Even though I was still vague about what TPS would do, I knew I wanted to take up the challenge and sped home that evening to relay to Arthur what George was proposing. Arthur backed me because, he said, it sounded enterprising. So I said 'yes' to George and gave in my notice at F.J. Parsons.

My new salary was fixed at £1,500 a year. So, on April 1st 1970, I turned up in Fleet Street ready to enter the wonderful world of public relations or press liaison as we also called it. If someone had asked me at the time to define 'public relations' I would have gone quiet. If someone had asked me how I planned to put together Recreation Manager for the printers in time for its monthly publication date, I would have had to change the subject. My learning process in PR and publishing was about to begin. George was going to have to be the teacher and I was going to have to learn fast.

We moved into our three rooms at 131 Fleet Street on a five-year lease in the early summer of 1970 and a 'sitting tenant' greeted us on the first day. He was Don Barlin, a photographer, who rented a desk and a telephone line in one corner of the small centre room, soon to become the reception. Don would become our resident 'snapper' who took most of the photographs at our press conferences over the following years. As our service got underway, these were generally held close to Fleet Street, then the centre for almost all the UK national, regional and international media. We would set up our conferences at two clubs at either end of Fleet Street, The Golf Club near Ludgate Circus and the Wig and Pen Club, where Fleet Street becomes The Strand, traditionally-styled and so called because its customers were from newspapers and from the legal world operating in the Law Courts opposite and the clusters of legal chambers in the area. Alternatively, we would book the elegant Waldorf Hotel in the Aldwych, the crescent above the west end of Fleet Street. Don would also be on duty at our increasingly frequent photo calls fixed all over London for our clients. It would be up to us to create a "fun" photograph of a client holding his latest brochure. TTG was our target and the photo would be used only if it were "lively" and if pretty girls in short skirts were in it. None of this was easy. Don's ability to think up the poses and keep everyone happy while taking the pictures was crucial.

Kay and the other girls who came to work for us found Don slightly spooky. He wore brown suede shoes, cavalry twill trousers and a blazer which, even then, seemed old-fashioned. But Don was reliable, professional and on hand – so he invariably got the job and became part of the 'family'.

While I was struggling to master magazine production, with Kay valiantly doing the typing for me, George was out and about acquiring several new contracts to kick-start our young PR business into action. One was with The Galleon World Travel Association, a union-based tour operator. Another, about which we were both excited, was with Cosmos Holidays, based in Bromley, one of the UK's top tour operators, then flying more than half a million people to holidays in the sun, mostly in Spain. Our brief was to handle the entire news output of this very aggressive company in what was becoming an increasingly cut-throat business. It may have been all nice and fluffy up front with great photographs of lovely family holidays in the sun at cheap prices but, behind the scenes, daggers were drawn – salesman to salesman, marketing man to marketing man. The competition was fierce to say the least and, as their mouthpiece, we were more and more in the front line.

We were to take care of day-to-day media inquiries, write press releases, organise individual press visits, take groups of media around, set up one-to-one meetings with senior company executives and create regular news stories. All this on a retainer fee of £3,000 a year and under the direction of their Marketing Director, Stevenson Pugh, a former Fleet Street journalist who had moved in-house at Cosmos and who terrified the life out of me.

Steve was a hard-nosed reporter turned Marketing Director, the sort who takes no prisoners and does not suffer fools gladly. He had no time for me, no doubt quickly judging me a bit of a wally. He made it clear he preferred to deal with George – to my great relief.

A third client was Rankin Khun, then a small, upmarket, long-haul travel company quietly opening up holidays in Hong Kong and points East. We also launched our Trade Publishing Service, a division set up to produce trade magazines. Among our early contracts, along with Recreation Manager, was Victoria Wine News for the High Street wine shop chain. As my knowledge of what to drink began and ended with Mateus Rosé, I could hardly have claimed to be a wine buff. Fortunately, this was a magazine for the chain's staff and what I needed to do was sharpen up copy and pick photographs to make an interesting read. And, slowly, I was getting the hang of the process.

It all sounded highly professional but, alas, it was no such thing. What it was, though, was fun! I couldn't wait to get into Fleet Street each day and we all happily stayed on late into the evenings. We all felt we were at the beginning of something. We weren't sure what but we sensed the business was going places and that eventually we, not our clients, would say where.

My job was a mix of whatever those contracts threw up from day-to-day and also to put together the unglamorous-sounding Recreation Manager, a lucrative and much-needed contract for us at the time. A Recreation Manager, I found out, ran the sports and social clubs for offices and factories throughout the country. They wanted the latest news on tennis court materials, bowling greens and football pitches, flood-lighting, sports seating and the whole area of "leisure". One of my first tasks was to meet a few of them to try to under-stand their work and their priorities. So off I trundled to factories such as Bryant and May's warehouse in the East End, buildings now converted into fashionable loft apartments.

The magazine may not have been The Stage, but I grew to love Recreation Manager and it was here that I finally got to grips with magazine journalism and production. We gath-ered copy from press releases and several regular contributors including Greville Janner MP, who wrote on legal matters. I'd feared at the start that we wouldn't have enough material to fill the magazine but we were inundated with features from all corners of an expanding leisure market. Each month, before travelling to Folkestone where the magazine was printed, I would sort and rewrite copy, lay out pages and scan in photo-graphs using the old method of covering them with thick tracing paper. I made lots of mistakes but the kind and patient Folkestone printers helped me out.

Over the next few months, George taught me to write in a short, sharp, succinct way; to construct press releases using three-line paragraphs and punchy headlines to attract the busy journalist; he helped me begin a media contact list and schooled me in talking to journalists. That was a short lesson. "Just be yourself," he told me, "and don't tell them anything you wouldn't be happy to see in print." It's a maxim I've held on to ever since, though I haven't always obeyed it. George told me: "What journalists want are the facts, just the facts, to the point, typed on one side of paper, so they can take the story forward. They want to speak to someone from the company or organisation concerned whom they can quote and who'll talk sensibly on that subject. And because journalists work on the move, they need a direct 'phone number and preferably a home number too. And most importantly, because they have deadlines to meet, they want it fast." That advice holds good today. I also had to learn to put a magazine together. My until then underused brain was being forced into action.

This was the beginning of the seventies. The media wasn't as leisure-orientated as it is today. Travel was covered in daily newspapers almost as an afterthought, to bring in a little advertising revenue. The PR industry was young; it wasn't socially acceptable to watch television during the daytime, breakfast TV had not yet started and round-the-clock radio broadcasting was a strange, almost dangerous concept. The idea of business executives being "disturbed" out of working hours in their homes by journalists or, indeed, a humble PR man was unheard of. So the launching of a PR newsroom dealing specifically with the leisure industry, staffed by young journalists with an aggressive style who were to be available 24 hours a day was, to many, a slightly alarming development.

One morning, George turned up in Fleet Street and announced that he had obtained a small contract for us to supply a weekly show business column to one of the many newspapers then delivered free to your door. This one was in south London and George, with a beam, said, "This is ideal for you, Jim." And so it was. I grabbed the opportunity to meet many of the stars of the day for coffee – among them Derek Nimmo, Brian Rix and Moira Lister – all then starring in West End productions. Also on the interview list was TV comedy actor Reg Varney and Peter Noone, lead singer with the then big name group Herman's Hermits.

With me feeling more settled and Arthur finding his work more challenging than in Glasgow, we made a joint decision to stop staying with friends. We loved 'camping up' with friends but trying to sleep on their floors was another matter. One weekend we sat in deckchairs in St James' Park, off The Mall, discussing our practically non-existent finances and agonising over whether we could afford the princely sum of £10 a week to rent a large flat at 80 The High, Streatham High Road, London SW16. It seemed exorbitantly expensive and would mean signing a proper three-year lease. True, the flat was magnificent with a large drawing room, dining room, two bedrooms, large kitchen and bathroom and the rent included central heating and hot water, a parking space for the Capri and use of the block's outdoor heated swimming pool. This was a palace by the standards of most rented accommodation in London and certainly grander than any place I had lived in before. We could have found something smaller.

Yet despite feeling nervous, we decided to go for it. It meant obtaining special permission from the letting agent for two males to take the lease. This may sound quaint now, but this was before the gay liberation movement had really taken off properly in the UK and it was a bold step. We succeeded.

Arthur summoned his furniture out of storage in Glasgow, what little there was of it. We set about decorating the rooms and Arthur's big orange sofa was re-assembled. In a few weeks, 80 The High became our first joint home. In Scotland I had to contend with the running damp on my bedroom wall. Here in glamorous south London, all I had to do was to evict a few hundred cockroaches who would creep up the kitchen pipes while we were at work during the day and be sitting, staring at us, when we came home in the early evening. We stayed there happily with, thankfully, a declining cockroach population, for the next three years.

As TPS was gathering business and its name was getting around, George continued to impress me as a journalist and PR. To keep his finger on the pulse, as well as to supplement his salary, he still worked occasional journalistic shifts on national newspapers. I began to notice however that he was less adept at handling people, at office procedures and communicating with the rest of the team and also at raising and keeping money. He would employ people to do things without working out if we could pay them or exactly what they would do. He'd hand me my monthly cheque but then tell me not to bank it. Kay got the same treatment. It was obvious, even to me, that the business was under-funded. George had invested his time and professionalism in TPS but it just wasn't enough.

The main problem, I slowly began to see, was that George had imagined doing more than just offering PR advice. He had envisaged getting stories out of his clients and selling them to newspapers. However, the concept was flawed because the newspapers would soon find out that these travel companies were TPS clients and refuse to pay for what could be seen as advertising plugs. The few stories that we did sell would not pay our wages: they made us tens of pounds and not a lot more.

With some trepidation, I suggested to George that we needed help with the financial side of the operation. So I introduced him to an accountant I knew: Arthur. To my great relief and, I suspect, to George's, the two got on well and George was very keen for Arthur to undertake all the financial aspects of the business during his free time in the evenings and at weekends when he wasn't working for Bass Charrington. Arthur had now to try to make sense of 'George's Great Idea' from a financial perspective and, to his mind, it meant going back to the beginning – virtually starting again as a PR consultancy pure and simple and painstakingly sorting out all the paperwork. And that's what we did. Arthur began sending out hand-written bills regularly and slowly bringing the books up-to-date. But he quickly determined that if the salary cheques given to me, Kay and others who were joining us were to stop bouncing, big changes needed to be made.

Saturday afternoon and all day Sunday were designated the 'TPS Bill Days'. Arthur would sit at his desk at home and hand-write all the accounts for clients on blue duplication books. As I hoovered and dusted, his shouted questions would rain down on me: "How many 'phone calls did you make last week?" "How many sheets of paper did you use?" "How many stamps did we need to send that press release?"

Arthur told George in no uncertain terms that if TPS were to become viable, the clients had to be charged the going rate for our services. He said we couldn't and shouldn't rely on newspapers to make our money. George was adamant that companies, at least the sort of companies he was talking to, would not agree to pay us proper monthly fees, simply because they wouldn't understand the concept of paying for a press and PR service. Yet other PR companies were up and running doing just that.

With hindsight, I can now understand George's reluctance. He just didn't want to become a PR man, to be "bought" by the clients. He wanted to continue to be a journalist but one who offered PR advice and services. But as it turned out, that's what we did do throughout the life of TPS: we took a journalist's day-to-day approach to PR with advice offered accordingly. What had to be changed was our charging system. And when George heeded Arthur's warnings and asked clients for modest retainer fees and increases, they agreed without hesitation to pay them. Arthur then drew up contracts for clients and devised a charge list of all the office tasks. This meant we would bill each client for almost every breath we took. It resulted in a very complicated billing system but our cash flow improved rapidly. For every telephone call, every envelope stuffed, every press release written, every Telex sent (there were no faxes or e-mails then) and every press conference arranged on their behalf, a special fee was created and, to our surprise and delight, they paid up without a murmur. And the more we worked, the more we got paid.

Cosmos, whose various directors, notably Wilf Jones and the genial Sidney Silver, paid us to arrange press conferences for brochure launches, at first annually and then for both the winter and summer brochures. These became major events on the travel and news media calendar as Stevenson Pugh had a keen eye for a punchy headline and, with our help, he would regularly produce "news". We would round up 40 or 50 journalists from the national daily and Sunday newspapers, the ubiquitous members of The Guild Of Travel Writers, then a far less organised group than today, and an extensive collection of freelance writers we'd collected along the way. They came to the chosen Fleet Street venue for "the story" and the drinks and canapés. I'd like to think it was in that order. For one Guild member, whom we didn't have the heart to strike off our lists, it clearly wasn't. He came to each reception wearing jackets with deep pockets, which he proceeded to fill with canapés. Presumably he was worried about his next few meals.

So, collecting a conference organisation fee wasn't a Herculean task, after all, given the average journalist's interest in food and alcohol. The conferences were always timed to start at 11.30am, running nicely into lunchtime. The worst that could happen was that a journalist would get drunk, needing to be bundled into a taxi back to his office. That happened often.

Cosmos ran away with big headlines and sold holidays as a result of these events and TPS became very popular with Cosmos and the media. We were also working very hard for what was still not a lot in return. We were, according to Arthur, still giving it away, "it" being our creative efforts, diplomacy, growing PR skills and long, tiring hours. Arthur's new regime was certainly having a positive effect on TPS's finances yet an immediate injection of cash was still needed. After much thought he came up with a suggestion of an arrangement to George whereby Arthur and I would take a shareholding in TPS for £1,500.

That's probably more than £15,000 at today's prices, a lot to hand over to what must have seemed a risky venture in uncharted territory. George agreed. All that was needed was for us to find £1,500. It was a huge amount and not even patient Mr Whitehouse, our friendly bank manager at Midland Bank in The Strand, had any bright ideas of where we could go to get it. Arthur began to look worried – again.

21

GERTIE TO THE RESCUE

ARTHUR'S WIDOWED MOTHER GERTIE (his father, also Arthur, died at the young age of 51) was to be our benefactress. She didn't know this until Arthur telephoned her in her Sandown Road home in Belfast and explained our situation. She listened and readily agreed. Thank goodness for mothers. Within days she had arranged to sell some of her and her late husband's hard-earned shares to raise the cash. She wanted nothing in return. She wouldn't hear of our paying her back with interest nor would she accept shares. Years later, she accepted a small portable radio as a gift but only after her arm was well and truly twisted.

Gertie was born in Dublin in 1908 but moved to Belfast shortly after she got married to Arthur's father. He was an engineer by trade and worked for the shipbuilders Harland and Wolff, eventually becoming a Shipyard Manager. He died with no pension and no life insurance so the cashing in of shares was a major consideration for Gertie.

With that act of generosity, Gertie, a warm and instantly likeable woman who always treated me as a second son, enabled Arthur's and my big adventure in the PR world properly to begin. Arthur began to work even more hours for TPS, running the office with Kay. George contrived to attract new clients and I pushed myself hard up the new learning curve of employee management while continuing to get to grips with journalism, PR and magazine production. But just as we thought we were about to overcome our problems and begin a new busy phase, we were hit, as was everyone else in the country, by the effects of both a steep rise in oil prices and the miners' strike which cut coal to power stations. It was the autumn of 1973 and the then Prime Minister Edward Heath put Britain on a three-day week.

Trains ran only intermittently, London traffic was solid as everyone took to the roads, power cuts were frequent and, this being the age of electric typewriters, our work was stopped as the typewriters went dead and candles had to replace electric light. Much of our income stopped as well.

To cap it all we still had writs arriving almost daily and several visits from the bailiffs. George had not paid the office supplies people, TPS had not put in its tax returns and had failed to pay National Insurance contributions for it staff. You name it and someone was after us. We were in serious trouble. I thought the whole business was about to go down the tubes. More worryingly, so did Arthur. So Gertie's money came just in time, but was it going to be enough?

It seemed to all of us that TPS's days could be numbered. We had lost money for three years running but had never had debts like this before. We owed about £2,000 and it seemed – it was – like a king's ransom to us. All our efforts seemed to have been useless. We could think of nothing else to do but to plead with our main creditor, the man from the Inland Revenue.

At work at Bass Charrington's in Tottenham, Arthur asked his manager if he could use his office in his lunch hour to make a private 'phone call. He got through to the man we needed to contact in the tax office, planning to explain calmly how dire were our straits and how we felt we could pull ourselves out of them with his help. He didn't manage to say that. Such was the strain he was under on our behalf, so important was this 'phone call, that Arthur, a man who doesn't show his feelings easily even to me, just burst into tears. Accountants aren't supposed to do that.

Yet Arthur's tears must have affected even the tough-hearted taxman. Hearing that we were a young company trying to get off the ground despite being under-funded, the tax man agreed to give TPS a breathing space and accepted a scheme whereby we paid £100 a month. When I heard this, I had to smile. We were now to run the company on tick. We knew all about tick in Gourock! There was never a time when Mum didn't have a running 'tick' bill in Colquhoun's, the grocery shop on the corner of Cove Road, and a few other essential shops around the town. I thought I'd left all that behind! Unlike Mum, we always paid promptly. Our monthly cheque to the taxman was one cheque we sent on time without fail, even if that cheque sometimes came out of Arthur's personal bank account – at least for the short-term.

22

OUR GESTETNER YEARS

AS WE CAUGHT OUR BREATH, a white knight was riding down Fleet Street and into number 131 in time to save us. This champion was a certain Colonel Clark – I never knew his first name – an ex-army conference organiser and an old contact of George's. The Colonel was 'old school' in his pinstriped suit with a fresh rose daily in the lapel and a 'mine's a gin and tonic' approach to life. He was blunt-speaking and to the point. He needed a firm to produce conference papers and copies of speeches reliably, on time and often at very short notice for his very busy business. We were running our PR service but we grabbed the opportunity even though we had no experience of this sort of work and no equipment on which to print it. He needed collators and printers. We would be those people.

We soon identified what we needed: a guillotine to cut paper and a Gestetner printing machine to print off copies of the conference documents – just what every PR company should have. Within days a Gestetner was installed in our tiny outer office. So our reasonably presentable reception area disappeared. It was turned into the print room. We had entered the print business. We congratulated ourselves and then realised that one problem remained. We had no one to operate the thing.

I had a brainwave. I contacted my old, useful friend Griff, the gas salesman back in Gourock. Well, doesn't every gas salesman long to become a printer? Griff had recently been in touch to tell me he was thinking of moving to London. Would the gas man cometh? He would. Griff knew nothing about printing machines but proved to be a quick learner after he joined us to work full-time with this wonderful, if noisy, beast. It often made office life difficult and he got used to pleading requests to switch it off so Kay or George or I could hear what was being said on the 'phone. But we all knew our pay cheques depended on it and it thumped away almost non-stop in the small middle room for the next few years – every printed sheet earning us money.

George, Kay, Griff and I took on these new duties together with our existing work. Arthur helped out in the evenings when he could. Kay typed the speeches and the schedules on to the special Gestetner paper and the rest of us proof-read, printed, collated, stapled and delivered. Many days we literally worked round-the-clock to service the Colonel's conferences. It was hard, unexciting but very profitable work and it saved our bacon. It had allowed us to catch up with our tax payments and, by the end of 1973, we felt confident enough to expand our office space by taking over the second floor of 131 Fleet Street as well as the first. We felt we were literally on the way up.

With this security for the business, I was freer to enjoy the social side of my job in PR. I've always been gregarious and soon found I liked gossiping to journalists, especially over lunch. I've always felt completely at home in a restaurant with a group of talkative journalists around me but I then had to get to grips with the social graces of entertaining at luncheon. At first this meant pretending I knew the first thing about food and wine. Not a lot of wine was consumed in working class Clydeside in the sixties. It was certainly never consumed at 47 Cove Road so I must have picked awful plonk on many occasions in those early visits to Fleet Street restaurants. But the mere fact that

I was being handed wine lists by waiters and smiling back at them when samples of newly-opened bottles were pretentiously poured into my glass for me to taste, seemed to work. For some reason I have never been intimidated by pompous waiters and I couldn't help smiling inwardly: if Gourock could see me now!

Back in the 1970s, Fleet Street lunches were still boozy, leisurely, most enjoyable events. I loved them. The puritanical culture which pervades most newspaper offices today, where lunch is a sandwich and bottle of mineral water consumed in silence at the computer, thankfully did not exist then. I would usually meet my contact at about 12.30pm at one of the Fleet Street restaurants now part of media folklore such as the informal Cheshire Cheese pub, the more pretentious Wig and Pen Club or the ever popular El Vinos, which famously enraged feminists by refusing to serve women or allow them to stand at the bar. We would have a gin and tonic at the bar, a bottle of wine with our meal and often finish off with a brandy, getting back to our desks at around 3.30pm or later. No one would bat an eyelid at this behaviour. Such a regime may not have been great for our livers and I'm still a wine philistine, though I know what I like and I can usually tell when a wine is corked. But I would argue that these long, boozy lunches didn't affect our overall productivity. The telephones would ring non-stop until about six and then most journalists and PR people would buckle down to a couple of hours of writing and 'fixing' stories, many of us leaving our offices late after what we usually felt had been a full day. And since the companies that employed TPS rarely, if ever, questioned our expenses, there was no anxiety about overspending. We didn't cheat because we didn't need to. Most restaurant bills, taxi fares, telephone costs and postage expenses were paid promptly, to our immense relief. And all of this expense was tax deductible. Those were the days!

Our clients were often inspiring and entertaining people too. Stevenson Pugh at Cosmos continued both to terrify the life out of me and to create some of the great travel PR stories of the early 1970s which TPS would push out to the news services, our journalist contacts and The Press Association. The stories varied of course. But they had one thing in common: the word 'cheap' always appeared in the first paragraph. That was guaranteed to grab the attention.

So as the three-day week ended, Steve devised a new line of 'cheapie' package deals. He found holiday havens such as Benidorm, Majorca and places on Italy's Adriatic coast, to be marketed as offering the exciting holidays in the sun that ordinary working people, notably miners, who were much in the news because of the revolutionary changes happening in their industry, could easily afford. Journalists loved the idea and we set up a whole range of articles on this theme and a press conference was called. There was a good attendance at our launch at The Golf Club, just off Fleet Street, and journalists seemed excited by the story. We sat back waiting to congratulate ourselves and for Cosmos to sell and sell.

Sadly, sex is even more important than cheap holidays to the British newspaper editor and reader. Thus a call girl called Norma Levy stole our thunder. The secret services revealed her links with a certain Lord Lambton and she decided to spill the beans over several pages of every newspaper. Our miners' holidays story was virtually dead in the water. It popped up as a small piece here and there but never grabbed the front pages as we'd planned it would. The story recovered its legs weeks later, when Norma's legs had disappeared from front pages, and eventually we caught up with the campaign. Unsurprisingly, the 'cheapie' brand became one of Cosmos' top sellers.

Meanwhile I was thrown in at the deep end with a few of Fleet Street's revered, feared and influential travel journalists and editors of the day. Elisabeth de Stroumillo was then Travel Editor of both the Daily and Sunday Telegraph and immensely important to all our clients. Her mainly middle class readers had plenty of money to spend on our clients' holiday products. Elisabeth was well known as the scourge of PR people. She didn't listen to long diatribes and you soon learned that before you telephoned her, you had to get your act together or the line would suddenly go dead. She did not suffer fools gladly but somehow she suffered me, probably because I was the new kid on the block, just starting out and obviously naive. And she did have a soft spot.

I had a much harder ride with Roger Bray, the knowledgeable and talented aviation and travel correspondent of the London Evening Standard. In recent years Roger has always struck me as a charming, mellow fellow. In the seventies he was brusque to the point of rudeness and to me, at least, terrifying. Because of his paper's late morning deadlines in London, he would often ring me at home at breakfast time and if I couldn't answer his queries or do as he wanted, which was often the case, he'd throw down the 'phone. As the weeks went by, I woke up to the fact that Roger and The Evening Standard were very important to TPS and our clients and I had to find a way of working with them to make things run more smoothly.

The solution was staring us in the face. We decided to persuade clients to allow me to give Roger their home numbers so if he needed early morning or indeed instant quotes at any time he could try us or try the clients direct. All this may sound obvious in today's world of spin and instant, 24-hour communication. In the early 1970s it was virtually unheard of to expect a client to talk directly to the media, certainly not before 10am or after 6pm. That was the whole point then of having PR advisors such as TPS.

Before direct contact could be suggested, though, we had to teach clients how to deal with the media and how far to trust them – and that meant instilling in them that you trust a journalist at your own risk. A golden rule is you never tell a journalist anything you don't want him to know or to print. There is no such thing as "off the record". If, however, a journalist abuses your trust or your openness, they are likely to spoil things for themselves for the future. They can no longer expect to be told things on an exclusive basis.

I concentrated on writing stories and getting positive editorial coverage for our clients, which, as any marketing manager will tell you, is usually worth far more than the most lavish advertising campaign. Looking back, I think part of the success of TPS in doing this was due to the fact that we treated journalists as people with a serious and often tough job to do. We put them in touch with our clients and asked only to be kept informed of how a story was progressing. Thanks to George, we ourselves operated like journalists and the atmosphere in our offices was like that of a newsroom, not a 'fluffy' PR office. We could often be heard fighting the case of the journalist when clients didn't want to speak to them. We always recommended that a client spoke to a journalist, however guardedly, as it helped build a relationship for the future.

I like to think that with our facts-based approach, TPS was responsible in a small way for raising the profile of the travel industry from its pre-1970s image of money-grabbing buccaneers. With one member of our staff, though, this relaxed, co-operative system went wrong and what resulted would have led to the loss of a major client and could have spelt the end for TPS.

In the early 1970s, the big five operators Clarksons, Cosmos, Horizon, Thomson and Global had captured half the package market between them. There were other companies making great headway, not the least of which was Intasun, started by Harry Goodman, a former boss of Sunair, which was bought by Cunard. An opportunist and a risk-taker, Harry made headlines in 1973 when he bought three new Boeing 737s, started Air Europe and began taking thousands of British holiday makers to Florida, a tour destination on which Thomson thought it had a monopoly.

With so much happening quickly we knew we had to take special care of Cosmos, our biggest client, to keep its product well before the media. So we advertised for an account director to help look after our important client. An obviously bright and outgoing woman called Rosamund Berne applied for the job. She had an impressive CV and I told her straight away that I thought she should be running her own PR company, not just taking a secondary position with us. She was extremely keen, however, and begged me to give her a chance. Eventually, while I still believed she should have been running her own enterprise, after she did a great deal of lobbying for herself and made numerous badgering telephone calls to me, I relented and TPS employed her.

Not long afterwards, Mike Imeson, the travel and transport editor for The Press Association rang me and said: "I didn't know TPS was handling the PR for Intasun." I was baffled. "We aren't," I said, thinking he was joking. Intasun, after all, was the arch rival of Cosmos.

"I've just had a call from your Rosamund Berne about Intasun. What's the link with Cosmos? Have they merged?" he went on, scenting a big story. I repeated that it was news to me and made a bee-line for Rosamund's desk, twenty seconds away, and put Mike's question to her.

"Oh, the link is just that I'm handling Intasun's PR", she announced breezily. Rosamund had taken my advice to become her own PR boss but had decided she'd operate from TPS offices and in our time. She was out of the door fairly swiftly. Had Cosmos learned that we were promoting a rival – and Intasun of all rivals – our contract would have been torn up on the spot. Rosamund went on to do as I'd advised – run a one-woman PR company.

That night I poured myself a gin and tonic and reflected on my good luck at having Mike as a good contact and at having saved TPS from what was probably – to date – the worst blow it could have suffered – now that we had settled down the taxman, that is. We'd averted a major embarrassment within the industry and the near loss of Cosmos, our most important client. I relaxed. We were safe now, I told myself.

23

HOME AND JESUS
THE NEIGHBOUR

ARTHUR AND I HAD DECIDED to take another important step: to become property owners. We sold on our lease on 80 The High, Streatham and bought our first house, what estate agents called a neo-Georgian townhouse near Croydon. The address was 3 Freshwood Way, Wallington, Surrey and the price tag was £17,000. The year was 1972 and developers were fighting each other to buy up the grand but hard-to-manage, old detached houses with large gardens in many of London's leafy suburbs in order to knock them down. On each cleared plot, clusters of Georgian style "luxury" town house boxes or flats could be built. One of these was our first house and we watched it go up almost brick by brick.

As a gay couple, we had no hope of a joint mortgage, so we pooled our money and opened the joint account we still have today. Arthur arranged a mortgage in his name; we had Arthur's mother's upright Bechstein piano crated over from Belfast and craned through our first floor "Georgian" windows. We decorated and bought furniture. In other words, we put down roots. The only snag was, they were deep in suburban Wallington....

It wasn't long before we were pulling them up. Commuting during the three-day week had been a nightmare and while suburban living had many advantages, I'd soon had enough of it, even though we made good friends of our neighbours –

the late John Walters and his wife Helen. John became the legendary radio producer who worked with the late John Peel on Radio One and Helen was assistant to the West End producer Robert Stigwood. Other neighbours were Diane and John Ogden. Later Diane was to work with us at TPS. We got on so well in the meantime that Diane volunteered to clean our house and do our laundry so we came home each evening to order and calm.

Yet I didn't want to stay on the outskirts of London. I didn't like suburbia. I wanted to be slap, bang in the middle of the capital. I'd left Scotland for the big adventure of living in the bustling, throbbing heart of London, not in pleasant, placid, neo-Georgian Wallington, Surrey. Arthur finally saw my point and, in 1974, we sold the Wallington house – and the large orange sofa with it – for £25,000 and moved briefly to a grotty top floor serviced flat in Craven Hill, near Lancaster Gate in central London. It was to be temporary and thank goodness for it was not an attractive place. It needed total refurbishment and Arthur could not help but compare it to the place we'd left, a spacious, light and modern three-storey house with parquet flooring and our idea of tasteful decoration. We were keen to find another house quickly so I began exploring different areas and found Notting Hill, west London. It was not as chic nor as expensive an area then as it is now but I liked its cosmopolitan atmosphere; the clusters of interesting shops and restaurants which were beginning to appear and, of course, its many grand Georgian and Victorian houses. We soon found 95 Portland Road, which was in a fairly run-down area on the wrong side of Holland Park Avenue, a mix of bedsit-land and solid, middle class family homes. Number 95 was a tall, skinny house with a basement, a ground floor and two other storeys. It had been converted into bedsitters and was half-way to being turned back into a whole house. The builder had run out of funds and enthusiasm.

At the estate agent's suggestion, we made an offer of £32,500 for a quick sale which was accepted. All it needed was for me this time to obtain a mortgage. Enter insurance wizard Joe Perry, of whom more later. Then we had to find a carpenter and knuckle down to a great deal of tiling, painting and wall-papering. Within a few months we had things as we wanted them. We liked the result so much that we stayed there 13 years. It proved a good base, being only a short walk to Holland Park Central Line station which took us straight through to Chancery Lane, a stone's throw from our offices in Fleet Street.

Mary and Jimmy made one of their first visits together out of Scotland to the new house in Portland Road. Mum wasn't impressed with the area. One evening I arrived home from the office to be greeted by her at the door. "Are you sure you're safe here?" she asked, cigarette in the corner of her mouth, "because there's a man across the road who keeps shouting out that he's Jesus." "Jesus" was a bedsit neighbour, harm-less and quite affable, who added to the interesting melange of life in this yet to be 'gentrified' road, now one of the most desirable in the area. We liked everything about Notting Hill, eccentrics included, a west London district fashionable years before we arrived, of course, and decades before the film *Notting Hill* made it internationally known.

We also liked its posher near-neighbour Holland Park and I got used to saying I lived in Holland Park 'but on the poor side – turn right off Holland Park Avenue'. Poor side or not, we enjoyed all the benefits of Holland Park proper, not the least of these being Lidgates, the 'By Royal Appointment' butchers. Here we'd regularly join the queue for the best in game, meat and pies and rub shoulders with illustrious neighbours including Lady Antonia Fraser, Honor Blackman, Una Stubbs, my heart-throb Russ Conway and Sir Robin Day among them. W11 had traditions and standards to uphold. It was a calming place to be.

That was not the case in Fleet Street where it seemed our world was turning very quickly. The seventies saw the birth of the British holiday industry as we all know it today. Without realising it, we were in there in the middle of all this change. Our fledgling company, still floundering financially and feeling its way, was involved in all the big travel industry stories. And they were breaking almost every day as companies either went bust, bought out competitors, launched a "new" version of the now established package holiday or sent holidaymakers to hotels which were unfinished.

George was in his element handling a good, hard trade story ideally involving trade politics, agents' commission or a new holiday idea. He seemed to have a telephone permanently stuck to his ear and would just love getting to work releasing the news to the media. He would also be ready, willing and able at any time to discuss the ins and outs of the story live on television and radio. Television was fascinated by this new industry. Outside the news and current affairs departments, in television features, first to cash in was the BBC's *Holiday* programme which began in 1969, produced by the late Tom Savage and presented then by Cliff Michelmore. It became a trailblazer. A key member of that team, and many other *Holiday* series, was Prue Gearey. She was to become a good friend and confidante as I contacted her regularly in an attempt to gain television coverage for our clients.

While George enjoyed the limelight, I was content to stay in the background, producing Recreation Manager, trying to keep the office running smoothly, and learning about PR in order to keep up with new rivals who seemed to be setting up in business more and more. At least writing got easier for me. Even I, it turned out, could put together three-line paragraphs to form punchy press releases.

It was a time of frantic developments in the British holiday industry. The government set up ATOL, the Air Travel Organiser's Licence and all members of ABTA, the Association of British Travel Agents, soon to become our client, were required to be licensed. ABTA also launched an independent arbitration system to settle disputes between members and customers, and there were many.

In 1971, the Government decided to abolish minimum price restrictions on breaks of seven nights or less, leading several operators to offer £10 packages to Spain. They sold like hot cakes. Horizon, another tour operator, launched Club 18-30 resulting in more young people breaking the habit of holidays with parents and helping to spawn the 'British Lager Lout Abroad'. Clarksons started amazingly cheap cruises, British Airtours and British Caledonian Airways were born, and Pan AM's first Boeing 747 arrived at Heathrow from New York. And another future client, Freddie Laker and his Laker Airways, was designated a transatlantic carrier by the government.

And it went on. Thomson started its ski holiday operation. BEA and BOAC merged to become British Airways. And, as the Arab Israeli war of 1973 lead to oil prices rising by 70%, the crash of Court Line and Clarksons was just around the corner. Rivals were to prosper. In 1976, for example, Thomson announced a big expansion of Wanderer holidays on the Costa Brava at prices starting at £39 and our client, Cosmos, launched a similar deal under the apt brand name, Cheapies. We seemed to be in the middle of all this news as the media usually rang us first when there was a travel story and, increasingly, if we couldn't help we knew someone who could. The 'phones would ring continuously throughout the day from early morning. Life was interesting and busy and business wasn't bad either.

In contrast to that turmoil, our domestic life had never been more settled. The move from the suburbs had been the right one. Friends enjoyed visiting us on Saturday evenings and sampling Arthur's increasingly adventurous cooking. On Sunday afternoons it was back to work. While Arthur wrote out TPS's bills in one of his many blue-covered duplicate books, I would continue to clean and vacuum the house from top to bottom.

24

REAL WORK AND A CRISIS

BY THIS TIME, WE HAD two sitting tenants in Fleet Street: photographer Don Barlin and newcomer Mike Lancaster, a sort of media and executive employment 'fixer', though what he actually did was always a mystery. What Mike had, it turned out, was the gift of the PR account which was to make us the envy of all our rivals and make George an even more well-known 'name' on radio and television and in the London PR world.

Mike's gift was the strong and influential Association Of British Travel Agents (ABTA). For some time, it seemed, Mike had attended ABTA meetings as a PR advisor. But as the travel industry expanded and several companies collapsed, resulting in newspapers carrying a series of doom-laden stories, ABTA executives realised they needed a fully-staffed back-up PR service to help with the media image both of the travel industry and of ABTA itself. We put in a proposal that was accepted. Mysterious Mike was a star and had delivered us our largest client yet.

Living now in central London, we were enjoying being close to so many good restaurants, theatres and cinemas. With our new mortgage, alas, we couldn't afford to visit many of them and anyway we were working until late most evenings in Fleet Street. We became creatures of habit, going to Geale's famous fish and chip restaurant in Notting Hill on Wednesday or Thursday evenings and on most Mondays to Monsieur Thomson's, a newly-opened small French brasserie in Notting Hill, now closed, alas. People in the office would usually know where to find us by telephoning us at home, Geales or Monsieur Thomson's. In that pre-mobile 'phone age, it proved a useful system on one night in August 1974 in particular.

It was the night the Court Line empire collapsed, taking major tour operators Clarksons, Horizons and Four S with it. An estimated 40,000 customers were stranded and altogether about 100,000 people were affected. As this was happening, Arthur and I were enjoying fish and chips at Geale's, excellent as ever. Minutes after the call came we'd abandoned our dinner and were back in Fleet Street manning telephones and organising press briefings because ABTA was at the centre of the affair. Journalists and TV crews from the BBC and ITV seemed to have set up home in our small offices and George became a familiar face on TV news bulletins while Kay manned the 'phones and the coffee machine.

This was our big induction into crisis management. Our little company became, for the first time, the centre of a major international travel story which affected millions of people. It was hard work, virtually round the clock for weeks, but we all loved it and the whole incident gave birth to a new PR service, TPS Crisis Management. It's now big business as is the training of company executives in the art of giving interviews to targeted media. "How To Handle A Crisis" became one of our most appreciated and lucrative services. We relished being in the middle of this major news story. Suddenly I had to become an instant expert on the British travel industry, became used to being quoted in the national media and added considerably to my contact book.

By 1974, Arthur was finding his job at Bass Charrington increasingly boring. By this time he'd transferred to the Baker Street offices, drove a company Ford Cortina and was considered senior enough to eat lunch in the 'Executive Dining Room' with its elaborate menu and full bar – but office life was certainly not as exciting as at TPS. Because the company made beer, his office fridge was full of the stuff and drinking it, throughout the day, was part of the culture of the place. But his working day seemed to lack the excitement and fun that packed mine. His workload was so light that he had even taken to bringing TPS's books with him and working on the accounts during Bass Charrington's time. Then came an announcement that changed everything. The company was to move its entire operation to Burton-on-Trent. Those employees who did not wish to relocate were to be offered generous redundancy deals.

Thoughtful, cautious Arthur did not need long to make his mind up. He decided to quit, stay in London and work with us at TPS full time as Financial Director – though he laughed at the grand title. He was understandably nervous that we'd be putting all our eggs in one none-too-sturdy basket. I was delighted.

Looking back, it is obvious that without Arthur's clear, strategic thinking and financial know-how, not to mention his willingness to roll up his sleeves and do whatever lowly job was necessary, 'George's Great Idea' would have fizzled to nothing within a very short time.

Until then I could not claim to have taken TPS forward in any new directions. George had been the driving force, Arthur the strategist, taking us forward together.

We were, however, soon to move into another area of the travel industry, one that I was to feel very comfortable in –

hotels. This was entirely due to a chance meeting with two men, David Bush and Chris Kyd, on a Cosmos holiday flight to Naples.

Arthur and I had decided we needed a break and did a deal with our loyal client Cosmos for a cheap week's holiday on Capri – testing the client's product, so to speak. As I boarded the plane, I noticed two men travelling together. I guessed they were a gay couple. Don't ask me to explain how gays recognise each other. Let's just say two men travelling together on a package holiday flight is a good start. (If that offends straight men who go with a pal on golfing trips, I apologise.)

I took a chance and mischievously took a copy of Gay Times – a relatively new and adventurous magazine then – out of my hand luggage. I held it prominently as I passed the men's seats and so gave them the signal, albeit a very clumsy one. This sort of behaviour greatly embarrassed Arthur and still does today. He is the least 'camp', most dignified man you could wish to meet. If a trap door in the aircraft's floor could have opened at that moment, he would have been very happy to parachute out. Luckily David and Chris reacted as I'd hoped, introduced themselves and turned out to be very good company and long-term friends. We spent most of the holiday together around the hotel pool and at the singer Gracie Field's holiday complex on the island.

Even more luckily, David, from Devizes in Wiltshire, was the head of PR for Grand Metropolitan Hotels, a chain built up from scratch by the late Maxwell Joseph after World War Two. (He used the small lump sum he and other soldiers received as 'demob' pay to buy small hotels and start his empire.) Chris was then General Manager of the tiny, bohemian Pastoria Hotel, just off Leicester Square in the West End of London. While its rooms weren't anything to write home about, it attracted a theatrical, unconventional crowd to its excellent restaurant and bar.

David was tall, blond and good-looking, though not in a classical way. He had a natural style and a graceful ease in talking to people that I, as a small town boy with a few rough edges yet to be smoothed, yearned to acquire. He was already a rising star of the British hotel scene when we met, having been in hotel advertising and PR for about ten years, and many of the innovative ideas in the industry had come from him. He had taken the "weekend break" idea forward and made it a huge success and was a deserving winner of many top awards in the hotel world. But he worked hard and enjoyed his life, which made him an entertaining companion. Conversations with David were always peppered with humour, most of it camp, with him lapsing into a Wiltshire accent to be even funnier. Professionally and personally, he was a role model for me.

25

HOTELS – A HEDONIST IS BORN

WITHOUT REALISING IT, I MUST have done a bit of a sales job on David during the Capri holiday because, back in London, he telephoned TPS and it was another meeting that was to change my life and the fortunes of TPS. David asked if TPS would consider assisting his office, then in Stratford Place off Oxford Street, to get media coverage for his hotels and a new creation they were launching in the burgeoning market in "weekend breaks". Grand Met Hotels and British Rail had already teamed up for the first ever weekend break, a package called Stardust Mini Holidays to London. The idea of tempting people to travel by train from different parts of the country to fill unused rooms of central London hotels was already catching on. In those days, many hotels were busy during the week with business people and travellers but empty at the weekends.

The Stardust programme was hugely successful and now Grand Met wanted to repeat this success with the launch of Camelot Country Mini Holidays, a similar programme for its motley range of hotels across the country. Many of the country hotels in Bristol, York, Edinburgh, Bath, Salisbury and Exeter were comfortable and efficiently run but they certainly weren't offering five-star comfort. However, I readily agreed and we quickly signed up with our first big hotel group, Grand Metropolitan Hotels, a prestigious name for our client list. I knew, however, I would need to call in a lot of favours and work very hard with the important Fleet Street travel writers to induce them to sample these hotels and write positively about them in their pages.

Travel editors are like the rest of us. They like the most comfort they can organise. The places we were offering them did not immediately present the height of luxury but the prices being charged for a weekend reflected this. Customers 35 years ago expected less than they do now. These were the days before hotels had spas, gyms and celebrity chefs. Camelot prices were in the middle to cheap range and this summed up the standard of some of the hotels in the programme. So I put on my best smile and telephone manner and started sending out invitations and meeting my contacts to persuade them to spend a few days in the country either on their own or in a small group led by me. I shouldn't have worried. They agreed with alacrity and acceptances flooded in for individual and group visits.

Hotels appealed immediately to the hedonist in me. They still do. While George enjoyed the politics of the travel business, I was far happier discussing hotel facilities, limited though they were in our early Grand Met selection. I also enjoyed seeing parts of the UK outside of London for the first time as I began to escort groups of travel writers such as Jill Crawshaw, now of The Times; Edward Mace of The Observer and David Ash of The Daily Express. I remember enticing travel editors including chain-smoker Adrienne Keith Cohen from The Guardian; charming Willie Newlands of The Daily Mail; the very grand Nigel Buxton of The Sunday Telegraph and we even tried coverage in The Daily Mirror by targeting its mischievous travel editor Paul Hughes, with great success.

More than anything it was a challenge. Back then it was extremely difficult, almost impossible, for a PR to get the name of a hotel on a television screen or in an editorial section of a newspaper. Mentioning 'brands' by name was a crime to most journalists and editors. Advertising departments were, and still can be, all-powerful and if you wanted to name names you had to advertise. Attitudes were slowly changing, but it was still a slog to win a mention for your client in an editorial column. Space was limited. Then a travel page was just that – a page – not the acres of space, sometimes whole supplements, it can be today.

Elisabeth de Stroumillo of The Daily Telegraph again became a prime target for me along with papers like The Sunday Times and The Daily Express. Even today The Telegraph is a magnet for the travel PR industry because it is able so easily to 'sell' holidays to readers simply by mentioning them. The instant response from editorial coverage in any of the Telegraph papers can be phenomenal and in the 1970s it was no different. So getting Elisabeth to visit The Rose and Crown hotel in Salisbury was like getting a member of the Royal Family to sample a pint of warm bitter in a backstreet pub. She needed a lot of persuasion and asked a lot of questions about the suitability of the place for her readers, but she finally agreed and had a passably good time, after which she wrote an excellent piece recommending this 'novel' idea of a bargain-priced inclusive weekend break in this country. Predictably The Rose and Crown was booked out for weekends ahead. My career in hotel PR had begun.

Elisabeth was and is a very grand lady with a well-pitched bark but only a small bite. She has corrected my grammar and general knowledge on every possible occasion over the past thirty years, taught me a great deal about lots of things, the media especially, and I've loved her dearly ever since our Camelot weekend break in Salisbury.

David Bush went on to give TPS the PR contracts for most of the major Grand Metropolitan Hotels of the time, including the Britannia and the Europa Hotels in London's Grosvenor Square and the Mayfair Hotel off Berkeley Square. He also took us into the restaurant PR area and, within a short time, I found myself promoting restaurants to yet another new media species: restaurant columnists, critics and – a new development – food writers.

We called each other every other hour of the working day and often had a working dinner in the evening. How good was I at restaurant PR, he asked. I gave my usual answer to this sort of question: "I can learn." "Great", he replied and suggested we meet that evening at The Boulestin, Covent Garden. "It needs help", he added. A few hours later, as I sat at what was then one of the best tables in London discussing what 'help' I, of all people, could offer, I couldn't resist the delicious thought that it had been only a few years since my global knowledge of the catering industry began and ended at Dom's fish and chip shop in Gourock!

Marcel Boulestin, chef and food writer in the late 1930s had died in 1943 but his restaurant on the south-west corner of Covent Garden had lived on. In its heyday, his restaurant was patronised by great artists, writers and musicians and is mentioned in many memoirs. Some of its décor was designed by Raoul Duffy and statesmen, crowned heads of Europe and the rich and famous, including stars such as Noel Coward and Gertrude Lawrence, were habitués. It had remained famous throughout Europe and America, but its paying clientele was shrinking. Fashions in restaurants changed less quickly then than they do today, but they were still changing. The informal brasserie style restaurant was just arriving. This, though, was a grand example of the formal and, as I would call it, "all flambé and American Express" style of restaurant. Max Joseph must have liked it because he had just added this trophy to his empire and had told David to "Get on and promote it". The death knell had sounded for such places and I sensed the market was moving away from The Boulestin. Nevertheless, I went eagerly to work to try to save it – anyway we needed the money.

So, I rapidly became a food and wine expert trying to talk knowledgeably to restaurant writers and critics on newspapers and magazines – who weren't numerous in those days – enticing them to sample a meal and write reviews of the restaurant. We also offered the restaurant as a venue for celebrity interviews. 'As Bette Davis revealed to me over lunch at The Boulestin...' was what we had in mind. Indeed many celebrities were quizzed and flattered by show business writers over lunch there and, many an evening, I found myself at the door to welcome them. We used it as the setting when we hosted what we pompously called 'Opinion Former' lunches, to which we'd invite sometimes important business people in the hope of spreading the good word about its food and service. I undertook to do all my client entertaining there so The Boulestin became my regular lunchtime caff. Yet the profits still did not improve and within a few years, to everyone's regret, particulary mine, it closed.

My efforts were recognised, however, and from them came a new contract from Grand Met to promote Le Coq D'Or restaurant just off Piccadilly, which was to become the massively successful Langan's Brasserie. It too was formal and staid and also not doing well when Max took it over. Again we tried in vain but Grand Met wasn't prepared to make the sort of radical changes to the décor and menu, nor to spend the money that was needed as I now felt confident enough to recommend. So again our efforts were to no avail. It was sold to the amusingly outrageous and talented Peter Langan. Out went the old velvet banquettes, the heavily sauced food and a wine list that was the envy of London and with it went the stuffiness. In came Peter, informality, a brasserie menu, comfort food, David Hockney paintings on the walls and Peter's legendary cabaret of odd behaviour. No wonder it made him very rich.

With David Bush's encouragement and some success literally under our belts – because we did eat very well on the Grand Met account – I began writing 'cold' sales letters to members of the RAGB, the Restaurateurs Association of Great Britain. I told them we were a new leisure news agency, which wanted to use our PR techniques on restaurants to achieve the same success that we were achieving for the travel industry. I was also able to talk of our (limited) success so far with The Boulestin and Le Coq D'Or, two big names on the restaurant scene. We expected most, if not all, of the letters to be chucked in the waste bins yet the response was overwhelming. Very soon we were to have a number of London restaurants on our increasingly impressive-looking books. New clients included Eric Armitage's restaurants in Notting Hill (now the Paul Smith shop) and Harrow (mischievously called The Old Etonian), and Pollyanna's, which was opening up a frontier for eating out in Battersea, south London.

With every elaborate restaurant meal we sat down to eat, we and TPS were expanding. We were certainly not complaining. After three years of losing money, the company had become profitable to everyone's relief. New people joined, the office was crammed with desks, thumping print machines, piles of paper, stacks of brochures and files. The telephone rang incessantly. The atmosphere was terrific but there was no getting away from the fact that we had outgrown 131 Fleet Street. So Arthur began the search for a new home for TPS.

26

JIM'S CHINESE WALLS ERUPT

ARTHUR HAD LONG BEEN SAYING that for TPS to succeed it had to grow. And around that time, grow it did at an impressive rate. One of the first new ventures was our acquisition of Fleet PR, owned by PR man Colin Hodgkinson, a contact of George's. His nickname was 'Hoppy' because he'd been a pilot in the war and had lost both legs in an air accident. He was very much 'old-school', polite, courteous and, like Colonel Clark, smartly dressed with a carnation in his lapel.

Hoppy wanted to sell his PR company and retire but he wanted to ensure the continued employment of his two bright young directors, Tony Ellis and Barry Cooper. One look at Fleet's client list, which included Laker Airways, the airline started by the soon-to-be-knighted Freddie Laker; CI Caravans – a sizeable international holiday company, and the Scandinavian shipping organisation Tor Line, was enough to convince us that Tony and Barry were indeed bright. Arthur arranged to buy Fleet PR for £1,500 and to give Tony and Barry a share in their business. We agreed to give Hoppy an expense account as part of the deal for a couple of years to smooth out any difficulties.

Buying Fleet PR was a defining moment for us as we realised we could now take on work for competing companies. We then set up TPS Group. Under this umbrella came TPS PR and Fleet PR as our second brand, part of our operation but separate. The industry called it 'Jim's Chinese Walls'

– the art of running separate companies from the same building with competing clients.

The move to introduce a second company into our relatively small group was greeted with some scepticism by both the media and our existing and potential clients. They all asked how we could possibly hope to operate the highly sensitive PR accounts for companies like Cosmos and their now arch-rivals Laker within the same building without a clash of interests. We had to come up with answers. All we knew was that we couldn't turn down a good business opportunity to add Fleet PR to our organisation. Equally we couldn't survive on the series of small retainers being paid to us by our existing clients.

The travel and leisure industry has always been notoriously mean to its staff and suppliers like us and, possibly as a result, many individuals and companies in the industry made a great deal of money. So we set out on a campaign to 'educate' the industry into believing, as we did, that our plan would work efficiently and that our system of 'Chinese Walls' meant that client confidentiality would be respected within TPS.

It took time but we convinced the sceptics in the end. Throughout the entire life of TPS and Fleet operating in this fiercely competitive industry, we only had one major instance where a client felt his price sensitive news was in danger of being leaked to a competitor. Anyway, when confronted with a choice, clients were just not prepared to pay us the right price for our exclusive services – they never did put their money where their mouth was!

That one painful occasion when it looked as though we were being disloyal came years later. It happened when a pair of our hotel clients both produced new brochures, copies of which sat in our reception during the same afternoon. And when one of the clients spotted a rival's material, a small volcano erupted. It was then that my acting skills, honed all those years ago for the Gourock Drama Group, served me brilliantly and helped save the account.

At the time Ladbroke Hotels and Holiday Inn Hotels were in deadly competition in many areas around the country as they developed new properties and each fought hard for the business and weekend break traffic, both local and national. I had taken the precaution of telling most of the Holiday Inn people that I was also working for Ladbroke but guaranteed confidentiality through the use of my 'Chinese Walls'. Somehow, one person not 'in the know' was the European Managing Director of Holiday Inn, Sigi Bergmann, a clever German businessman, and a chap well-known for flying off the handle on a regular basis. He was the one person above all who should have been told of the Ladbroke Hotels PR account win immediately. Somehow I had managed to persuade myself that he did know and I think it is called, on reflection, not confronting the issue.

It was he who unexpectedly strolled into our office that quiet afternoon to tell us, I learned later, that our contract was to be renewed on improved terms. He arrived just as our receptionist busily stuffed envelopes with the two sets of brochures ready for the post and, because our reception area was small, he could hardly avoid spotting the brochure for Ladbroke Hotels. The enemy!

Sigi raged, Sigi shouted, Sigi erupted and then Sigi stormed out saying that he was returning to his office and would be confirming our immediate dismissal by fax. As I returned from lunch in my usual good humour – though thankfully after only half a bottle of wine – chaos, panic and the fax greeted me.

Everyone was interested in Sigi because not only was he an important client, he was also the lover of one of our senior account directors – the strong-willed but charming redhead Anna Fox who, conveniently, handled the Holiday Inn account. (The reason for Sigi's visit to our offices was no doubt only partly to announce our account renewal.)

If Holiday Inn fired us it meant the loss of over £50,000 a year – a substantial fee now but huge then – and also three people's jobs. So I immediately tried to telephone Sigi. He refused to speak to me. I then began calling other "tame" Holiday Inn executives asking them to intervene on our behalf. No luck. Suddenly everyone was "in meetings".

There was only one thing for it: to get into a taxi and turn up at his office and beg. I grabbed Arthur to show how seriously TPS were taking the fax and told the taxi driver to step on it. The ride through central London and halfway down the M4 to Holiday Inn headquarters near Heathrow at Windmill House – known to insiders as Treadmill House – was one of the longest I've ever taken.

When we arrived, Sigi still refused to talk to us, let alone see us. We sat tight outside in his secretary Jeryl's office and, after about an hour, she signalled to me. "Right Jim, I'm going to open his office door and you are going to walk in and sit down – I've positioned the chairs", she whispered.

In we went. Sigi exploded again, showering me with expletives, calling me all the names under the sun – many in German but I still knew that I was being insulted! Nothing I said seemed to calm him. This barrage went on for more than an hour with the ever-patient Jeryl supplying regular pots of coffee both to sustain us and to eavesdrop. She was giving Anna and the others back at TPS minute by minute bulletins.

Finally my amateur acting skills were summoned up. I became the hapless victim of a terrible mistake. I hadn't realised that the two companies were in such competition. Ladbroke had not been bothered about us handling the Holiday Inn account – so what was the problem? Tears began to roll down my cheeks as I argued all the reasons I could think of for not being sacked.

Sigi relented. "Fuck off back to your office and get on with your work," he said. He had made his point and the whole episode was never discussed again. By the way, he and Anna were married and later split up, to no one's great surprise. We continued to work for Holiday Inn for many years.

Fleet PR's arrival brought us a new level of professionalism. Tony Ellis, then in his mid forties, was a consumer specialist, brilliant at PR and also a wise man. He was working in areas where PR had been around for years and he taught us a great deal which we were able to use in the travel industry. He showed me that a PR's work is not only about getting press coverage, it's also about listening to clients and trying to solve their problems. Press relations, Tony made us realise, was only a small part of PR.

Barry, on the other hand, steeped himself in the politics of travel and looked after Freddie Laker's affairs personally. We all liked Freddie, who often came to our offices. He in turn was the ultimate PR man, the Sir Richard Branson of his day, a great self-publicist. Freddie was on first name terms with most of the travel journalists, the news editors and picture editors. He knew the media crew at Heathrow and Gatwick airports and, not surprisingly, what he paid Fleet PR was peanuts compared with the value in man-hours, effort and editorial coverage delivered. But as Freddie launched Skytrain, his cheap flights to America, Barry held his hand. And, with our 'Chinese Walls' in place, Freddie was happy to allow Barry to look after his holiday company interests – including Laker Airways – even though it was a rival of Cosmos, which we of course also promoted. The 'Chinese Walls' of TPS meant that we could represent a stable of clients whose interests would not clash even though their day-to-day media affairs were being handled in the neighbouring room or on the next floor. We always felt strongly that we had the ability to keep secrets. And we did. Especially from each other.

Over the years, other PR consultants working in the travel and leisure sector have followed suit. Indeed all the really big communications groups use this formula, forming parallel companies to handle competitors. Most found they had to do this. I always maintained that provided each team could be trusted with confidences and price-sensitive details, the fact that the ever-expanding TPS Group had a second brand led to an even deeper involvement with the media and it could only mean a better service for clients. Between the 'Walls' we did share media contacts – to the benefit of everyone. Journalists began to find that by ringing one number they could be passed from floor to floor and account team to account team for the latest news. Often, in a round-up column of travel news in a newspaper or magazine, TPS and Fleet clients would be the only companies mentioned.

27

QUALITY PRINT

TONY CONCENTRATED ON CI CARAVANS and the offshoots of that account which included Auto Homes and a firm making chemical lavatories for caravans, the much-joked-about Porta Potty (now bog-standard!). The fees Tony was charging made Arthur wince with embarrassment at first and then realise that again we were still undercharging on many of our accounts. Our philosophy until then had been, like many supermarkets, 'pile 'em high and sell it cheap'. That was to change. We have always had the work ethic and believed that the harder we worked, the more we got our hands dirty, the greater would be our profits. To an extent, that too was to change. We now had a more structured business in terms of billings and fee structure and, with Tony there to advise, we looked forward to a steady and profitable expansion. Sadly Tony, a heavy smoker, suffered a sudden brain haemorrhage and died, throwing us all into yet another crisis.

By this time, our valuable contract with Colonel Clark and his conference papers had come to an end, but so profitable had that work been that it was George's idea to make our small printing wing, which now produced all our press releases and letterheads in premises we rented in Charlotte Road in the East End, a much bigger operation. We decided to relaunch it as TPS Quality Print. This new venture would benefit from our work with our clients and would also try and secure general printing work. Knowing next to nothing about printing, well nothing, we bought a four-colour printing machine at a cost of about £3,000. Arthur, the world's least pushy person, then became a super salesman-cum-co-ordinator between the print-works and these clients as well as continuing as Financial Director of the Group.

The project got off to a good start. George was, cleverly, able to direct many printing contracts our way, including the annual, inches thick Convention Handbook for ABTA which listed all the delegates and events at the annual ABTA jamboree, a great money-spinner. And Norfolk Capital Hotels, a Grand Met division, gave us a contract to print brochures for their hotels and their weekend package literature.

Our former neighbours in Wallington, Diane and John Ogden, had by then become residents of Holland Park, a move aimed partly at shoring up their troubled marriage, as we were later to learn. We gave Diane a job first as office manager and then, because she was Miss Efficiency personified, we sent her to help run the printworks down in the East End. It was to change her life in more ways than one.

Husband John, who had just been made redundant by Volkswagen had returned as marketing manager for Renault Cars and he assigned to us the contract to print high quality brochures for new models. We also developed a lucrative rela-tionship with Joe Perry (Holiday Insurances Limited) to do both his PR and the printing of his multi-sheet contract forms.

Today, few people question the wisdom of travel insurance but, in the 1970s, only the cautious-minded or seasoned trav-ellers regularly took out policies. Yet with so many tour operators flying by the seat of their pants and with news-papers reporting daily how groups of package holidaymakers were left stranded or made victims of bungled travel

arrangements or half-built hotels, the need for insurance policies was suddenly obvious and the government began to take
steps to regulate the business. So, as the press coverage in both
the travel and consumer sections expanded and stories about
travel companies regularly hit newspaper front pages, we now
became the principal spokesman for the holiday insurance
industry. Insurance expertise was now added to our growing
list of talents.

Forever the hedonist, I stuck to hotels and restaurants, finding
insurance matters only slightly less boring than travel industry
politics. One good thing to come out of our work with Joe Perry
was that he was able to set me up with my first mortgage on
95 Portland Road.

Meanwhile, TPS Quality Print was proving a bit of a
misnomer. There were frequent emergencies requiring
whoever was available to rush over to the printworks and
spend all night fitting pages into ring binders or checking
the sequentially numbered pages of Joe's proposal forms, all
in a feverish dash to meet a deadline. It didn't take us long to
realise we were amateurs, our equipment was never exactly
what was needed, our colours rarely matched up and Brian
Kalmann, our print manager, though enthusiastic and a
thoroughly nice man, was incapable of presenting anything
without an ink thumbprint on it.

On top of this, I had to deal with yet another staff problem,
one that was acutely embarrassing for everyone concerned.
Diane Ogden and Brian had a good working relationship in
the print department. I didn't realise how good until I called
into our office late one evening, intending to return brochures
and press kits after a press reception, and heard rumblings
and voices in the top office. It didn't sound like a burglary but
I felt I had to investigate. I climbed the stairs and discovered

the pair engaged in activities clearly unrelated to colour proofing or typesetting. Soon after this, Diane's husband John also found out and turned his anger on Arthur and me, insisting we must have known about the situation for months. We hadn't known or even suspected and it was probably a sign that he came to believe us that we continued to print his Renault brochures! Diane and Brian eventually married and have been happy together for more than 25 years.

Our contract with ABTA was proving financially rewarding, guaranteeing us several thousand pounds each month, very big money in the late 1970s and far larger than any of our other clients. The ABTA contract was also continuing to build our reputation with the media and within the travel industry. As ABTA news was of international interest, our list of press contacts grew to include not only trade and travel writers, but also news editors, picture desks and feature departments, all to the benefit of our clients.

So much was happening in the travel industry at the time. As the media had finally woken up to the fact that their readers, viewers and listeners were fascinated by the latest offers, company developments, collapses and rescues, we continued to find ourselves at the centre of the news.

28

HELL IS A TRAVEL AGENTS' CONVENTION

TWO EVENTS IN THE TRAVEL CALENDAR – the annual conference of the Association of British Travel Agents and the World Travel Market – rated as my personal periods of hell each year.

I was unfortunate enough to work at 25 ABTA conferences held in places ranging from Bournemouth to Miami. Our job was to promote the event and man the press office. I wondered what it was all about the first time – and I still wonder. Every year some country is daft enough to subsidise the event in the belief that by gathering a mere 1,000 or so travel agents, a positive effect on its future tourism figures will be achieved. In most cases it had no effect whatsoever. Usually the attendance at the event was about 2,000, half of whom were hangers-on and suppliers, advertising agencies and PRs like me – all looking for new business.

We would send a team of five or six people each year at considerable expense to both our clients and to our nerves. For three or four days, life would begin at 7am and end way after midnight. Our time would be taken up with client breakfasts, photo calls and one-to-one meetings between clients and journalists attending the event from the trade and consumer press, lunches, more press conferences and interviews and elaborate dinners staged by our clients, tourist offices or the host country. Our main aim was to gain "advantageous" editorial exposure for clients, mainly in the form of so-called creative photographs of them doing silly things in silly hats, the sillier the better but always holding the all-important brochure. One middle-aged female marketing manager, who should have known better, regularly wore hot pants just to get her company into the daily trade papers with their limited circulations among delegates.

We would advise clients not to attempt to release any serious news at these events because nobody would pay attention to it. Most potential readers were suffering from serial hangovers anyway from the receptions and parties of the previous evening. But clients had to justify their attendance and coverage, any coverage, in the daily trades was a way of doing just that. National journalists would be running round chasing the few available senior executives to get a quote on this or that and we'd be chasing either the executive or the journalist – hoping to put them together at some point and earn our fee. All this might, with much luck, result in a paragraph in national media like The Times or The Telegraph. In between all this chaos, we might try to catch a discussion session or two on subjects important to the industry about which we needed to know.

Rarely did anything come of any of these presentations. We all knew it was madness but the asylum had to be attended. One quote from our partner Barry Cooper seems to me to sum it all up. Standing by the lift during one conference, going up to his room to change for a black tie dinner, he was heard to say, "If anyone finds Barry Cooper can you say I'm looking for him?"

I suppose some business must have been done between tour operators and agents. Certainly people met and talked (and almost instantly forgot who was who) and lots of food and drink were consumed. But in 25 years, TPS never obtained a single piece of serious business from our attendance at this ghastly event – perhaps that was a reflection on us…

One early ABTA conference held in Athens was another nightmare. As the Association's PR, we were much involved in the event's organisation. One job was to arrange the cabaret for the black tie dinner on the final night. At the time I was taking tentative steps into setting up a show business PR division and had not yet learned that artistes are a different species from the rest of us, or think they are. Their egos, and the egos of those who serve them closely, tend to be more fragile than those of us ordinary mortals.

Anyway, an early client in this area was Peter Walsh, a pop promoter impresario with artists including then newcomer Billy Ocean and the 1960s pop group Marmalade under his wing. I spoke to Peter about the cabaret and it emerged that he could not only rustle up an orchestra, he could also, allegedly, conduct it and, more importantly, he could get us the top crooner of the day, Matt Monro, as star of the evening. The bookings were made, pronto. It had all been so easy. Too easy, it turned out. Diminutive and amiable, Matt was so co-operative. His minder, on the other hand, was the opposite. He was also suffering self-esteem problems.

This came to light as Peter, twenty or so members of the orchestra, Matt and his minder stood by reception at the Hotel Grande Bretagne, Athens as I attempted to check them all in. The minder soon began giving me a hard time, making a fuss about the type of room he and Mr Monro should be allotted. He wanted everyone to know they were entitled to the biggest and best available. I, meanwhile, was trying to juggle dozens of requests and keep everybody calm. The minder persisted. My patience wore out. I lost my cool and had a 'hissy fit'. "Don't talk to me like that", I snapped at him. He lunged forward, one massive arm raised, fist clenched, as I realised my mistake in a split second. It was only the tiny, nimble-footed Matt, jumping between us, that saved me from at least one black eye. Everyone and everything settled down and the evening's cabaret went off with only a few hitches. The orchestra played brilliantly and Matt crooned away but I have never been convinced that the conductor could conduct!

The World Travel Market (WTM) meant another trip to hell but this one happened at home in London's Olympia over three days in November and I could get back to sanity and my own bed each night. The same mad process as at ABTA conferences would ensue. Bemused, bewildered PRs chasing, in a most undignified fashion, a few paragraphs written by frazzled journalists in the daily travel press issues which were only ever read by those at the event. Again everybody was trying to justify his or her existence. Clients would arrive by the 747-load from around the world – ostensibly to attend the Market but actually with a more pressing agenda: to Christmas shop in Harrods and buy Burberry. So cars and chauffeurs had to be organised for Ambassadors and other senior tourism officials; clients, usually marketing directors, had to be pampered with media meetings, lunches and dinners and, because representatives of countries and companies often sought to justify their visit by fashion-parading their PR consultants, the occasional pitch had to be scribbled on the back of a fag packet in a taxi and then presented.

Relations with rival PRs always became strained during ABTA conferences and the World Travel Markets. Only three days were available in which to promote clients and we all pushed and shoved for the attention of journalists and for potential new business. I was once pinned against a wall by two butch female PR competitors for having had the audacity to hold a breakfast press briefing that clashed with theirs. I survived, shaken. About fifty PR agents would be working the event and we, by far the largest group with the highest profile, 15 or so attending staff and the most diverse range of clients, were more likely to cause a clash than most. I generally frowned on socialising with rivals. We had a large group of talented people by then working in our four divisions and we didn't want them to be poached. I know all is fair in love and war but I preferred low-key meetings with media contacts to lunching with the competition who would merely pass on exaggerations and lies rather than the exact truth about any situation. I knew because I was doing the same.

While the conferences were misery, our ABTA contract was important in that it took us to the forefront of the news about the whole industry. Stories about travel companies were beginning to lead the main news bulletins and, because the stories were usually negative, it was our job to help put a positive spin on them as best we could and assist in getting George into television studios as an ABTA spokesman to try to limit the damage. George always performed with great professionalism and enthusiasm. But he was more and more elusive, either "in meetings" or simply not able to be contacted at the telephone numbers he gave us. The ever-faithful Kay did her best to locate him when we needed him but his personal life was complicated and he did not make himself as available as a press and PR officer should be – 24 hours a day. It did not look good. It also upset clients who were happy to deal with me or other members of the team most of the time but, when things got really serious, felt they *had* to speak to George.

Things gradually came to a head and ABTA finally brought George into line – not an easy task. It was agreed that George would attend all meetings of their Regional and National Councils so that he would be completely in the picture about what was going on and we'd know where he was – at least most of the time. About a year into this arrangement, ABTA executives asked if George would work in-house full time for them at their Newman Street offices off Oxford Street. He was happy to do so and we were content because the TPS offices in Fleet Street seemed to run more smoothly when George was away. I was able to get on with the management of the group, the team weren't confused about to whom they were answerable and gradually George's day-to-day contact with our Fleet Street operation was reduced. This was essential, if for no other reason than our other tour operator clients were major ABTA players and they *did* want to see through those 'Chinese Walls' and hear all the ABTA gossip first-hand.

I also learned quickly that PR advisors should never get involved in the politics of their clients. If they dabble in company power struggles and end up on the losing side, they'll almost certainly lose the contract. We were to learn this the hard way. In the meantime, there were other events about to plunge us into despair and threaten our survival as a company. All this as we were in the process of moving shop.

29

STOPPING THE TRAFFIC

IT WAS IMPORTANT THAT WE stayed as close as possible to our Fleet Street contacts. Our physical proximity to the media world, then located in and around EC4, was, along with our journalistic experience (such as it was in my case) and our ability to talk media language, what our clients paid us for. Journalists can be lazy and if there were two or more press launches on the same day – and there generally were – they tended to go to the one happening closest to their desks unless the "story" that was being launched was of major news value – then they'd travel virtually anywhere.

So I was delighted when, in late 1974, Arthur found number 75 Carter Lane, a street just the other side of Ludgate Circus, running more or less parallel with Ludgate Hill. It was an area of former warehouse buildings which were being refurbished and used as offices. The development was giving the existing pubs and shops a new lease of life. We were able to take a long lease on a small but smart building, with a basement and three floors and we were still only a stone's throw from Fleet Street.

The actual day of the move out of Fleet Street turned into a comedy in five acts. I managed to miss this kerfuffle of course – as I missed all our subsequent office moves – by accompanying a group on a conveniently created press visit abroad so, with George working at the ABTA offices, it was left to Arthur to direct the huge operation with his usual quiet authority.

He reported later that he felt as though he was having a series of heart attacks. The second floor window-frame on Fleet Street had to be removed and out came our enormous amount of printing equipment, the giant Gestetner machine on ropes followed by the enormous guillotine – stopping the Fleet Street traffic. Down the narrow stairs came the desks and other office equipment that the team of now fifteen people had needed. Slowly, between urgent calls for assistance from Charlotte Road and from George at ABTA, the new, self-contained home of TPS was taking shape up the road. Big, airy, open-plan offices on each floor like newspapers' news-rooms were soon buzzing with activity.

I've always hated "selling" but, in PR, you have to keep selling your services not only to expand the business but to replace clients who might or do fire you – fickle is the word. I wrote a letter to Cathay Pacific Airways and Ted Smith, then the airline's new general manager for Europe, rang me back himself to discuss our proposal. We chatted for about ten minutes and, soon afterwards, we met for lunch during which we agreed a deal. No 'pitch' was required; no elaborate pres-entation needed to be rehearsed. Ted and I hit it off immediately and the deal was struck. We would hold the contract – one of our most prestigious – to represent Cathay for over 25 years. Ted was also to become a life-long friend.

Our brief was to promote Cathay, 'the British airline based in Hong Kong' as they liked to be called. British maybe – its parent company, the Swire Group was based in London – but it had a strong Asian feel to it with mainly Hong Kong Chinese cabin staff. And, as time went by, as the shrewd Swire brothers, John and Adrian, saw the way the politics of the region were going, they allowed the Chinese mainland government to take an increasingly large shareholding. TPS helped it grow from an off-line regional Asian carrier, that's airline parlance for an airline without a direct route into London, to one which had twice daily flights from London to Hong Kong and then onwards to San Francisco, Los Angeles and Vancouver as well as a host of Asian cities on its "local" route.

At first we targeted the travel trade media, particularly Travel Trade Gazette and Travel News, but I gradually persuaded the airline to attack the consumer media so that businessmen would begin to request that their agents book them on Cathay Pacific out of Hong Kong rather than the competitors. In the early seventies, travel agents were all powerful and trade PR had to be handled with great care so as not to upset them. We must have been doing something right because in no time word had spread and we had a number of clients in Hong Kong and Asia. Looking back, I can say that one "cold call" to Cathay Pacific turned up trumps. It also meant that through that one letter a continuous stream of free airline tickets had begun to flow – some of them for me…

30

GAYS IN BUSINESS

MOST GAY PEOPLE IN BUSINESS in the seventies and early eighties didn't broadcast their sexual orientation. They kept quiet about it. Or tried to. I don't think I ever made a secret of being gay and, if I had, I doubt I would have succeeded for very long. My manner has always been slightly camp – it has been known to worsen or get better, depending on your view, as the day goes on so it wouldn't have taken people long to reach the right conclusion. There were and are lots of gay people in the travel business, of course, but most of the big international travel and hotel companies are run by men who seem, on the outside at least, to be rather butch. In Hong Kong, where homosexual acts are illegal and where we had a lot of business with a number of clients, the question of my orientation never arose, certainly never with the mainly ex-English public-schoolboys who dominated the early management staff of Cathay Pacific Airways. For most of my working life, I've had to sit and listen to men talking about women and sex without contributing and without the subject of gay relationships ever coming up.

It certainly never helped to be gay in the business to my knowledge, other than in that one fortuitous meeting with David Bush, and there was no hidden gay network that I was aware of – though I can't say how much it hindered us. I suspect the damage wasn't great in financial terms, but we rarely socialised with clients and media people as a couple. Arthur and I would keep our work and our private life separate as far as possible. It wasn't hard because Arthur didn't come into contact with clients or the media often and those clients who did meet him seemed to accept him without prying deeply into our private arrangements. Not that our home life was one long gay party, quite the opposite. We were two very conservative people. We didn't go to gay clubs. We usually worked until about seven thirty then took our two Labrador dogs – who spent the day at the office with us – for walks before we went home. There we ate something, watched the television news, fed the cats and did other domestic things. So, during the week, it wasn't hard to pretend we were anything other than regular blokes!!

At work, being naturally sociable and gregarious, I was always 'front of house' at the trade events we organised, doing the 'fluffy' bits, while Arthur, no lover of small talk, stayed in the background unless we needed his support. Even then he'd keep well out of the limelight. At weekends our lifestyle became, perhaps, a potential problem. We were out of the social loop.

Today, public relations people are definitely *in* the social loop and it's quite chic and respectable to have a poof or two at the dinner table. Social evenings and weekend house parties to which spouses and partners are invited are frequently arranged. It's accepted that to operate most effectively, you should be close and familiar with senior people on your client list.

Back then I doubt such gatherings were as frequent. Nevertheless, in our case they were non-existent: we were never invited together. I knew of a couple of people who were clearly unhappy in my presence and others who, I sensed, would not want me to handle their account. I felt sure this was because they didn't like gay people as a general rule, though perhaps they simply didn't like me as an individual. I'm sure some PR women too suffered this sort of prejudice just for being female. But when I look back and consider how open and sociable our industry is and was then, compared with others, the way Arthur and I failed to be ourselves to the world at large strikes me as regrettable.

When invited to a launch party or an evening gathering back then, I tended to ask one of the TPS 'girls' to accompany me. I suppose some people thought – "Lucky bugger, surrounded by so many glamorous girls!" – for we somehow managed always to employ exceptionally attractive women. Others probably thought, "He's a poofter really but we mustn't mention it." It would be different today. Now if asked if I have a wife or girlfriend, I would not hesitate to say, "I'm gay and have a partner." Society has changed its attitudes greatly and I rarely need to make such an announcement. Arthur and I have grown older, more confident and successful and our friends and employees referred to us as 'Jim and Arthur', knowing we were partners in the office and at home. Most people who meet us must, I feel sure, at least consider the possibility we're gay. It's a consideration often made about men over 40, who have never married and who don't talk about liaisons with women.

One hugely important client and his wife once invited me to bring a guest to their home for dinner. I took our female office manager. I had never discussed my home life with him so I was stunned when he announced, a few days later, with a knowing wink, "My wife says you're a fairy, Jim." How right she was.

He was not being insulting. It was his clumsy way of trying to make me feel more relaxed but, instead of admitting I was gay, I changed the subject with a shrug. To me then, clients were too important to the business to risk upsetting and I just couldn't bring myself to relax completely as far as my orientation was concerned. The business had to come first, we had fought too hard to get where we were. Perhaps if I had been honest and open, things would have been different. Perhaps I would have had a far deeper involvement with people in the travel business. Who can say? In today's climate, where gays are accepted by and large and require and get no special treatment, I would behave differently. In the seventies, things were less clear. Every client or journalist who thought about it must have concluded I was gay. But the subject was never raised. I never encouraged a discussion. And I now feel that was a mistake.

Life has changed so much in the last 30 years or so but, what's interesting to me, is that the meeting habits of gay men seem not to have changed much – even in the Internet age when contact can be so easy. I'll bet experimenting schoolboys still meet behind the bicycle sheds to play around as we at Gourock High did, trying to shock and thrill each other. When I was rushing across London recently to go to lunch, I needed to pee and went into a gents' loo at the end of Carnaby Street, opposite the stage door of the Palladium theatre. It was full of young men looking for sex. Old habits seem to die hard.

The one thing that has changed is the arrival of a vast range of 'counselling' services for young gay people to help them 'adjust' to the life they have been given. Perhaps I was lucky, I've always been thoroughly adjusted to my maladjustment, and was never offered, nor needed any help or counselling.

I've no wish to undervalue the traumas that some young people still go through with friends and families when they realise they are gay. I can speak only for myself. Something made me go out as a young teenager and seek older men for company. Something made me decide that this was the life I had to lead and lead it I did without reference to anyone else. And I know, sadly, that I live a life still deeply disapproved of by many.

I'd advise any young person who is gay to try not to agonise. If your parents are upset and seem disapproving when you "come out", consider that they may be genuinely worried for you, believing that your life will be harder, more lonely and complicated and that you may be victimised for your sexuality. You may feel that such fears are exaggerated but parents of young people tend to worry – they see it as their job. I'd say give them time, prove to them that you're coping as a gay person and that you're not being ostracised.

I'd also say always be aware of the dangers, especially when cruising in open spaces in the dark. Learn what concerns and bothers other gay people by reading publications such as Gay Times or Attitude and checking the net. Then perhaps venture into a few gay bars. You don't need to conform to anyone else's standards. But generally smile, say 'hello' to people and get on the conveyor belt of life.

Well, it worked for me.

31

ALL IN A PR'S DAY

WORK WAS NEVER BORING, but sometimes our wonderfully theatrical publicity stunts almost went disastrously wrong. One of those was the major launch of Cathay Pacific in the UK when the airline began flying out of Gatwick to Hong Kong via Bahrain. To emphasise the airline's Asian connection we hired a large Chinese lion dance team from London's China Town to perform on the tarmac as the aircraft arrived. We found one with a high reputation for authentic performances. The plan was for me to stand at the bottom of the steps up to the door of the aircraft, heading the welcome party and introducing everyone to the Swire brothers – Sir John and Sir Adrian, senior executives and a posse of journalists and for the lion dancers to be performing in the background.

We duly gathered, all ready to greet the group of Hong Kong VIPs off the flight. I'd prepared a short welcoming speech and I knew there would be a couple of speeches in reply.

The aircraft arrived, the steps were wheeled to the door and, as the guests walked down, the dancers began smashing their cymbals together and making their strange, fabulous, synchronised movements. What a noise! We watched appreciatively… and watched… and watched. The ear-splitting noise went on … and on. I signalled to Nina Gardiner, our Cathay account director, to get it stopped. She rushed over to one of the dancers and I saw her gesturing, talking, waving frantically and looking worriedly into the face of the coloured mask. Soon she came back almost in tears, frustration written all over her face. She shouted to me that she'd just been told that once the lion dancers begin, they go into a deep trance from which they can't easily shake themselves at will. We hadn't realised this, of course. The dance could go on for hours. It felt as if it already had. I fidgeted, coughed and made excuses, the journalists sniggered, the Hong Kong guests looked bemused – they undoubtedly had seen this situation before. And the photographers caught it all. As I began to visualise my sweet, young contract with Cathay floating up into the clouds, Nina, never one to accept defeat readily, then strode out in front of the lion dancers and banged on the costume head repeatedly, shouting "Enough! Enough!" in exasperation until all went quiet. The arrival and consequent coverage was deemed a huge success and we all lived to write another press release.

At other times, our mischievous enthusiasm to promote clients got me into very hot water. One of these happened at Badminton Horse Trials where Cathay was sponsoring a horse ridden by Maureen Piggott, daughter of jockey Lester. Show jumper Mark Phillips, then married to Princess Anne, was also there, as was the Princess, and, on behalf of the airline, we were offering champagne and a lavish buffet in the enclosed area for travel agents and guests. We welcomed VIPs, friends in the trade and journalists and all was going smoothly. In the tent next to ours, a car manufacturer was entertaining guests who included a well-known woman broadcaster. Through the canvas walls I happened to hear this broadcaster telling someone that she gave guided tours of Gatcombe Park, Anne and Mark's marital home, "usually when the Princess was away". This struck me as a delicious nugget of gossip and a way to get a mention of Cathay into the newspaper diary columns. So I rang our contact on the William Hickey column on the Daily Express and dropped the names of the broadcaster and the royals into the conversation. Next day the story, with its implication that a royal marriage was in trouble (which was true), was on the front of the paper. Buckingham Palace's press office issued fierce denials and worrying threats. They contacted the airline to demand how the story came to be written. The car manufacturer did the same. I had to pacify a whole stream of angry clients, Palace and car PR people while claiming I had no idea at all how this scandalous rumour originated! I'd like to say I felt guilty and remorseful for embarrassing so many people. I'm afraid I thought it was all highly amusing and I couldn't help noting that the publicity for our client was excellent as Hickey also mentioned the Piggott horse and the sponsor – Cathay.

Another PR problem, not our fault for a change – but one that also had a funny side – was a less than uplifting involvement with a world-renowned religious festival. Cosmos had sold a package of coach travel, hotel accommodation and arena tickets to people travelling to the Bavarian Alps to see the 1980 Oberammergau Passion Play, a solemn event which, once every decade, dramatises the bitter sufferings of Christ with tableaux and performed scenes. Many of the devout travellers had booked years in advance and were understandably excited about the trip. To Cosmos's horror, they discovered at the last moment that there had been massive double booking and entire coach loads of people could not be accommodated. Their fury and disappointment filled acres of newspaper space. Although we tried our best to cool the situation down, Cosmos could do little but offer grovelling apologies and free tickets for the next Oberammergau festival... in ten years' time!

I've done strange things for clients in my time. I've sent flowers to clients' mistresses and I've taken clients' wives to lunch to cheer them up – after their husbands made them miserable by spending time with the mistresses. But perhaps the strangest was the request to test a hotel suite for Lady Thatcher, then in the early years of her premiership. Our client was David Arscott, head of European sales and marketing for The New Otani Hotel in Tokyo. This enormous hotel, with around 2000 rooms, which prided itself on being able to pipe birdsong to each and every one them – bathrooms and loos included – was to accommodate the Thatchers for four nights during an economic summit. The hotel's management wanted to know exactly how to look after her. I suggested the easiest solution would be for them to ask Downing Street for a briefing document. "Certainly not", came the reply back. They insisted I get every scrap of information I could glean on the Prime Minister's preferences in terms of colours, furnishings, food and drink. They planned to refurbish the royal suites in her honour and provide two, one for Lady Thatcher and one for her husband, Sir Dennis.

I put the requests to Downing Street anyway who could barely stop yawning. "For security reasons," they trilled, "we do not release such details." All they would tell me, off the record and in hushed tones, was that she would be travelling with a hairdresser and enjoyed a little whisky at night before retiring. Any good brand would do.

The New Otani insisted I get on a BA flight to Tokyo at the double to brief them directly. Which is what I did. I spent five days in the hotel waiting for the meeting during which I would put forward my suggestions. Eventually, after a long wait, the meeting took place and lasted less than an hour. I viewed the suites, which they had indeed re-decorated to their own bland

and unexceptional designs. I returned to London. The summit took place without a hitch. Lady T. was happy. The client was happy, which was most important. I'd done my job.

The New Otani account stayed with us for 17 years. The contract was renewed automatically most years but, on one occasion, they asked again to see me personally in Tokyo to re-negotiate. I spoke no Japanese. They spoke no English. The "negotiation" took place in the hotel's Whisky Bar. A contract agreed, somehow, I staggered to my room hours later having satisfied myself that the Japanese like whisky as much as, if not more than, we Scots.

During this time, our restaurant PR division was appointed by Steak Nicole, a small restaurant in Wilton Road, Victoria, owned by one Norma Des Jonquières and her French husband Guy. It had a simple menu – lightly cooked steak, a "secret" sauce and superb French fries, based on an idea from a Parisian restaurant. Our campaign turned out to be hugely successful – it seemed that Londoners were ready for an informal steak bistro – but the restaurant caused Arthur even more distress than his appeal to the taxman two years earlier.

We managed to get a glowing review of the restaurant in The Daily Telegraph, a perfect vehicle to generate interest in the place. The chef's "secret" creamy mustard sauce was highly praised with the result that customers were soon queuing outside and the place was full every night as the news of this delicious dish spread. Yet, months later, the business was still losing money. Norma appealed to Arthur to look into her accounting system and to keep the accounts for the next few months to see if he could find out what was going wrong.

Very quickly it became obvious to Arthur that someone was on the fiddle. That's not uncommon in the catering trade where a lot of cash changes hands and supplies are delivered throughout the day, especially at a time then when account-ancy systems were not as sophisticated as they are today. But this was a serious shortfall. A few discreet enquiries and a period of watching the restaurant closely by Arthur, revealed that no one was stealing money but that one of the waiters was smuggling slabs of best quality beef out of the premises almost as soon as it came in. He would wrap the meat in cello-phane and dump it in a dustbin by the back door for his accomplice to collect. With this going on there was little hope of the restaurant ever making a profit.

Arthur told Norma about this and assumed she had passed on the bad news to husband Guy, who was funding the busi-ness and would act on the information. She hadn't and didn't. Norma, it seemed, preferred to tell Guy only the good news. One day as Arthur was leaving the restaurant, a frustrated Guy rounded on him, accusing him of being "one of the sharks surrounding us" and, in effect, suggesting that he was involved in the losses. It was a harsh and unfair accusation and Arthur was very upset. When I heard about the accusa-tions, I immediately jumped in a taxi with all the files under my arm. Arriving at the restaurant minutes later we both confronted Guy in no uncertain manner with the evidence on paper, much to the surprise and entertainment of staff and customers and the embarrassment of Norma. Guy was humbled and apologised profusely. We decided that from then on we would not get involved in restaurants, other than as PR advisors or as paying customers.

The restaurant PR division turned out to be one bedevilled by bad debts or by restaurateurs who did not pay their bills and wanted to give us meals in lieu of our monthly retainer fees. We'd accept wine in part-payment but when you're asked to eat your way through several thousand pounds worth of starters and main courses, it becomes too difficult. We'd try to eat at those restaurants as much as possible and offer meals at them as incentives to the team but we soon learned that PR man cannot live by food alone.

32

A DEATH IN THE FAMILY

THE STEAK THAT WALKED SEEMS funny in hindsight. What happened at about the same time to David Bush, my first big PR client and my mentor in hotel PR, does not.

In the mid-seventies it had almost seemed as if David called me every hour on the hour. That is what you expect from a busy client, as the Grand Met hotels, restaurants and mini-holiday account was turning out to be. We were already handling over ten different products within the main account and David and I had a great relationship as friends and in business. He admired the work we were doing and the results we were achieving for his department. He was happy to use our services and recommended us to others as often as possible. He was a conscientious and, at times, over-anxious marketing manager, under pressure from his immediate bosses on the Grand Met board of directors to keep delivering results.

We were now a major part of his small in-house press and PR team and, partly because he was a great motivator, we were delivering. All seemed to be going smoothly and I was enjoying life as a hotel and restaurant PR, until the day in 1976 when I didn't take his call. It was early afternoon and I was in an internal meeting. I could easily have interrupted it to talk to him but I decided not to. He was told I was busy but would ring him back. I never spoke to him again.

That evening at about seven, still in the office, I took a call from a mutual friend and learned that David had thrown himself in front of an underground train at London's Earl's Court station in the middle of rush hour. No one knew more details. I was in shock. We were all in shock. I had never before experienced the death of someone I knew well and liked immensely. Sinclair, my half-brother, had died suddenly on Christmas Island in the Pacific but, by then, we were not really close and the event happened on the other side of the world which made it seem somehow unreal. This was different. David had been a short taxi-ride away and I hadn't taken his last call. He must have needed me.

I was shocked to the core and I am haunted to this day by that call I didn't take. It might have been a cry for help. We might have met and discussed his problems. It could have saved David's life. I will never know.

The news shook the industry and particularly our office. David had been very popular. Any of us would have done anything for him – he was that kind of person.

A few weeks later, after the funeral, there was another shock. It was alleged that David had apparently been embez-zling Grand Met funds through his marketing department. All his marketing suppliers and associates, including TPS – and Arthur and I in particular as known close friends, would be put under suspicion. Had we been in cahoots? We hadn't been but we were to be investigated.

Internal enquiries by Grand Met's Chief Executive, the late, French-born Eric Bernard, were coming close to accusing David of serious fraud and presumably he knew it. They may have tackled him about it in person and thus provoked his suicide. If the chance that our good name as a company might be besmirched was a worry, there was something that affected us immediately that was worse. When David died, Grand Metropolitan Hotels owed us a total of £10,000 on different accounts. Because of the embezzlement charges, all David's departmental accounts were frozen and suppliers' contracts suspended. Our financial stability was again under threat and a major part of our business looked as though it was about to disappear.

The investigations proceeded aggressively and we found the process, over a number of meetings, highly embarrassing and downright frightening. We were a young company just starting up in what was a hugely expanding market and already we had a major scandal in our midst. The internal inquiry finally announced its findings and TPS and David's other business associates were cleared of all suspicion. But it didn't mean we would get our money without a struggle. After months of letters going back and forth, Arthur began to believe we would never be paid the outstanding £10,000. Then we received a summons from Bernard to attend with our documents for a face-to-face confrontation.

I clearly remember the Frenchman examining each invoice and exclaiming as he turned each page: "Zis iz rubbish!" Nevertheless, to our amazement and delight, he finally said: "I will pay them." We shook hands and I left the Grand Metropolitan Hotels' offices in Stratford Place for good, we had also been fired! Ironically, almost 10 years later, my 'phone rang and it was Eric Bernard asking me to advise him on marketing pitches he was making in New York to potential hotel clients. He had left Grand Met and had become a hotel consultant. We flew to New York together and he put me up at the smart Pierre Hotel for a week. The David Bush incident was never discussed.

Even more incredible was the fact that one of the executives who walked into our suite in New York as a potential client turned out to be one of my lovers from Glasgow all those years ago who had gone on to great things in the US hotel industry!

As a result of David's death, there was a new regime in Grand Met's PR department and we lost a major contract for a part of the leisure industry that truly excited me – hotels.

For a while, we retained our deal to promote the subsidiary company, Norfolk Capital Hotels. This was an uphill struggle because many of the hotels were shabby and in need of total refurbishment. We did our best for several years but gradually this account also faded away.

Even now, 30-odd years later, I miss David. I think of what he would have achieved and how we might have helped him – if, perhaps, only I had taken that call.

33

A PLACE IN THE COUNTRY

ARTHUR AND I NEVER EXPECTED to see that £10,000 from Grand Met so, to reward ourselves for enduring the traumatic aftermath of David's death and the loss of the account, we took the 'executive' decision to buy ourselves our first decent car: a second-hand white Daimler Sovereign which was to be the first of a series of Daimler and Jaguar cars to which we were to treat ourselves thereafter.

It was in that particular car, however, that we began tootling around East Anglia at weekends in search of something we then felt we needed: the weekend country cottage. We didn't need a country cottage, of course. We weren't country boys eager to go hunting, shooting and fishing. My accountant partner had said it was good money management to put some of the money we were now making into bricks and mortar. Thus began our period of second-home ownership.

So on one glorious Saturday morning in 1977, not a cloud in the sky – unusual in itself in East Anglia – we toured around Suffolk with an elderly gentleman estate agent called Mr Turner who showed us a number of properties which failed to excite us. Then he took us to a place called Hickbush which had only seven houses. Mr Turner was an extremely agreeable chap who seemed able to cope with the fact that two young poofters were excited by what he called "a most bizarre little hamlet". At the end of a rough track, passing a grand old English oak on the brow of a hill, was Howe House – an oak-beamed, three-bedroom retreat with its view down a valley of pure Constable country. Within moments of seeing it, we fell in love with it. As we looked around the bedroom on the first floor, Arthur said to me, "I have GOT to have this house." We discovered soon afterwards that from the living room underneath, you could hear every word spoken in the bedroom. No wonder the vendor felt confident in sticking rigidly to his asking price.

Anyway, we had bought the place before finding out about the acoustics and spotting the enormous pylons dotted across that valley – oh how blind a buyer can be. We were soon arriving from London with a bewildered, highly-strung bit-Persian cat called Lucy who would spend the weekend tip-toeing around the garden, eyes wide with terror at every sound, and then could never be found as we prepared for the return journey on a Sunday evening.

Our neighbours in the "bizarre hamlet" were charming, interesting people. One was broadcaster Douglas Stewart who, for many years, presented BBC Radio Four's nightly news programme *The World Tonight* and his wife Margaret. Others were artists and teachers. We thoroughly enjoyed their company for the three years we owned that house and so did the many visitors who came up from London and met them.

Why did we sell? Partly it was because it was easy for us. Gays are rarely restricted by children's schooling and that may explain why so many of us move house so frequently. We have merely to pack the pets and off we go. Partly it was because we foolishly thought we should keep the house "quaint" and not install central heating. Consequently it was the coldest place on God's Earth, I swear. It didn't put us off the country, though. After three years our confidence as week-enders was boosted and there was no stopping our acquisitiveness in the house-buying market. We'd work long hours Mondays to Fridays with little social life, knowing that the more money we made, the more we could keep. Come Friday at six, we were off.

Our next stop was a long, low farmhouse atop a hill just outside Sudbury. The house was called The Hays so, inevitably, we became known as The Gays At The Hays. Then it was on to Guist Hall, a truly splendid Georgian pile, built in the late 1700s, in the depths of Norfolk. It had high ceilings, gracious rooms and a classic green baize door behind which lay the kitchen and staff wing. All this wee boy from Gourock had to do was to find the staff to go with it.

I wasn't a complete novice. We'd employed daily cleaners and, on many occasions, caterers for parties in London. We'd also hired a succession of gay men who looked after the London house and then they'd drive up to Suffolk to attend to that house and garden. All of these proved disastrous. We naively thought that by employing gay people found through the Situations Vacant columns of Gay Times magazine they would be more trustworthy and sympathetic. Wrong!

We'd worded our advertisements foolishly, we finally realised – and we were supposed to be marketing whizz-kids. This was the 1970s, the era of Kenneth Williams-style innuendo. "Man required for house duties. Butler, cleaner, gardener etc." we put. Oops. It was probably the "etc." that led to the many strange callers I answered as I vetted the applicants. Did I want the house to be cleaned by someone in the nude, was one query. Another turned up for interview in full butler suit – black jacket and pin-striped trousers, wing collar, the lot – after having taken most of the evening to find our remote Suffolk home. He sat answering our formal questions about his experience but it became obvious he thought there was more on offer that night than just a job.

One man we hired had a nervous breakdown and his lover turned up in London looking for him in the middle of the night. Another was discovered entertaining his "gentlemen callers", quite possibly *paying* gentlemen callers, in our homes in London and Suffolk.

But, with Guist Hall, we were progressing. We had to have a person or a couple to look after the place during our weekday absence but, as we learned with our first hiring, you can't always rely on references from former employers. Some employers, we again naively discovered too late, write glowing testimonials purely to get rid of hopelessly inefficient people. The first couple we took on were highly recommended – by a well-known family in Scotland – for just this reason.

Doris and Tom were cousins. She was rather grand but a good cook. He was downright lazy. He spent half the week in bed and blamed the weather for the fact that he hadn't cut the grass or disturbed a weed in the garden. We knew it could rain a lot in East Anglia but, to listen to him, there were monsoon seasons. Doris had claimed at the interview that she liked cats. But Lucy, our beloved old moggy, disappeared for the first time soon after Doris's arrival. The animal turned up, thin and bedraggled, scratching at a window on a Friday evening two months later. The following weekend, Arthur found a note from Doris to Tom instructing him not to let the cat into the house under any circumstances after we left for London on the Monday morning. When I tackled her about it, things ended in tears. I asked them to leave but they "squatted" in their quarters until a lump sum persuaded them to go on their way weeks later.

The next married couple to take on the job were quiet, unas-suming and hard-working people, it seemed. All went well until several husbands in the village discovered that our in-house husband was paying far too much attention to their local wives. So they were off on their travels. We later learned that our female guests had suffered from our man spying on them from the bushes whenever they used the pool.

Ronald and Michael were like Julian and Sandy in the radio comedy *Round The Horne*, camp as a row of tents, wildly amusing, often amazingly enterprising but completely erratic, neurotic and exhausting. We romped from drama to drama every weekend. Ronald smoked and drank too much and often the food only just landed on the table, sometimes barely cooked or, on a really bad day, undercooked. They too blamed the weather for forgetting to cut the grass. If our dogs and cats, who lived there full-time, could have talked, they'd probably have told stories to make our hair stand on end.

Still, they were honest and usually worked hard. But after having fired them once and relented, I knew they had to leave when we witnessed one of their rows at a time when their rela-tionship had reached a very low ebb. We had battled the traffic up a congested M11 to Norfolk after a tiring week in the London office and were sitting quietly on the terrace sipping our first gin and tonic of the weekend, winding down and watching the sunset.

Suddenly we could hear curses, the sound of crockery flying and knives being brandished. Michael, the younger of the two, had apparently taken a new lover and had been sneaking off at night to secret assignations in a nearby village. (All this in strait-laced Norfolk or, as it is sometimes known, "No-Fuck"!) Arthur and I had to hold them apart. Later we decided we'd reached the limit with them. Our weekend retreat was turning into a battleground.

The pair promptly split up, were soon reconciled but not before we sent them packing with mixed feelings. We always remember the laughs they gave us during our time together, not least the final story they told against themselves. They went on to apply for a position in the south of England with a well-known pop star and his American wife. They apparently passed all the interviews and other tests, including a medical (which, given Ronald's drinking and chain smoking was astonishing), conducted formally at a smart Knightsbridge hotel. Then the wife asked them to take a handwriting test. Her graphologist would, she claimed, be able to tell by this if employees and employers would turn out to be compatible. The boys misunderstood and thought they had to write something that would endear them to the new boss. They wrote, "We really want this job." Wanting wasn't enough, though. Their writing revealed their turbulent natures to the expert who declared they weren't a good 'match' and under no circumstances should she work with them. Exit, flouncing, two baffled prospective housekeepers.

TRAVEL PRESS SERVICE

THE VOICE OF TOURISM

Principal: GEORGE MATHEWS, NUJ. Guild of Travel Writers

LONDON: THE ADELPHI, JOHN ADAM STREET, W.C.2 · tel: 01-839 3721 · telex 263303
BROMLEY: SUITE 4, 19, BROMLEY COMMON, BROMLEY, KENT. · tel: 01-464 5457

Please reply to **Bromley**   Office

25th February, 1970

Mr. J. Dunn
80 The High,
Streatham High Road,
London, S.W.16.

Dear Mr. Dunn,

This is a formal note to set out my offer of employment with
Voice of Tourism Limited the company which is now being formed
to operate Travel Press Service, Travel Publicity Service
and a number of other similar enterprises.

Your appointment would be as editor of Travel Press Service
but, of course, initially as in any new venture, we will be
"jacks of all trades".

Your salary will be £1500 per annum with a review on October
1st, 1970.   A bonus scheme will be paid annually in December
will be introduced.   Four weeks holiday a year (April 1 to
March 31) will be granted, but I would ask you, if possible,
to take this in two seperate fortnights or weeks.   Hours
would be from 9.30 to 5.30, Monday to Friday, with perhaps occasional
homework in an emergency.

As explained to you, the date of commencing employment with this
company will depend on when you can be released by TTG
Publications.   I am endeavouring to aim for March 16 at the
earliest and March 31 at the latest.   During the interim,
if you can provide some off-duty help it would be appreciated.

Your place of employment would be 9 Great Chapel Street, London,
W.1. with perhaps occasional days in the Adelphi, John Adam
Street, London, W.C.2.

Perhaps you would be good enough to send me your formal
acceptance of this offer.

Meanwhile I am pursuing the matter of your pension scheme
transfer.

I look forward to working with you.

Yours sincerely

GEORGE MATHEWS

P.S. Initially I will be sole director, but I am prepared to offer
you up to 50 £1 shares in the company out of my holding of
600 - 60%; no doubt you will let me know in due course whether
you would like some.

Job offer for TPS – how it all started

Our first house in Wallington near Croydon. The white Capri is in the garage

(Above)
George Matthews

(Left) My first package holiday flight. Then you always wore a tie to fly... a sombrero was de rigeur

Shopping... the early days

David Bush

In the garden at one of our first clients, The New Otani Hotel, Tokyo

Gracie Fields in Capri with one of my journo groups – that's me back right

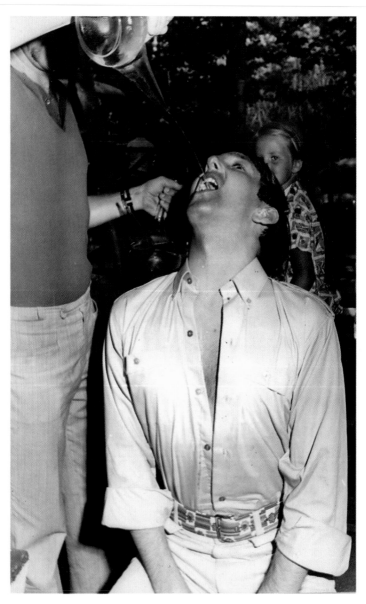

The PR man always had to try things first...

In India...

With Korean guards on the border with North Korea

With the late, great travel writer Peter Chambers of the Daily Express walking the Great Wall of China for the first time

Visiting Soweto in South Africa was one of the most moving experiences of my travelling career

First visit to Moscow...

A Travel Trade Gazette cutting with the TPS team celebrating ten years in business

'Mr Benidorm' in action

Mary and Jimmy at our first house in Suffolk, Howe House in Hickbush

Dad on the roof terrace of our first house in Notting Hill, London. Then just beginning to be gentrified, Dad thought the area was 'a dump'...

The Hays, Suffolk – we were known as The Gays at The Hays...

Guist Hall, near Fakenham, Norfolk where we lived at weekends

With Arthur

Arthur's mum Gertie with 'Bella' our old Bentley in the mid 1980s.
Without Gertie's early financial help, the Bentley wouldn't be there

Waiter services are included in the day-to-day tasks of the travelling PR man

Jim and Arthur with lovely friend, the late Robert Carrier (centre)

Mum and Dad in later years

Arthur in our beloved Venice

Jim and Arthur in Norfolk with the dogs Daisy, Dolly and Tinker

34

GEORGE'S BOMBSHELL

IF DAVID BUSH'S DEATH AND THE Steak Nicole fiasco weren't upsets enough for TPS – in addition, of course, to the day-to-day dramas surrounding clients, staff and temperamental media – an unexpected event was to deal a body blow to the company and result in another departure from our ranks.

George had continued to enjoy his time as a media figure and rightly so. He was much sought after because he had his finger on the pulse of the industry and was frequently lunched by the great and the good. And, as one of the three equal partners, he was able to help make TPS profitable by selling our printing and PR services to companies and bodies with whom he worked at ABTA.

What George was doing at ABTA apart from running their in-house PR was a mystery to us back in Carter Lane for most of the time. It was very much his business and his alone. We would hear rumblings from time to time about the precarious nature of the ABTA account, as George reputedly got involved in taking sides internally, but we never knew the true situation. As I've said, it's not a good idea for an advisor to get deeply involved in a client's day-to-day business politics and office power struggles. I always try to stay out of company gossip because you never know who is going to be promoted from below and that person could become your future client. At Cathay Pacific, for example, a secretary suddenly became the marketing director. Luckily I had always got on with her well and our contract continued to run.

George became so engrossed in ABTA affairs, however, that he began to see his role as one of influence. PRs should be impartial and offer advice to the client on the basis that if they take it, fine, if they don't you still have to run with their alternative decisions and present those in the best light. That, I believe is the PR's job. George, it seemed to me, got too bogged down with the politics of the travel industry, taking sides and forgetting that we were only paid advisors. In PR, as in other industries, there is always a competitor sitting in reception, ready to take over the account. And this is exactly what happened.

George reached a point where he could no longer support others within the ABTA secretariat over what was no doubt a very important issue at the time. It resulted in his resignation of our account with little reference to us. ABTA, a powerful body and an impressive name on our client list, said goodbye to George and to us.

When I heard this, I hit the roof. Why hadn't we been consulted in more detail? We tried to re-present a tender to ABTA but they were not interested. George cleared his office in Newman Street and prepared to join us back at Carter Lane.

But what would he do now? Our business had changed dramatically and irreversibly in the four years he'd concentrated on ABTA affairs. New, thrusting, female account directors had taken over our work with Cosmos and taken it in new directions. We were emerging as a full-blown PR agency where, it seemed, everyone had titles. Titles are great motivators, I was told, and it appears to be true. Everyone should have one. So TPS account managers, executives and directors were born. The new young team, including me, were less concerned about the politics of the industry and got on with the job of launching new holidays and resorts, writing press releases and – above all – organising press visits to hopefully obtain positive coverage for our clients. The name of the game was now 'coverage sells holidays', which meant more business for TPS, which meant good bonuses. Also ABTA was boring. Endless committee meetings. So much detail. It was much more exciting to write about the vast number of new holidays our clients were launching. After all, the world was truly opening up – we were promoting holidays to the Far East, Australia and all over the Americas. We became totally geared to maximising media coverage for our clients' products, vitally important at a time when the industry was expanding so rapidly that travel companies were often under-financed, and selling more holidays through our efforts was the only way that they could justify paying even our modest fees.

The set-up was new to George. Most of the other faces in the office were new to him too. Arthur and I tried to work out a division of labour but George solved the problem himself. He didn't want to go back into PR, he told us. He wanted to set up a group of print shops. Thus TPS Copy Print was formed.

To us it seemed a backward step for George. To my mind he could have gone on to become one of the great spin doctors of his generation. But it seemed, however, that he'd run out of enthusiasm for PR, the long hours, the endless meetings, the politics and the pressure. So he put all his efforts into setting up his first print shop, selling photocopying and stationery around the corner from Carter Lane and the business began moderately well. After six months it seemed he hit a financial problem. We knew few details: Arthur did not deal with the accounts. He met George to discuss the future and George announced he felt he had grown apart from TPS and was willing to sell his shareholding. We agreed on £3,000, the amount he needed in his current financial situation.

I sometimes wonder if the split made George feel bitter. He was an ambitious person, but not a businessman at heart. He was a fine, creative journalist who could pluck notions from the air and make things happen. I've a suspicion he thought that Arthur and I would run out of ideas, come a cropper. I was sad to part company with the man who'd somehow seen potential in the floundering young Scottish trainee he'd met at F.J. Parsons and who had given me the chance to spread my wings. For that and much more, I'll always be grateful to him. But his departure finally gave Arthur and me the freedom to control TPS – the company he'd first dreamed up and we'd all worked so hard to develop.

35

TAKING OFF FOR THE WORLD

THE DEPARTURE OF GEORGE WORKED to bolster my position at TPS and my confidence in general. I settled down with Arthur to running a business that was our own and I was sublimely happy in my career as a PR man with, I felt, good and improving contacts throughout Fleet Street. I was still learning the big things – how to manage a team and run a company successfully – and now, for the first time, I had to learn by trial and error how to pitch for new business.

The PR world was changing rapidly, becoming more competitive, and I saw that we needed to polish our techniques and become much more professional – as opposed to enthusiastic amateurs. It was certainly becoming a dog eat dog world as we fought to keep accounts and land new ones as fickle clients terrified the life out of us by threatening to shop around if we were the slightest bit inefficient – as we often were.

At any rate, we could no longer rely on the 'old boys act', a quiet drink, a talk and exchange of ideas. Now people were looking for sophisticated presentations, flip charts, slides – remember them? – and some infernal accompanying 'document' that summarised our campaign.

I'd always enjoyed searching out and meeting new journalists and potential clients and when companies began to ring me, instead of George, to ask me to come along and talk about how we might help them, I was delighted.

What pleased me most though, was the opportunity to travel, for free, on behalf of clients. I grasped this chance with both hands and soon found myself travelling extensively in the UK, then for Cosmos to mainland Europe and then for Cathay Pacific, hosting groups of media people to all its destinations from Bahrain to Australia.

Why would clients pay for my travels and those of my media parties? Because getting a journalist or broadcaster to mention a client in favourable terms in a newspaper or magazine travel article can pay handsome dividends. That mention can sell more holidays, hotel rooms and airline seats than a costly advertisement perhaps ten times the size of the article. Even the best written descriptions in an advertisement are less convincing than a brief third-party endorsement by a journalist who is assumed to know what he or she is talking about (though may not). So inviting journalists to 'test' a holiday resort or hotel by accepting all-expenses paid jaunts and then keeping them happy on those visits, became an important part of my life and of the service we offered. Almost invariably I enjoyed the trips, even with the long hours and having to deal with the irritating, greedy and accident-prone people that some of the invited writers turned out to be.

So, the charlady's son from Gourock who, a few years earlier, had never travelled further than Glasgow by British Railways, as it was then known, found himself becoming an international traveller. And loving it.

Mary and Jimmy had never shown any enthusiasm for travel, although I always suspected that, given the chance, Mum would have been off like a shot to far flung places – great floppy hat or French beret and a packet of cigarettes in hand. I did, however, persuade them to take coach tour holidays in the UK to south coast resorts like Weymouth which they enjoyed. They would sit happily on the prom, they'd tell me, Dad with his pint and 'chaser' and Mum with a cup of coffee or, at most, a glass of creamy Advocaat. One year I persuaded them to holiday on a Cosmos coach around Europe visiting France, Spain and Italy. Dad was highly suspicious of the whole idea. On their return he announced, "Never again, James, son. Ah, they're awe robbers. Every time 'a changed money they robbed me." So that was the end of that.

My job was about more than just travelling, of course. It was also about "hosting", whether it was simply organising a cup of coffee for a journalist and the client he or she came to interview or fixing a lunch at The Ivy or any other good restaurant in Britain.

When Jeremy King and Chris Corbin took over The Ivy in Covent Garden in the late 1980s, I wasn't the only PR to spot that they were going to turn this faded, jaded 1930s eatery into one of the most glamorous restaurants in Europe. So, along with a few hundred other advertising, marketing and PR colleagues, I started booking myself a table for lunch or dinner. I'm still eating there. I had so many Ivy experiences – first night stars applauded on arrival, the buzz of recognition rippling through the place as the newest soap star or scandal-prone footballer or starlet appears, the sudden hush as royalty is ushered in or the sound of Madonna having a party upstairs. You name it, it has happened while I've been there. The Ivy is usually a client's first choice. Most couldn't wait to get home to tell "the wife" they sat inches from Dame Maggie Smith or Lord Snowdon or a cabinet minister. Grumpy clients were always soothed there by Mitch, the maître'd, and his team and disputed PR accounts were always smoothed out there. On a few memorable days, I'd have both lunch and dinner

there and, on occasions, a great day would begin with breakfast at The Ritz, lunch at The Ivy and dinner at another of
Jeremy and Chris's restaurants, The Caprice, off Piccadilly.
Once its reputation took off, clients would ring from Los
Angeles, Memphis or Hong Kong asking us to get them a table
at The Ivy. Jeremy and Chris have now decamped to the
equally successful Wolseley and St Alban restaurants but my
heart belongs to The Ivy.

As an agency, we always believed in the importance of
regional media and the team would regularly "hit" Birmingham,
Manchester, Liverpool, Glasgow, Edinburgh, Cardiff and
other big cities. Our "Media Roadshows" would blitz a city so
that a client could give radio, TV and print media interviews
that we'd set up in advance. With the expansion of local radio
in the 1980s, I also found myself suddenly becoming an expert
on giving radio interviews and, far more difficult, responding
to listeners' awkward questions during the now much-used
"phone-in" programmes which were just beginning. Bob
Holness, who presented the morning show on LBC with
colleague Douglas Cameron, became a friend. We would regularly troop along to the studios, then off Fleet Street, to give
interviews on the state of the travel business that day,
bringing in the names of our clients as much as possible, of
course.

Peter Hobday, who went on to become one of Britain's top
broadcasters, presenting the BBC Radio 4 *Today* programme,
also became a firm friend from the time I dealt with him on
The Director magazine and emerging stars such as Michael
Aspel would compere travel industry evenings for us at the
Grosvenor House hotel. With Capital, the new pop music radio
station, we introduced a regular champagne and flowers

competition on the Gerald Harper Sunday morning show, giving listeners a chance to win a weekend break in the country. This would be a run-of-the-mill promotion today but then it was new and daring.

At times, we needed to be ruthless. For instance, while our client Cosmos was the overall number one tour operator during the late seventies and eighties, it fell behind Thomson in its sale of package holidays to Tenerife. I needed to change this by getting favourable articles written about Cosmos holidays on the island. I decided to send one account director to live there for a month, during which time we arranged flights and accommodation for a continuous stream of journalists so that the media would be bombarded with plugs for Cosmos.

Nina, the Cosmos account director, had to turn on her welcoming smile and keep it fixed. Day in, day out, night after night, she had to show journalists the sights and host dinners with tourist board officials and hotel managers. She had to make it all seem like fun, no mean feat since the cultural surprises of Tenerife are severely limited. She came home complaining that she never wanted to set foot in the place again and, worse, had gained a stone in weight from eating the rich local delicacies night after night. But the ploy worked. Cosmos conquered the island and Thomson became mere also-rans.

Taking groups of British and European media people to Hong Kong, Bangkok and other places in the Far East became a regular occurrence. Our work with Cathay Pacific also helped expand our client list in this part of the world as big names such as The Mandarin Hotel, Hong Kong; The Oriental Hotel, Bangkok; the Hong Kong Tourist Association and Holiday Inn, Asia soon followed. We weren't so daft as to think they brought their business to TPS just because we were brilliant PRs. No, we had access to complimentary aircraft seats on Cathay Pacific out of Gatwick every day to enable the media to visit their hotels. And that was a strong attraction.

36

TRAVELS WITH MY JOURNOS

AND SO MY LIFE BECAME one long press jaunt. I wasn't complaining. In some ways it was good for me to be apart from Arthur, to spread my wings and take care of press groups abroad, my way, while Arthur stayed in London and kept a beady eye on the company. He also looked after our homes and our animals. I missed him, of course, even though we spoke every day by telephone. But, as things turned out, after living and working closely together for a decade, I spent most of the 1980s and 1990s living out of my Mulberry soft bag, hopping on and off aircraft for long flights to exotic places. Certainly, during this period, I had the better half of the bargain.

I loved the work. It usually meant spending up to two weeks with the same small group of people working from after breakfast until midnight. I soon learned to draw those time limits. Even today I have an abhorrence of public breakfasts – breakfast should be eaten in peace, I say, not as another dinner party with non-stop chat. I took breakfast in my room instead. The advice I gave my team was go to bed at midnight at the latest, no matter where you are in the world, because if you stay up longer, you'll probably regret it. Just think, you'll have had pre-dinner drinks, a lavish meal, after-dinner brandies and then a 'nightcap' in the bar with your journo group. Everyone is pissed – including you. What they get up to is their decision. But you're working the next morning – so go to sleep! So if anyone in my team claimed to be exhausted after being "up all hours", I have to say I was rarely sympathetic.

Like all my colleagues, I would always try to find the right mix of people when organising these events, being sure to include people whose company I knew I liked, then asking around at the planning stage for suggestions of other journalists. This was an opportunity for some to suggest that their friends (or lovers) were invited, I could never be completely sure. Usually, then, my companions on these jaunts would be parties of between six to ten travel writers from newspapers, magazines, radio or TV companies. I called them "my" journos because I always felt like a mother hen – I *was* mother hen – responsible for their welfare for every moment of the trip. Most of them began the trip excited, pleased to be out of their offices, perhaps away from their families, away from the usual grind, willing to be bossed around a bit by me and to keep to the itinerary for the pleasures of being pampered and paid for.

Many journalists have low opinions of commercial PRs – they consider we have "sold out", lost our journalist's zeal for 'The Truth' in the process of polishing our clients' egos and selling their products. Similarly, many PRs despise journalists, and consider them freeloading oafs with pretensions as creative writers and power without responsibility. Yet I can honestly say that with a few exceptions – and I'll come to those later – I liked and admired the journalists and broadcasters we invited and many have remained friends.

I wanted my journos to like the places I was showing them because I liked them, not only because I was paid to like them either. I genuinely enjoyed exploring new places. But, if I'm honest, I revelled in the luxury I'd never imagined existed when I was growing up in Gourock. I never went 'native', never roughed it, even though many people were dirt poor in most of the Asian countries we visited. It was a rare occasion when, on entering an aircraft, I had to turn right into the rows of economy seats. I flew business or first class. On arrival, I was rarely housed in just one hotel room. There was usually a suite waiting for me. Abroad I was a VIP and it was a part I loved to play. I always knew it was an act, though, knew I was there because of the client and the media. Mary's words, "Whitever, always keep yoor feet on the grun!" would ring in my ears if I lost sight of that. She, incidentally, would listen intently as I told her of my latest trip and about the country. She'd take a puff of her cigarette and say, "Well, James, jist you be careful..."

When people asked me about my job, I'd usually say, "Well, Mondays are always good". That was because Monday mornings with the media could find me snorkelling on the Great Barrier Reef in Australia, or swimming off Cape Town in Camps Bay – very cold – or game-watching in the Kruger National Park, trying to spot the Big Five, so that my journos could take home their coveted certificate confirming the sightings.

One Monday I might have been climbing the Great Wall of China – I visited this magnificent construction twice – or sitting on less famous walls by the side of the Yangtze River in the centre of Shanghai, helping locals with the faltering English they'd learned from listening to the BBC's World Service radio – and this was well before satellite TV brought them Madonna and The Simpsons.

Another week I'd be deep-sea fishing on Lake Michigan, near Chicago, trying not to be seasick (usually not succeeding), or shopping in Hong Kong, or dancing to the Vienna Philharmonic Orchestra in the ballroom of the Hapsburg Palace or – and this I *really* adored – travelling in India, especially strolling through Rajasthan in the heat and the dust.

It never mattered how often I'd done these things before. I would be introducing journalists to them for the first time which added to my enjoyment. Life seemed to be one long adventure.

It was always enormous fun to arrive at Los Angeles airport, and herd my group of bleary-eyed British journos, slightly the worse for wear after 12 hours of airline hospitality in Business Class, through customs. I'd arrange for them to be steered towards those naff white stretch limos and, as they fumbled to put away their passports and blinked in the daylight, they'd be greeted and escorted by the "stars" of Universal Studios theme park – a client. These might be Lucille Ball or Charlie Chaplin lookalikes, or actors dressed as other favourites, who would warmly shake their hands and chit chat in character during the entire ride into town.

While in Los Angeles once, a couple of journos in the group asked to visit the locations for the film *Pretty Woman*, then out on general release. So I duly organised a trip to the shop in Rodeo Drive where Julia Roberts was filmed, then a visit to the Beverly Hills Hotel room where the bed scenes were shot. And, yes, there was an opportunity to bounce on the very bed where Julia and Richard Gere did the deed. Simple treats for big boys and girls. And all part of the PR's job.

The three years in which we worked for this Hollywood theme park were quite magical. We helped to launch such attractions as 'E.T. – the Ride'; 'Back to the Future', a hair-raising back-projection ride across rooftops and up and down city streets and the 'King Kong' project which had the monster attacking New York. And to cap it, we'd frequently share an evening drink in the hotel bar at the Sheraton with

Telly Savalas, the *Kojak* star, who took a suite there when he was working in Hollywood, making sure my journos were never short of good copy.

Imelda Marcos's famous shoe collection delivered another news angle. On a visit to the Philippines with a group of young travel writers, the highlight was a private viewing of the Palace of Ferdinand and Imelda Marcos, the country's former first couple, soon after they fled – reputedly taking with them $6 billion. Some of this money is only now, 20 years later, beginning to return to the country. Their hurried departure from Manila – a great bustling, traffic-clogged, polluted metropolis – meant that Imelda had to leave behind around 1,200 pairs of shoes, which encouraged millions of shoe-loving women not to suppress their desires. What struck me was that the Palace has been turned into a museum displaying the extravagance of the Presidential couple but the footwear collection, I noted, included some very scruffy pairs and none of the private apartments were at all elegant – without exception they were tacky and in need of a good coat of paint. That, of course, was in the early days as we were among the first to view the apartments. Perhaps it's got more chic since then.

Of all the countries I visited, though, only one stole my heart: India. There is still so much of that continent for me to see but wherever I am in India, I am in heaven.

I knew it on the first night of my first visit. It was a dozy snake that did it. We were booked into what turned out to be a glorious hotel, the Rambagh Palace, a former Maharajah's palace with all the original suites made available to paying guests – not forgetting its glamorous Polo Bar. As the Indians love their whisky, it serves an array including Balvenie, Ladyburn and Glenfiddich amidst its cream and green colour scheme with photographs of British royalty like King George

V who, it is said, was so worried about India that he took his own cow from Windsor Great Park because he had no faith in foreign cream!

On the first night, there we all were on the terrace recovering from the long flight, enjoying a sundowner and soaking up the sights, sounds and smells of this remarkable country. A tiny Indian in a turban padded barefoot across the terrace clutching a lidded basket and sat down cross-legged on the lawn facing us. He took out a small pipe and began to play one of those haunting Indian tunes, as if serenading the basket. We all looked, waiting for something to happen. Nothing. More playing. Nothing. Finally in desperation he whacked the lid of the basket severely with the pipe and gradually, and very sleepily, a massive snake pushed upwards and wobbled its way heavenwards – seemingly in time with the music. A huge smile swept across the face of the little man and, with a nodding of his head, the show began.

From that evening onwards I was in love with India and the Indians. No matter where I was, I was mesmerised. I could be walking around the majestic, marbled Taj Mahal thinking pure thoughts or watching the young men who loitered in dark corners, offering romantic favours to tourists, male or female, and having less pure ones. I always smile to remember the photograph of Princess Diana sitting in front of the Taj Mahal. It went around the world conveying the message that she was a woman alone, seemingly abandoned by her husband. Prince Charles may not have been there but I knew that when that pose was struck, she was probably only a few metres away from young men who would have been very happy to say hello to her.

Sex is never very far away in India. Boys and girls always seemed to be giggling and offering "jigjigging". At The Temples of Khajuraho, a punishing but rewarding rail and road drive from Delhi, sex is everywhere. The Temples are a legacy of the Chandela Rajput and have outstanding – perhaps that's the wrong word – images on stone of group sex, bestiality and homosexuality. There's a man pleasuring three women, another showing the positions of the Kama Sutra. What becomes very obvious to the alert tourist is that some locals are also on hand – you can take that literally – to service visitors in discreet corners. On at least one trip there, our coach was delayed as we waited for writers to return. When they finally arrived they were looking decidedly sheepish.

India's cities fascinated me. I could be striding through the gutters of Calcutta with my group or through the streets of Bombay at dawn, mingling with the street people performing their ablutions as they began the day. I could be touring the superb Lutyens buildings of the Delhi government headquarters, haggling in the markets or watching a traditional dance of welcome at a remote and run-down palace, hearing from the local Maharajah about his relatives in Slough.

On a couple of occasions we joined hundreds of other Western tourists for the annual Pushkar Camel Fair in Rajasthan. Here the animals are paraded, traded and sold. About 200,000 traders, devotees, musicians, comedians, story-tellers, saints and charlatans set up camp around this small town. Many of the traders are Hindus and bathe in the waters of the town's sacred lake on the morning of the festival of Kartik Punmiina, which falls at about the same time. After the day's business, the whole encampment turns into a riotous festival of lights, music and dancing as traders sell everything from Indian silks to horses and, of course, the camels.

Tourists were fortunate enough to be housed in large, comfortable tents with a central toilet area. But the locals slept in the open by their horses and camels. In the morning, I would take a camel ride and enjoy watching the whole valley coming to life from my vantage point atop this huge beast; an almost biblical scene of hundreds of Indians squatting in the sand, washing and busying themselves in readiness for the day's work.

The charm of India can come at the price of uninvited visitors. One night I snuggled down in my bed in a hotel near the Taj Mahal for some much needed sleep. Just as I was dozing off, I heard a persistent scratching noise. I lay awake in the darkness and listened until I could stand it no longer. I reached over quietly, switched on the light and there, in the corner of the room, was the biggest rat I had seen before or since looking back at me in surprise. I froze. After several terrified seconds, I picked up the 'phone nervously and dialled "0". Eventually – things never happen quickly in India – someone answered and within minutes of receiving my garbled, probably hysterical message, room service arrived and the rat was chased back out through the French windows whence it had come. Smiling room boys, nodding their heads from side to side, assured me in that ages-old Indian fashion, "Don't worry, Sir, rat gone to bed".

The rat was almost acceptable in comparison with the travelling companion I acquired once in Bangkok after another night on the town. I'd packed the journalists off into tuk-tuks – the small, unstable, three-wheeled taxis used by the locals and by tourists with a taste for danger – and slid gratefully into a far safer, regular taxi and headed for our base, the Oriental Hotel. As I settled, I noticed a slight movement behind my head on the back ledge. I turned slowly and there, curled up, seemingly asleep, was a huge, thick snake. I screamed at the driver to stop. He did so eventually and reluctantly. I dived out, threw some money at him and fled as he shouted, laughing, "No problem, sir, no problem – it's my pet".

Once I'd started leading these press visits, it didn't take long to feel that I was a "seasoned" traveller. I stopped being self-conscious about being foreign and just went ahead, listening to advice about local customs so as not to give offence, but concentrating on savouring each new experience. Travelling with those who were more inexperienced could, however, present occasional dilemmas. Deep in India, our group chose to stop for a picnic just off the main pot-holed road, near a small village but in open countryside. Our drivers parked the three air-conditioned Mercedes hotel cars and we all got out, stretched our legs and settled down on luxurious Indian rugs to eat the welcome lunch which the hotel had prepared for us.

As is usual in remote parts of India, the Middle and Far East, we gradually attracted a small crowd of young onlookers who appeared, as if out of nowhere, and stood silently watching us. Eventually I went forward to the oldest and offered some food. He politely refused but still stood while we continued eating and drinking. Suddenly, one of my group – a young feature writer on a regional newspaper who was travelling in India for the first time – got up and rushed back to her car. She looked distraught. I followed her thinking she felt unwell, not unusual in India. When I tried to speak to her, I received a tongue-lashing. "I don't know how you can all eat and drink in front of those starving people," she spluttered indignantly. "I'm too upset to talk – leave me alone!"

So I walked back over to the group and, to my amazement, found a cricket match between the journalists and the local boys in full swing. It turned out that the locals had been politely waiting for us to finish our picnic before asking our group to play. They'd refused our offer of food partly because they didn't fancy it but also because they had plenty of their own.

37

SHEEP'S EYES AND SHOPPING

SYRIA IS A COUNTRY THAT has fascinated me in different ways over the years and when its young, forward looking Minister for Tourism – yes there is one – asked us to help them in the early 1980s, I certainly met some weird and wonderful people there. One night, watching the sun set, I listened as an eccentric travel writer sang her heart out in the magnificent ruins of Crac de Chevalier after telling me that she was convinced I had been a Crusader in a previous life. And that was before the first drink!

That evening, an elderly Bedouin appeared out of nowhere – again they always do – to sing for us and sell us hand-made trinkets at about 50 pence each. My group disappointed me by buying nothing but were happy to listen to his fine voice. It was left to me – as was so often the case – to buy something and save face. I always try to support local tradesmen as I travel, even if I throw away the cheap items before I pack to leave. It's an honest exchange, especially if I've bartered the price down a bit, and it doesn't seem patronising to me.

Thinking on your feet is a useful skill in PR and it can help in many countries. Once in Syria, near the ancient city of Palmyra, I thought I'd lost the knack. When sheep's eyes and a set of sheep's testicles were cooked for me and presented with aplomb to the "important team leader" at a roadside restaurant stop in the desert, I was temporarily stumped. In a flash of inspiration, I suggested to the chef that our hard-working local driver needed them more than I did. I quickly passed the dish to him. He was very grateful and devoured them instantly.

Room service in Syria had proved very satisfying for one gay journalist who'd earlier made eye contact with a room waiter. After a very pleasant interlude, the waiter left and my journalist apparently settled down to a quiet evening in his room. Shortly afterwards the doorbell rang and, when he opened the door, another waiter was smiling in anticipation. The journalist duly obliged. After the third knock on the door, the journalist put up a "do not disturb" notice. Room boys, and occasionally maids, offering sexual services are an occupational hazard or perk to the traveller, depending on the way you look at it. I've come across it in most parts of the world.

Travelling to Damascus by Syrian Air out of Heathrow was reasonably comfortable during our work for the country but, when it came to our return journey, I had to break my usual habit of well-ordered, gentlemanly behaviour. We arrived at the airport to find that there were no reserved seats and about 100 people had already collected at the gate entrance – and this was pre-easyJet! I gathered my group of travellers and instructed them: "Right, team, it's war. Go for it! First on, bag seats for the others!" So, when the gate was opened, we pushed and shoved in a very un-British way but we made the flight and got our seats.

I had no hesitation in agreeing to work for the Syrian Ministry of Tourism in Damascus, despite the country's complicated political situation and its opposition to the Western powers and Israel. I've always accepted the view that tourism has a trickle-down effect; the more groups of Westerners are able to travel, spend money and mingle, the more international understanding is helped and struggling economies are boosted. Also, I have a rule: never knowingly turn down business.

The greatest perk of my travelling years was the opportunity that arose for shopping. This activity came easily to me. Perhaps because as a young boy I never had enough money to buy things and grew up in second-hand clothes, patched and mended by Mary, I became a shopaholic as soon as my bank account allowed; in all places, in all languages, addicted and incurable. To me, retail therapy is one of the greatest cures for tiredness, boredom, disappointment, almost everything. I became known among some travel writers as "Ship-it Dunn". If I saw it and liked it, I bought it, never worrying about how I was going to get it home.

So, in a remote part of China, for example, when I spotted a pair of 18th century cloisonné vases or reasonably priced, hand-painted, Victorian-period blue and white china, I'd airily order it to be "shipped" or I'd carry it myself. As we would be travelling in the expensive end of the aircraft where the baggage allowance was generous, this usually meant only occasional aching arms and slight embarrassment. After another China trip, I bought so many ornaments and artefacts that every one of my journos had to help carry something. We made a motley band of removers and shippers going through customs but, to their credit, no one seemed to mind.

Our local "minders" – people from the client's own PR department at base who would meet us at the airport and be with us throughout our visit – were a mixed bunch. On principle, I seldom argued or upset them because I knew I'd need their co-operation for this and future visits but, one day in Los Angeles, I had to put my foot down. This minder, a briskly efficient American PR woman, blasé about her surroundings and nicknamed Barbie by the group, was driving us on a guided city tour which included Rodeo Drive – that great American shopping street. I instantly noted it was sale time! And it said 20% off at Ralph Lauren! As my fellow shopaholics and I realised our guide had no intention of stopping there, despite hints and anxious stares all round, I made my way forward in the coach and suggested to the driver that we stop. Silence greeted me. I tried again. Silence. Then she said, "We haven't got time." What? "We've always got time for a Ralph Lauren sale," I said. "Please stop. Now. We'll be half an hour." Needless to say, we were much more than half an hour. But I knew all good things had to end and, before our schedule was completely ruined, I raced around the store dragging myself and my guests away from the "20% off" tags.

Guides or minders were often the bane of my existence. Whoever trains guides at the Great Guide Academy should be shot. They are taught a certain script and most never adapt it. They make no allowances for the specific needs of different groups, especially journalists. They tend to concentrate on ancient history and never think of telling groups about life in their country at the present time. My journos often played a game of asking questions which would purposely take the guide off his or her well-worn path. Such games rarely worked. The patter would continue, as if delivered by a robot.

But there were exceptions. In China, marvellous Mr Woo travelled the country for five days with us, lightening the boredom of long coach journeys by singing, beautifully, arias from all the best-known operas. In Damascus, Syria and Caracas, Venezuela, we were provided with security guards, armed, who stood alert at either end of our hotel floors. These soldiers were jolly characters, who were most grateful for our tips and cigarettes. But somehow, walking the streets of Caracas with armed guards at the head and tail of the group, made it seem scarier than it would probably have been otherwise.

It was also scary once in Mexico. Without my noticing, the earth moved for me in Acapulco where I was staying at the 5-star Las Brisas hotel up on the hill overlooking the city and the bay. (It was here that the fashion of floating bougainvillea petals in private swimming pools before your early morning swim was launched. Now every boutique hotel worth its name fills your bath with petals.) I was attending the annual Association of British Travel Agents' (ABTA) convention and, after a late night doing the rounds of the cocktail parties, dinners, meeting clients and contacts, I fell into my bed and went instantly asleep. At 3am I found myself sitting bolt upright, not in bed but on the tiled floor of my suite. Odd. Half asleep, I stumbled to the terrace window and below me there was Acapulco in complete darkness, no street lights, nothing. There'd been a massive earthquake but it had lasted only a few seconds. I stumbled back to bed and went straight to sleep. The next day I learned that had not been a wise reaction: the authorities had been so concerned about aftershocks that they had evacuated all the high-rise hotels around the bay. Most of the other ABTA delegates had sensibly left their rooms and slept or continued partying on the beach.

On the whole, I had a good run with foreign police and officials. I was in a slight panic once when I was "arrested" in Jakarta while my name was double-checked. There must be a terrorist somewhere in the world with the name 'Dunn'. While I languished in an airport office, my group was being garlanded, welcomed and eased into air-conditioned limos which sped them to our plush hotel. My mind raced as I imagined all the problems that might follow if I were not around to carry on organising the trip. I hoped someone was missing me. At any rate, I was soon "released" when the mistake was confirmed and I caught a taxi into town. And no one missed me.

You will have worked out by now that PRs and their journalist guests are spoiled on press visits. Everything happens like clockwork – at least that's the plan. Luggage is taken from you at the airport carousel by the waiting drivers, if not by me, and limos or air-conditioned coaches await. At the chosen hotels there are always liveried porters and smiling general managers in the lobby, usually proffering a glass of bubbly to help with the jetlag. You are then whisked off again, this time to your allocated rooms or suites on the best butler-patrolled floors.

It's at this point that trouble can start. And journalists can be very troublesome. Their egos are sometimes fragile and size does matter. If a room one journalist is allocated is smaller than that given to another, worse still if the occupant is a competitor, problems may arise. The Rambagh Palace Hotel in India, for example, has a limited number of suites. Who should get them, who should get the rooms – pretty spacious and luxurious but not quite suites? It was a lottery and the result tended to be a few miffed journalists with the PR having to sort it out. But, as I soon learned, you can't keep everyone happy all the time.

It was writers who were deputising for their editors or who had little actual travelling experience that usually gave us headaches. Luckily, professional travel writers can cope with most travel hazards – delays, missed flights, bumpy car journeys, bad food and stomach upsets. To them it's all part of the job. But even experienced writers have off-days. A veteran female writer who was freelancing a travel piece once had, literally, hysterics in front of me at an airport in the middle of China in the early hours of the morning. She was tired, we were delayed and the Chinese staff simply refused to give us any information about take-off. It was all my fault – of course!

It's always the PR's fault. Be it the timings, or lack of them, the standard of the food, choice of restaurant, the length of press briefings, you name it, it's our fault. A young journalist from one of the top regional papers called me in my room one morning to tell me that she couldn't work that day as she had been awake all night due to jetlag. This was in Hong Kong, which is eight hours ahead of the UK. I was momentarily lost for words. I pointed out that I didn't think she had much of a future as a travel writer if she couldn't cope with time changes. Enter on the coach at 9am sharp, one sleepy trainee travel hack.

Jetlag can be a pretty awful affliction, I admit. I suffered whether I was travelling east or west. That wave of nausea and exhaustion which sweeps over a group at about four in the afternoon in Hong Kong – especially after a good lunch – can, however, have its funny side. On one occasion we were enduring a boring after-lunch briefing from our client, the Hong Kong Tourist Association, in their offices overlooking Hong Kong harbour. The building has round porthole windows and because of this, it's known locally, and without ceremony, as "The House of 1,000 Arseholes." The tourism executive was droning on, spouting statistics of tourist arrivals and departures and the number of hotel beds available at any one time in the territory. I glanced away from my client, on whose every word I had been hanging like an obedient PR, to look at my group. One was fast asleep and the rest had heads lolling from side to side, eyelids drooping. I felt it necessary to ask a question – loudly – and end the session.

A senior Scottish journalist caused me considerable trouble and strife when he travelled with me to write a piece about the Philippines. On our way home, we'd stopped off in Hong Kong. I took a call in my room at The Mandarin from the hotel back in Manila and learned that the Scotsman had, in true pop group style, completely trashed his room. He'd ripped curtains and bedclothes and damaged furniture and the television set. The repair costs would probably amount to several thousand pounds. I'd noticed earlier on the trip that the writer drank heavily but, on this occasion, he had obviously soaked up the local hospitality just too much and run amok. What should I do? My advice to the hotel was to forget it. If tackled, he would almost certainly deny causing the damage and the resulting upset could easily spread through the rest of the group who tend to stick together when there's trouble. The hotel manager, with understandable reluctance, took my advice, bore the costs and officially "forgot" the incident.

This journalist thus made it to The Black List. Every PR has one. On the list are people who will not be talked to or taken anywhere again, usually with good reason. To get on the list a journalist may have committed one of many "crimes". He or she may not have bothered to write a piece following a visit or they may have written unreasonably about the area or one of the clients. Sometimes coverage didn't appear as extensively as I had been led to believe. One well-known TV producer accepted free flights and hotel accommodation in Hong Kong, saying that my clients would be credited prominently at the beginning and end of each of the six programmes. Yet there was no coverage at all in the first episode. Embarrassment all round. However, a frantic call to his home immediately after transmission led to the "mistake" being rectified for the second and subsequent shows. Result: happy client. But, as I often lectured new PRs, this was proof that nothing could be taken for granted. Even after promises you always had to check. Belt and braces has always been one on my many mottoes. As an airline PR, I was let down quite a few times over the years by journalists who took seats to exotic destinations on the pretext of writing articles. In spite of follow-up calls and a lengthening black list, this certainly continued to happen once or twice a year.

My job soon brought me into contact with the then doyenne of gossip columnists, Betty Kenward – or Mrs Kenward to you and me. She wrote the famous Jennifer's Diary in the glossy Harpers and Queen magazine. It was a turgid monthly "report" – basically a list of names – of the people she had met at a busy round of *the* parties the previous month. I took a call from her one day: "Yes Betty," I said. Oops! I don't think anyone had called her by her first name – ever. Anyway she wanted – surprise, surprise – a first class ticket to Hong Kong to report on the stuffy (my word!) ex-pat scene there. After that, we met for lunch on a few occasions and, despite my best efforts to relax the atmosphere, these were extremely stilted affairs. She was always "Mrs Kenward" and, as this nearly 70-year-old lady approached the table, I almost felt myself bowing in her presence. She was of another age with her bouffant hair, powdered mask-like face and eyebrows painted just a little too high. I think she felt she was the Queen Mother, at least she dressed like her, in large feather hats and afternoon frocks and matching coats. "My feet barely touch the ground from May to October", she told me as she fixed me with a steely stare and described how she "did" the London season. We hosted Mrs Kenward regularly to Hong Kong – her flights, her hotel suites and her limousines – and received excellent editorial coverage in return, for the simple reason that I was able to check the columns in proof before publication and change copy if necessary.

Giving free airline seats or hotel rooms to journalists was always a risk. Would they produce copy to pacify the client? In the majority of cases they did. Recognised travel editors were, of course, bona fide but sometimes journalists who had no connection with travel sections would slip through the net. One travel editor was discovered sending his friends, who weren't even journalists, on free trips with the promise of coverage. Luckily we were soon on to him, complaining to his editor, with serious consequences for him.

Another editor at the same game was very important to me and my colleagues and I went along with this scam to my continued regret. I discovered it only after I had agreed at least two complimentary visits for his mates. I took the decision to continue in the interests of the client's future editorial prospects but, shortly afterwards, the editor disappeared to the suburbs and now ignores me sheepishly whenever he sees me.

Bad manners can also result in a ban. Not always, though. The disappearance of the thick fluffy bathrobes from all ten of the rooms allocated to the journalists in a Munich hotel was noted just as the group was drinking farewell schnapps in the lobby to the accompaniment of a very loud and enthusiastic oompah band. My advice to the hotel manager in Munich was similar to that given to his colleague in Manila. He was told the bathrobes were probably packed in the luggage we could see before us in the lobby ready to be transported to the airport. "Let them go", I said. The alternative was to ask all the journalists to open their suitcases there and then or to charge the cost to their credit cards. This would leave a bad taste and ruin what had been a successful visit to promote the hotel and the city. He sensibly agreed. On the coach to the airport all was revealed. A mischievous journalist had spread a rumour that "Jim said" they could all take their bathrobes from the rooms!

Food is an obvious danger area when you're travelling far and wide and are responsible for other people's stomach linings. I must be blessed with a cast iron digestive tract. Whether my food comes from a back street stall in Marrakech, Jakarta or Bangkok or a smart international hotel with a top chef, I'll eat it and I've only rarely suffered the gripes. I learnt, however, to avoid stomach bugs in India by travelling with a good supply of Glenmorangie whisky and water biscuits. While I enjoyed my Indian meals, I always had a good stiff whisky on retiring. If, however, there's a bug about you'll catch it, is my theory.

At a sensitive police check in India where my luggage was searched, I had to give up my precious, partly drunk, bottle of whisky. Otherwise, it was made very clear to me by the policeman's unmistakable eye movements that I'd be delayed, considerably.

Indian tummy bugs are a subject the late TV presenter, Anne Gregg, knew something about. Once, while we were making a 10-minute slot for BBC's *Holiday*, she arrived looking as glamorous as ever and took her allotted position aboard an Indian dhow, seated serenely amongst silk cushions, as it sailed around the Lake Palace Hotel in Jaipur with flocks of green parakeets flying overhead and dancers and musicians playing for us. What the TV audience never saw was that Annie had to rush below deck to the loo every few minutes between takes.

In Cairo I caught hepatitis at a hotel near the Pyramids but that, and the occasional bout of diarrhoea, are the only health problems I've had in 40 years of travelling, covering more than three million air miles. On that Egypt visit, the whole group came down with severe diarrhoea and stomach pains after eating in a hotel and the journey home was a nightmare. We could never be very far away from a loo either at the airport or on the aircraft.

Airline food is quite another kettle of fish, meat or vegetables. I am on record as saying, and it's true, that I adore airline food but I once got myself into hot water over the first class menu on Cathay Pacific. On one particular flight, I was served up a dish of avocado which, as I put it to the client rather harshly, reminded me of cat sick. I didn't think its look or taste was appealing or appropriate for an airline. Well, my comments provoked the proverbial to hit the fan and memos were fired like bullets from the client to the catering company at Gatwick. Instead of taking it on the chin and simply altering the dish or substituting another, the catering company rang me and insisted I should have contacted them directly. What did I know about food anyway? Did I realise the trouble I had caused with such a major customer? I tried to explain that I saw it as part of my duty to comment not only on the food served, but also on all other aspects of the service in first class, which is highly competitive and where customers expect only the best. Voices were raised. Nerves frayed. Tempers were lost. The avocado dish was withdrawn.

Much more serious problems seemed to befall my colleagues, though. For instance, I never had a journo die on me although this event was something I sometimes fantasised about. But colleagues have experienced this and it's a traumatic event. One journalist died of a heart condition in his bath after the rest of his group had left for London, just after having enjoyed an apparently pleasant evening meal with the hotel PR. Other members of the team have had to airlift home heart attack victims and casualties from ski trips. One even found herself in jail, with her group, in Africa. A policeman stopped them and asked about their "business". The reply that they were journalists puzzled him. Unsure of just what journalists were, he threw them all in jail while he gave it some thought.

I've also had to deal with rogue journalists, those who don't like the other members of the group knowing what they're up to, particularly their activities in the trouser or skirt department. Those were the ones I had to worry most about, especially in places like Kuala Lumpur, Jakarta, Manila and, of course, Bangkok. I didn't mind them keeping quiet about their proclivities, of course, but it was alarming when they'd just disappear without reference to their hosts, their itinerary or to me.

On one trip to the Far East, one of the group disappeared for several days immediately after a visit to one of the naughty areas of Bangkok. He went off, I later discovered, with a local girl he'd met then, three days later, he re-appeared at the hotel to say he had changed his return flight and would be staying on. It turned out that he eventually married another Thai girl. Much as I wished him joy, I didn't relish the job I had to do of explaining to our client how I'd lost one of the party to a Thai-style romance and got no coverage for my efforts.

38

THE NAKED LADY OF
HAMPSTEAD

WE WERE ASKED TO LAUNCH a new hotel in Cyprus – The Amathus Beach – to the UK travel trade and holidaymaker. It was a one-off project, unlike a usual PR campaign, which can – with luck – run and run. We always welcomed these projects however because they were lucrative: we could charge by the week and they could be slotted into the team's existing workload. It was profit added direct to the bottom line.

I was therefore happy to escort six senior travel writers to Cyprus along with representatives from tour operators and British Airways, the airline supplying the flights. The whole affair was designed to give everyone a relaxed few days looking at the hotel, which was under construction, exploring some of the island's tourist attractions and enjoying delicious food and wine, which can be difficult on that island. All went smoothly. I remember great conversation, good fun and the group arriving back at Heathrow the best of friends vowing, as ever, to keep in touch.

A few weeks later I was to pay a price though. Now I have always got on very well with women. Most gay men do. After all, we have something in common – an attraction to men. We always preferred to employ women at TPS, finding them more efficient, conscientious and less likely to waste time empire building than many male PRs.

On the Cyprus visit there had been three female journalists and I got on very well with all of them. One, a leading Fleet Street writer, who'd been sent to Cyprus for an influential Sunday broadsheet, invited me to lunch a few weeks later and I accepted. It's not unusual for the PR to be invited out after a trip as a "thanks" and I enjoyed such occasions. Some of my best friends in the business came about as a result of meeting on a media visit. This was not one of them.

Off I trundled to the chosen lunch venue, the French House in Soho's Dean Street. There we re-ran all the great gossip first exchanged under the Cyprus sun as better wine flowed and we both became nicely tipsy. As the pub was closing at three, my hostess suggested that we continue our talk over yet another bottle at her Hampstead home. I readily accepted because I can never resist nosing around someone's house. We poured ourselves into a taxi and headed north.

I had no inkling of what was to come. I had always made it clear that I lived with "Arthur, my partner in TPS", and let travel industry gossip do the rest. Alarm bells sounded faintly in the taxi as my hostess sat much too close and her hands seemed to be all over me. "I'm gay, remember?" I said with a laugh in as casual a manner as I could manage, putting her hands back where they belonged. " Let's not worry about that", she sighed.

Through my sozzled awareness, terror was creeping up. I knew there was no such thing as a free lunch, but surely... surely not? I was a drunken damsel in distress, a damsel who didn't want her virtue compromised but wanted to hang on to valuable coverage for my client, the hotel in Cyprus, even more desperately. How to escape from the clutches of this albeit charming creature without losing what I hoped would be an approving travel article?

The groping continued throughout what seemed like a very long cab ride to Hampstead and, when we finally arrived at the house, I took some deep breaths, tried to sober up and turned on my most affable, diverting PR man talk. We staggered into what was a stunning contemporary home overlooking the Heath. My hostess disappeared into the kitchen to get the wine. I shouted, "Why don't we just have some black coffee?" No such luck. She appeared with a tray of more wine and glasses.

I was standing looking at the view of the Heath as she put the tray down and, to my horror, knelt before me and started to undo my fly. "I really must get back to the office", I gasped, grabbing the zip and pulling it back up.

"Wait a minute, I have to go upstairs," she said ominously. A few minutes later, I heard her call, "Jim, come here!" My blood froze. I went to the bottom of the stairs and looked up. There, stark, staring naked was my female travel writer. She started slowly down the stairs towards me. "I really, really have to go now", I blurted, panicking, bursting out of the front door into the street, running and hailing a taxi a few hundred yards later.

Should I ring the next day and apologise, try to make a joke of it? Too embarrassing for both of us. I decided to lie low, fully expecting that I'd blown the chance of good editorial coverage for my client. But I was spectacularly wrong. A few weeks later a huge piece appeared, rightly waxing lyrical about Cyprus and the hotel and, in the post, came a note wishing me 'all the best' with a copy of the glowing article. Phew! The client was happy, British Airways was happy but I've always felt rather guilty at letting the girl down badly......

This wasn't my only narrow escape from a sexually challenging female. Perhaps in those early days of more open attitudes, a few women felt that they could "convert" me or that I was secretly bisexual. They couldn't and I'm not.

On another occasion, a secretary turned up at my hotel bedroom door after midnight, clearly drunk, asking to be let in. When I did so, she made a beeline for the bed saying she was afraid of sleeping alone. I had to ask her to leave very firmly. A few female travel writers have invited me home "for lunch" with a smile, but generally most women get the message pretty quickly and we all remain "girls together".

TPS was always lucky in that we managed over the years to employ many great female PR operators and I like to think that we made work fun. I always enjoyed finishing in the office early evening and moving on to the local wine bar either in Fleet Street or latterly in Victoria. It would be very relaxed. One evening, as I was into my second glass, a question put by one of these colleagues almost made me choke.

"How do I pleasure a man?", she asked. Blimey! Sex guru to women was not a sideline I'd ever thought I'd take up. After a few minutes' thought, I said, "Well, listening to male journalists around the world, I'd guess you do it with oral sex. In addition to the usual." The table broke into laughter, as did other drinkers nearby. I then had to quietly try to explain the art of oral sex, or, as it turned out, enhance and correct the knowledge that already existed around the table among the girls, as the wine flowed.

39

SEX IN A FOREIGN CITY

THE SEX DRIVE OF THE AVERAGE media member – so to speak – seems curiously to surge on trips abroad. It probably happens to most people away from home. At nights, even after long, hard days when everyone proclaimed themselves to be dead tired, I'd invariably hear doors opening and closing as members of a group got to know each other better or invited guests into their rooms. This was frowned on by the hotel management, if and when they found out about it, fearful of late-night trouble from unsavoury characters met perhaps in the lobby or, worse still, in the street. I learned how deep is the disapproval when, on one visit, my Hong Kong hotel room telephone rang at about 1am. One of my group was in a panic. He'd met a man and a woman in the hotel bar and invited them back to his room. They'd been spotted by one of the 'floor boys', butlers who double as night security people on each floor, who'd reported three people going into the journalist's room to his boss. The boss then followed a security procedure whereby he 'phoned the journalist to ask if he was all right. I had to impress upon the journalist when he rang me that, whatever happened in the room, if indeed anything had happened, it was at his risk and his responsibility. He accepted this and nothing untoward occurred. Well, he didn't get mugged anyway. But the 'incident' was raised the next day at the hotel's regular morning management meeting and I was formally told that "entertaining" had taken place in one of my group's rooms. It's always the PR man's fault.

There were many gay men who came on my visits abroad, I'm delighted to say. Usually they were armed with the excellent Spartacus Guide, which gives invaluable information about haunts in cities around the world listing bars, cruising areas, cinemas and clubs frequented by gays. As usual, I was mother hen for the trip and I would always tell them to be doubly careful about pick-ups because they could often be targets for robberies. Most of them didn't need to be told this as they were already streetwise, but the scene varies throughout the world and I always wanted them to be careful at least, as it would have to be Dunn to the rescue when things went wrong. I was often impressed watching the skill of other people's pick-up techniques. One writer managed to spot and make an arrangement with a bell-boy – or bell man, in this case – at the hotel in the brief moments between checking in his luggage and taking the lift to his room. He came back down to the lobby in minutes and told me he'd made a rendezvous for seven that evening. Now that's what I call a fast mover. Female writers were always that much more discreet about their assignations.

In many Arab countries harsh penalties – including death – hang over men found engaged in homosexual acts. That doesn't stop young Arab men in Bahrain from trying to stop passing cars and offering sex. I was told by a couple of gay men on one press trip that often straight Arab men would want to be given oral sex in cars. In Morocco it seems that almost every man is available for sex, so long as a "little present", usually money, "backshish", is offered at the end.

Gay men don't have to go abroad to get into trouble with the police, of course. I was once telephoned by a near-hysterical media colleague, a man I'd got to know well over several years, who had just been arrested by a plain clothes police officer in a notorious public lavatory in London's Green Park underground station. The charge was "importuning in a public place". He had been loitering too long in the loo hoping to meet someone and his bad luck was that a copper had been on entrapment duty and he'd been caught. My friend was calling me from Vine Street Police Station in the West End to which he'd been frog-marched under threat of being hand-cuffed if he made the slightest trouble. He was interviewed, given police bail and told to attend Bow Street Magistrates' Court the following morning. I met him at the police station, a respectable middle-aged man in a smart, conservative busi-ness suit, and walked him back to his office. On the way I had telephoned his solicitor friend for advice. The advice was, "Turn up, plead guilty, pay the fine straight away." The fine was £800, which he paid in cash the next morning. The shame was far greater.

One request that floored me was from a client, the head of a major American hotel group, a married man with two children. He wanted me to organise some 'female company' for him when we attended a press event that I was running in London as part of a European media tour. I felt like saying "no" immediately because I had no idea of how to go about such a task. Male company, yes, no problem. But girls? Where to begin? But I knew a man who did. He knew of an escort agency. This was, of course, before the advent of the web, which revolutionised the world of sex contact. The whole thing backfired. The woman duly turned up at the executive's hotel room but, ten minutes later, so did her pimp demanding money and threatening trouble. Result? Embarrassed PR man and Chief Executive. My pimping days were over!

One thing I could always be sure of during a press visit was that everyone, including seemingly high-minded journalists, would want to visit the red light districts after the official part of the itinerary had been completed. In Bangkok, one of the famous districts for live sex shows, brothels and lap and pole dancing clubs (with names like Pussy Galore and The Big One) is Patpong, where everything closed strangely early at midnight – at least it did in the 1980s. So there was usually pressure on me to streamline the obligatory official dinner where the general manager would greet everybody and have his say about the delights of his hotel.

It was not polite to admit that this was the reason for leaving the dinner table so promptly of course. I would have to tell the manager that the journalists were tired and wanted to go to their rooms for an early night. I know he knew this wasn't true and knew from experience where everyone was heading. We would then gather outside my room or in a corner of the lobby. On occasions, when we had been spotted by our hosts from the hotel or the Tourist Office, I've even taken a group down the staff lift and packed them into taxis and they'd disappear. All in a night's work.

Once inside one of the bars, we would begin ordering the highly-priced drinks while watching the sex shows. These tended to consist of the usual dancing by naked girls interspersed with a performance of the heterosexual sex act on the bar counter. This was spiced up with a few stunts including one in which the young girl demonstrated extraordinary muscle control with a ping pong ball! We would all usually gawp in amazement and then they would drift out leaving me to pay the bill, which usually totalled several hundred pounds. If I was unlucky, I would find them heading into another bar to sample the performances there. I was always a willing participant, happy to take them around the bars. I knew it was my expense account that they were after. When it came to filling in my expenses sheets to present to the clients as pro-forma invoices, I was grateful for Arthur's invention of the 'merge' system. This allowed me to be unspecific about the places where drinks for the media were bought.

Sex in the air has not been a big issue for me, unfortunately. The Mile-High Club has only functioned once, as far as I know, when I was travelling. I was in a packed first class cabin on a flight to Asia and little did I realise that across the aisle, under the blankets, as the rest of us were tucked up trying to sleep, one of my group was quietly joining that famous club. This most discreet, senior gay journalist informed me of his membership as we disembarked. "It was very sudden", he said, "it just happened, there were no crew around and the timing was perfect". I can't pretend I didn't feel fleetingly envious.

Working abroad with celebrities can sometimes present other varieties of ego problems. I met Michael Parkinson, the sports journalist and television chat show host, in the early 1980s when his career was taking a bit of a back seat. He had stopped his peak time BBC chat show and was living part of the year in Sydney with his wife Mary and part of the time in England where he presented a popular radio programme for the London station, LBC. A fan of that show, we suggested to his producer that he broadcast live from Hong Kong daily for a week. The producer thought it a great idea and proceeded to link us with the local Hong Kong radio station to provide the facilities and track down suitably interesting guests visiting or living in the territory for Michael to interview. For my part, I undertook to make the first class travel and accommodation arrangements. I was due in Asia with a media group during that time anyway. What I was gaining was a chance to promote our clients, Hong

Kong as a tourist destination, The Mandarin Hotel and Cathay Pacific, to a target London morning audience.

All went smoothly and Michael and his team were excellent company over dinner at the Mandarin's plush Grill restaurant and at the Captain's Bar, then a lively social centre for ex-pats. Smoothly, that is, until Michael's return journey from Hong Kong. He had chosen to travel home to London on a Friday night, the busiest of the week. Having a free ticket meant he was at risk of being 'bumped' off the flight to make room for a paying customer or a pilot or member of his family needing to return and always given priority by the company – this despite my efforts to see that he travelled home on schedule. The inevitable happened and Michael was told he could not proceed to fly home as planned. As there was only one flight a day, it meant he had to return to the hotel and start his journey again on the Saturday evening. The star was not happy. Loudly not happy. The next time I saw him was at The Ivy restaurant in London. I bounded up to him to be met by an exceedingly cool Mr P. On subsequent occasions when our paths have crossed, he has pointedly looked the other way. Such are the joys of PR!

Clients were occasionally troublesome too. Always troublesome, now I come to think of it. One of our airline clients – over the years we handled the PR for six airlines – was a very stuffy stick-in-the-mud. Once when flying with his wife on a long-haul journey to Hong Kong, he happened to glance across the aisle in first class and spotted a captain's wife flying home on a complimentary ticket and breastfeeding her baby. An old-fashioned man, he decided that other passengers must be hugely embarrassed. On arrival he immediately sent a memo to all airline heads of department and to us to say that, in future, no baby would be allowed to set a bootee-d tootsie in first class and there would certainly be no breastfeeding in any section of the aircraft. A New Man he was not. We decided that it would not be sensible to release this new ruling to the press.

We've all had to suffer the airline superbore. The person in the next seat who insists on talking, no matter how much you try to look the other way, read or go to sleep. On one long-haul flight, I had one of them. Worse, this one not only talked incessantly, he also drank incessantly. Finally I got to sleep but was awakened at one point by the chief steward telling my neighbour that he was to be given no more to drink by order of the captain. At this he erupted angrily. Thank goodness, alcohol got the better of him eventually and he passed out. When I arrived at my destination and reported the incident, I was shocked to discover that my hellish travelling companion had been an off-duty airline pilot!

My addiction to travelling encouraged me to create a competition which would not only give me more reasons to hop on planes but would also help young, aspiring travel writers. The Young Travel Writer of the Year Award was taken up instantly by The Observer's enthusiastic travel editor, Desmond Balmer, and ran for a number of years. The idea was simple. You had to be no older than 25 and to submit an essay of 500 words. Writers of the best six pieces chosen by Desmond and me were taken by us to a Cathay Pacific destination where we would also stay with one of our hotel clients. The only hard part was reading the hundreds of entries. Some years there were more than 500 and the writing standard was usually high. Then, once again, the Mulberry bags were packed and off we all flew to places like Hong Kong, Beijing, Sydney, Saigon and Manila. This last journey was filmed for the BBC's *Holiday* programme. We were very proud of the competition. It discovered some excellent young writers and even helped establish successful Fleet Street travel editors such as Cath Urquhart, James Bedding and Max Wooldridge. We also spawned the successful author Colin Bateman from Northern Ireland. Apparently, a character from one of his books, which have all sold very well, is a camp TV presenter called Jim....

40

ON A BED WITH A PRINCESS –
AT WORK WITH THE ROYALS

YOU MEET ALL SORTS IN PR work, including people you'd rather avoid. But meeting members of the Royal Family always gave me a buzz. I've always been a committed royalist and seeing how alternative systems function has confirmed my views. None of the heads of government departments I encountered over the years in Asia, for example, impressed me greatly and all have been intent on bolstering their own positions by manipulating the media – local and international.

They also seem to have as many unnecessary chauffeurs, limos, secretaries, security men and houses as people often accuse members of our Royal Family of having. If there's one thing a President or senior government official loves, it is to appear in the local press or on television pictured with a group of visiting journalists, apparently promoting tourism but actually promoting themselves. The journalists generally politely comply, though they are usually uneasy about seeming to endorse politicians and their regimes.

Abroad, I'm frequently asked what I think the Queen thinks about this or that, whether Camilla Parker Bowles will ever become Queen or whether Prince William rather than Prince Charles will succeed the throne. I have absolutely no idea, of course.

It's been enlightening to sit at various tables around the world where the only Royal Family to be discussed has been the British one. Even when there have been Spanish, Dutch or Swedish journalists, it's the British royals that dominate the conversation. Admittedly our lot have had a turbulent few decades but there have also been "scandals" and gossip amongst European royal families well worth talking about. Yet somehow they never attract as much comment as the British versions and foreign royals, of course, do not have such an inquisitive media.

I've been involved on a number of occasions with various royals, including the recent recruit, Sophie, Countess of Wessex whom I first met when she was working as a busy, young PR consultant around London and very effective she was too. Once, before her engagement to Prince Edward was confirmed, she approached me with her then business partner, Murray Harkin, to discuss us taking an interest in the company. I told her that, in my opinion, she would have to resign from her PR work in the commercial sector when she got engaged then married. I felt that there would be clashes of interest but Sophie thought differently and assured me that her future commercial PR work had been "sorted out" with the Palace. I took no pride in reading about her subsequent embarrassing difficulties. And, as the media hounded her when she was "turned over" by a News Of The World scam – it alleged she had promised Arab clients contact with the Queen – and reported her belated decision to quit, all of her friends in the PR world felt great sympathy for her.

In recent decades, commercial PR people like me have begun to be directly involved in the organisation of royal visits if they involved a client. Following the media expansion and the development of an overpowering and, some would say, unhealthy interest in all things royal, Buckingham Palace officials realised that they had to get their own media relations in order. It was decided that their PR department had to work with the outside consultants.

This is what led to my first visit to Buckingham Palace. I was invited by one of the Royal Family's close advisors to be briefed on arrangements for a "Night-Of-Nights Gala" taking place at one of our client's hotels in London, the St James Court, just off St James's Park. What was very special about the event was that almost the entire Royal Family, led by Her Majesty the Queen, were going out for what the tabloids would call "an Indian" that evening.

The Indian hotel group Taj Hotels and the owners, who were also our clients, were hosting an Indian banquet to celebrate the anniversary of their country's independence and the Royal Family were to be honoured guests. This was to be the ultimate in glittering occasions, covered by the world's media, all arrangements at the hotel handled by TPS working with the Palace press office.

At these big royal events, the Palace press office is always very much in control – at least as far as it can ever be. The press officers usually arrange what is known as the Royal Rota, allocating which outside media group may cover a royal visit which can often avoid the paparazzi scrums we have seen. This means that one press company, maybe News International or Associated Newspapers or the BBC, is selected to cover the story on behalf of all the other media. The rules are not always obeyed and journalists sometimes turn up en masse if they think there's a particularly big story in the offing. Often they are accommodated. My experience was that Buckingham Palace officials were always open to suggestions and were thoroughly professional with a no-nonsense attitude.

I'm not going to claim that I'm close to any member of the Royal Family. Far from it, I never believe people who say they've "met" a particular royal and then go on to give the impression that they are now the best of pals and that a shooting weekend at Balmoral is on the cards. Royal meetings are still very carefully staged, despite our egalitarian times, and for anyone to receive more than a few words, if that, out of the royal mouth is a major breakthrough. Right or wrong that is a fact. Anyway, in royal matters I believe that "them that know don't say and them that say don't know...." So I always smile when people say they've been to Highgrove, Prince Charles' Gloucestershire home, and had a walk in the garden. I'm afraid that's no big deal. If you're a member of a major gardening club or charity you can apply for just such a visit.

The late Princess Margaret was great fun though, I can tell you that for certain, even though she had the reputation of being a bit sharp and sour. When she opened the new Holiday Inn in Glasgow, the first in Scotland, it was my job (we were the company's UK PR consultants by then) to be on hand to give her hosts, the hotel's general manager, The Lord Provost of Glasgow and others, a rest from what is always stringent royal protocol during an official visit.

Without warning, the client signalled to me and ushered me forward to take over for a short period as we stood waiting to go into the formal lunch. What on earth could I talk about? I tried lamely, "Did you enjoy your trip, Ma'am?" She looked up at me in complete bewilderment. "What?" she said with a smirk, "I wasn't aware I had fallen", and turned to her security officer who, robot-like, lit her cigarette. I looked at the Princess and I burst out laughing. "I meant your journey up to Glasgow, Ma'am. Was it comfortable?" She looked at me intently this time, then said, "I take it you have never flown on a royal flight?" I nodded and she continued, "Well, then, if you had you would realise that they are extremely uncomfortable and this morning's was no exception". So that was that.

At this point, one of the organising team, a scatter-brained woman, rushed up to us and, quickly curtseying to the Princess, said, "I'm desperate to find the Lord Provost, he needs to lead us in to lunch, everybody's waiting." Princess Margaret drew slowly on her cigarette and, pointing the holder towards the crowd of pre-lunch drinkers, drawled, "I think you'll find him over there, he's the one with the large gold chain around his neck".

The Princess impressed me on that visit. She not only spent time with all the official guests at the lunch and during the tour of the hotel but also made time to meet all the "below stairs" team, the cleaners, cooks and maids. In one bedroom, as we toured, I sat on the bed and tested the springs. "What's it like?" she asked, as she sat down beside me. Almost instantly we were bouncing on the new bed, laughing.

What was really touching about her was that on her arrival, as she stepped out of her car, she heard the Glasgow Police Pipe Band playing welcoming music. Instead of just walking straight on to the official line-up, she paused for a few minutes to listen, just long enough for the band to notice, so delaying the finely timed proceedings. It showed to me that she had appreciated the effort made for her.

I'd met Princess Margaret years earlier when I had gate-crashed a cocktail party at a big travel industry dinner-dance at the Grosvenor House in London. I recollect, just about, that I had accepted the hospitality of a few too many clients that evening. Looking for a colleague, I somehow found myself in the room at the hotel where the event was being held.

I walked straight in and was immediately approached by two women: the Princess and singer Joan Baez, who had been supplying the cabaret to a noisy, rude audience of rowdy travel agents and their dressed-up wives. The Princess asked who I was, introduced Joan Baez and the three of us chatted away about the evening.

To say I wasn't popular with senior members of the travel industry on the organising committee the next day would be an understatement. The guest list in that room had been carefully chosen and there had been fierce competition to attend, especially from the wives. My intervention meant that as we three talked for so long, many of the chosen ones missed meeting the Princess – not a smart move on my behalf as a humble consultant.

Prince Charles asked me to "organise" a glass of white wine for him "please", when I found myself arranging the opening of a salmon-processing factory in Scotland – as I say, never knowingly turn down business! The factory was owned by Ian Anderson of Jethro Tull fame and his financial advisors (who also worked for another of our clients) had been the people who had asked us to handle the media at the opening event. All went well until the Prince had performed the opening ceremony and, as he was going into lunch with local dignitaries, the owner of the hotel shouted, yes shouted, for the Prince to sign her guest book! After a withering glance from the royal eyes, her guest duly obliged.

My only claim to having "talked" to the Queen came during an assignment in Manchester when she was opening another Holiday Inn, this time the converted Midland Hotel. She asked me where I would like her to stand for the unveiling of the official plaque and photograph. The resulting picture has gone down in the annals of PR photography as one of the dullest and most boring. It's just the Queen unveiling a plaque, that's all, no flowers or stage setting. Again, not one of my greater moments.

By far the most memorable of my royal events occurred at a World Travel Market in London. A young Princess of Wales was extremely nervous as she spent an afternoon 'opening' the Market and touring some of its stands. We were all on hand to guide her through the massive crowds that had gathered to see her. It wasn't long after the "fairy tale" wedding and this was one of her first official engagements on her own with only equerries in attendance. You can imagine the atmosphere. This brand new British Princess, strikingly beautiful to boot, doing her royal duty, mingling with thousands of visiting business people and hundreds of journalists from around the globe.

It was our job to promote the fair and to look after her during the visit. A "walkabout", agreed in advance with the Palace, was underway. The rapt expressions on people's faces – particularly travel agents from Thailand, where their royal family are considered Gods, and from Japan, where royalty is similarly revered – not to mention clearly-impressed journalists, will live with me for a long time. Chatting with an equerry over the buffet lunch later, I became aware that Princess Diana's arrival was creating this level of excitement all around the world. We weren't to know then that 'Diana Fever' was not just a passing phase but would grow and continue up to and after her death in 1997.

Not all of our royal PR work was this easy, though. Norton Romsey, Lord Romsey, then one of our partners in a video production company and a personal friend of Prince Charles, asked us to run a discreet campaign to promote Broadlands, his house in Hampshire, one of "The Magnificent Seven" stately homes in Britain. It was well-known that Charles and Diana had spent the first night of their honeymoon there in a magnificent four-poster, though in what I judged was a comfortable but rather austere bedroom.

We got to work but, to no one's great surprise, despite previous assurances that staff would be helpful, not one Broadlands person would talk about anything of interest to a journalist, particularly not THAT honeymoon. The House Manager, who had previously dabbled in PR for the estate, resented the arrival of these 'jumped up' PR people from London and was totally non-cooperative. Despite the historical importance of the house, we just couldn't persuade newspapers or magazines, and certainly not the tabloids, to write about the place. The campaign fizzled out.

We were similarly stumped when the Duke of Roxburghe asked us to publicise Floors Castle, his magnificent pile in the borders. Guy, the Duke, wanted us to launch his 'boutique' hotel Sunlaws, which is on the estate and, at the same time, try to attract publicity to bump up visitor numbers to the castle.

Promoting the exclusive hotel was easy – we got coverage in all the target glossy magazines and it is now a leading British hotel, renamed The Roxburghe Hotel and Golf Course. But an interview I'd arranged with the Duke in one of the main rooms of the castle backfired on me. A journalist decided she didn't, after all, approve of all the castle's splendour, despite having previously assured me that she would write a sympathetic friendly-aristocrat-relaxing-at-home article. I'd been naïve. Thereafter we conducted all interviews with the Duke in his office in the stable yard.

Without knowing it, the late Diana, Princess of Wales and the young Princes William and Harry helped us considerably in our promotion of a new hotel and timeshare development called Craigendarroch near Ballater in the Scottish Highlands.

I heard that when Diana stayed at nearby Balmoral she regularly brought the boys, then small children, to the Craigendarroch indoor pool for early morning swims. Sometimes they were there on their own, sometimes they joined in with other children. The words "Pool by Royal Approval" flashed before my PR's eyes. I couldn't resist it. We placed the story with one or two feature editors in the nationals. The client, who'd disapproved at first, conveniently looked the other way – looking rather at increased timeshare sales – and the story appeared in all the nationals, main regionals and, of course, all the Scottish papers.

It put Craigendarroch on the map. This was in the early days of the timeshare industry and developments had a bad name as many were associated with cheaply built blocks of flats and high-pressure selling methods. But this was different. Here were attractively designed 'luxury' chalets, each with expensive sound systems and first class furniture and fittings in spectacular countryside. The royal story resulted in the travel media reviewing their fixed ideas about timeshare properties.

We were the first PR company to achieve positive coverage for a timeshare development on BBC TV's *Holiday*, as the programme sped north after seeing the Diana story. And our success led to us being offered other property and timeshare business in Portugal and Spain – naturally, we took it on.

Diana continued to use the pool despite the occasional press intrusion. Craigendarroch was, after all, only a short drive from Balmoral, which, by most accounts, wasn't her favourite holiday haunt.

On one occasion, during a visit I made to Ballater with a group of travel writers, we foolishly decided after a good Saturday night dinner, to get up and attend church early next morning. We would thus be able to do some Royal Family spotting and get a close look at the weekend guests, the then Prime Minister Margaret Thatcher and husband Dennis. I remember little of the service except how dreary it was and how sorry I felt for the small battalion of young soldiers sitting in the pews in front of us. They looked even more hung-over than we were.

41

RED NOSES ALL ROUND

IN THE ELEVEN YEARS AT Carter Lane in the City before we moved to Grosvenor Gardens, near Victoria Station, in 1986, TPS grew up. When we moved in to Carter Lane, we occupied about half of the available space and we let out a couple of desks on the top floor. By the time we left, we not only filled the building but we had also taken two floors in the building opposite. Our staff of 15 had grown to a gang of 40 and we had acquired our first computer. We were also handling the PR for some of the biggest names in the European leisure industry including Holiday Inn Hotels, Ladbroke Hotels and several regions of Spain. Most importantly, Arthur hired the incomparable Elizabeth Platt as his bookkeeper and assistant. This splendidly loyal and bright woman ended up as the Finance Director .

We had also gained an entertainment division and suddenly found ourselves in show business PR. It amused me to think that I had been in London for little over a decade and, from knowing nothing about journalism, the media and PR, I now found myself – as if by magic – an "expert" and a "consultant" on a whole series of industries: travel and hotels, tour oper-ation, trade relations, restaurants and now show business!

The man who took us into showbiz was Jason Pollock, who came from a background of promoting West End shows. He persuaded us to launch an entertainment PR division with a colleague of his, Phil Symes, a music PR who'd been working with a large agency. At first we called it Pollock Symes Associates and then PSA. This was fortunate because Jason bowed out after six months (to join the new breakfast TV company, TVam) and Phil took over the helm. PSA neatly became the initials for Phil Symes Associates and together with colleague Angie Errigo – now a top London film critic – and a small team, he went on to expand this new division.

Early clients of PSA included The Northern Ballet Company, Barry Manilow, Simon and Garfunkel, Paul McCartney, Adam Ant and the rock group Queen, whom Phil had represented during the late seventies. Our work involved arranging press interviews, usually in the Grosvenor Gardens offices, overseeing arrangements for concerts and tours, publicising record releases, handling any news stories connected with the clients and generally giving PR advice. Barry Manilow was especially concerned that he could be advised at any and all times of the day. In this distant time before mobiles, he insisted that Phil and his assistant leave telephone numbers with him every evening so that they could be reached from the moment the office closed, through the night and until the next morning's opening. Barry often tested these numbers to make sure he did indeed have 24-hour representation. Paranoid or what?

By the mid eighties we were organising many high-profile music and film projects and even handling the PR for the young David and Elizabeth Emmanuel who had secretly designed the wedding dress for Diana, Princess of Wales and could not take advantage of the fact until after the wedding when the dress stunned the world. Arthur was not impressed, however, mainly because of the modest revenue that was being generated by the division. Celebrities, we discovered, tended to be people who expected all those they worked with to be star-struck fans and work for next to nothing, preferably nothing. It was as if they believed it was a privilege for a PR company to represent them.

On the other hand, our other clients loved the fact that we had "stars" on our client list. It was as if some of the glitter was rubbing off on them. I was grateful for the occasional pair of complimentary tickets to previews and premières but was disappointed that this division was not making much money. Happily Phil was not deterred. He was the consummate PR man who left all the money matters – such as they were – to others. He enjoyed the company of enthusiastic, talented beginners in the entertainment industry and gained satisfaction, though little money, from helping their careers flourish. He welcomed new challenges such as that presented when we were approached by a small, emerging movie company, Palace Pictures, formed by Nik Powell who had launched Virgin with Richard Branson.

With him we went on to publicise several of their innovative and controversial movies, including the hugely successful French language film *Diva; Angel,* the first directed by future award-winner Neil Jordan, and the horror film *The Evil Dead.* This was initially banned on the grounds of obscenity and generated the whole debate about "video nasties", but it is now hailed as a classic of the genre. We also launched *Blood Simple,* the first film by the brilliant Coen Brothers; *The Company Of Wolves,* and several notable British films including *Wish You Were Here*, starring Emily Lloyd and *Scandal,* a dramatisation of the Profumo affair which rocked

British politics in the sixties, starring Joanna Whalley as Christine Keeler.

For this, Christine Keeler herself agreed to do a bunch of interviews at our offices.

Undoubtedly it was fun, though I was slightly taken aback when I encountered Miss Keeler, the notorious former call girl, waiting in our reception. The same shock came when Buster Edwards, one of the Great Train Robbers, arrived there for interviews with Phil Collins, who played him in the film *Buster* which we were launching. When we came to publicise *The Krays*, the movie about the notorious Kray twins, Phil announced that the proceeds of the première would go to the Taxi Drivers' Benevolent Fund. Both Reggie and Ronnie Kray began contacting us from prison asking for tickets for friends and dozens of five feet wide, broken-nosed, cauliflower-eared gentlemen turned up at Grosvenor Gardens also demanding tickets. Telling them the event was sold out – as it soon was – did not go down well. Phil had to beg for tickets allocated to other groups to satisfy this unnerving extra demand.

After this success in promoting movies, our show business division was approached by new television production companies Hat Trick and The Callender Company who went on to great success with a Channel Four series, *The Last Resort*, featuring the then unknown Jonathan Ross. I wonder what happened to him? Other TV "unknowns" who came to our offices and were signed up were Vic Reeves and Bob Mortimer and, later, a budding, little known actress who we agreed to represent for a tiny fee without any great hope of her gaining future fame. Then, one night, she appeared with her boyfriend, actor Hugh Grant, at a première, wearing a dress with large safety pins up the side. Press photographers went to work.

The next morning Elizabeth Hurley had "arrived". Phil then decided it would be a good idea for her to get to know the editors of some of our national newspapers and arranged a drinks party. It was Stuart Higgins, the then editor of The Sun, who later repaid the favour by tipping off Phil that a story had just come through that Hugh Grant had been arrested in Hollywood for an indecent act in a car with a prostitute. When a brave member of our team interrupted Elizabeth's lunch at Daphne's Restaurant to break the news, the 'phone could be heard to fall from the shocked actress's hand. Soon Elizabeth and Hugh Grant were communicating – but only through separate telephones in our offices. A few hours later the press inquiries began. A long night's work lay ahead.

A more satisfying project began when the organisers of the new Comic Relief charity appeal came to us to handle the event's publicity after its first year, the start of a nine-year association. It was in Grosvenor Gardens, at an ideas meeting, that Phil suggested, off the top of his head, "something silly to enable millions of people to participate". How about a red plastic split ball on a piece of elastic? Thus the Red Nose was born and since then this simple, brilliant toy has become an instantly recognisable symbol of the fund-raising.

At the same time PSA continued to handle stage events, among them the musical Buddy about the late singer Buddy Holly. I don't remember this but Phil insists we were offered the choice of shares in the production as payment for our PR work or a monthly fixed fee of £500. He remembers Arthur advised we accept the fixed fee. Since Buddy went on to be a hit, ran for 13 years in the West End and is performed all over the world, we should probably have taken the shares. But who knows? Years earlier we had made money from backing the Andrew Lloyd Webber hit *Evita* but lost some in a box office disaster called *The Case of the Oily Levantine,* starring Hywel Bennett. It lasted about ten minutes in the West End – you can't win them all!

42

LUVVIES AND A TRIBAL CHIEF

WITH PHIL'S ENTERTAINMENT DIVISION taking off but showing small returns for long hours of hard work by him and his team, we began to look around to see if there were other areas of PR in which we could expand and grow our company. We took the view, somewhat conceitedly, that a good PR could promote anything if they had creativity and researched the right contacts in the industry and the target media. We were not always right.

Our restaurant PR work gave us the idea of taking a look at the food industry. Could we help there? Could we make money? I had met the late Robert Carrier, the restaurateur and doyen of food writers, and we sat down with him to see if we could cook up a new division. We thought we could and we called it Prime Communications. It didn't really take off until many years later and under a different team. We found that the food industry at that time was well served by good PR companies and consultants and they didn't need us – not even with Bob's proven success.

If Prime Communications was less than a big hit Original Image, formed a year earlier, was turning out to be a real mistake, the one company in TPS's history that was to become a serious loss-maker and to cause our greatest heartache. It came into being after we met a young television producer who had "a brilliant idea". I have always been fascinated by television and we certainly made it work in promotional terms for our tourism clients over the years.

Television producers were becoming more approachable around the end of the 1970s, especially in the top travel programmes. Today, many series, both factual and drama, are sponsored by commercial companies but, back then, television was only slowly and nervously waking up to the fact that the PR industry – not to mention the advertising sector – could be useful and save them money. Budgets have always been tight, but the production teams were allocated more time then than they are now to make each programme. We always had to be careful of course. With BBC film crews, we had to watch that they weren't seen to be in our pocket – although they certainly were during filming as we usually paid all the expenses. Flights, hotels, cars, drinks – you name it, it usually came out of our PR budget.

We took full advantage. We'd meet producers and researchers every few months over lunch with our array of brochures and put ideas into the pot. Once we got the green light – confirmation that they were interested in a particular film idea – we'd go off and arrange flights, hotel accommodation, transfers, meetings with tourist officers and book all the restaurants. We knew that the most important people on a shoot were the scriptwriters and the cameramen – words and pictures – and we made every effort to help them as much as we could. And we never forgot that meals were very close to most cameramen's hearts. Then we went to work cajoling directors and producers to increase the on-screen visuals for our client in order to ensure that their name and product were well to the fore in each film sequence. These usually lasted about eight minutes, so the 'plug' for a client was sizeable. Later editions of *Holiday* on BBC1 included segments lasting only about five minutes – too short in my view because of the large amount of information which needs to be conveyed to the viewer. Consequently, many programmes are now garbled and I wonder what good, if any, they do for the travel industry, not to mention the viewer. Certainly their power to 'sell' holidays has diminished and indeed *Holiday* is no more.

Our involvement never guaranteed editorial approval of what went on air however, but the results were usually satisfactory and I always enjoyed working with the travel programme presenters, some of them television's big stars of the day. Cliff Michelmore, who I'd watched on *Tonight* with Mum all those years ago in Gourock, was courteous and charming and time spent with Judith Chalmers on ITV's *Wish You Were Here* was always a hoot. Taking Judith on a private tour of developments of two resorts in Majorca, Palma Nova and Magaluf, was like accompanying the Queen on a royal visit. People left the beaches and the sea and lined the promenades to applaud and cheer. It was no surprise that she has become the 'national treasure' and travel icon that she is.

Wish You Were Here began on ITV in 1974 and, at its peak, was watched by 19 million viewers. Judith has visited 120 countries, reporting on travel every year up to the present day. The only exception was in 1975 when the pound was so low that it was thought to be in poor taste to broadcast the programme.

Working with the late Anne Gregg on *Holiday* was always a delight and she too was recognised everywhere we went. In India, filming an item in Udipur, lights and cameras were set up for a shot of elegant Annie walking between the pillars of the Lake Palace Hotel, a glamorous dress flowing in the breeze. It was to be a romantic sequence, silent except for soft background music. The director called for hush and then "Action!" Annie began slowly walking. Suddenly, out of nowhere, came a cockney screech: "There's Annie Gregg off the 'oliday programme! What you doin' 'ere, love?" Collapse, into giggles, of production team.

During this period we had also formed a good working relationship with Roger Ordish, producer of *Jim'll Fix It*, the hugely popular Saturday evening programme hosted by Jimmy Savile – soon to be Sir Jimmy – which, at its peak, attracted around 10 million viewers including children of all ages. What I saw was a perfect vehicle for films about 'fix-its' involving holidays and travel and a way not only to get to a family audience on a Saturday evening but perhaps to business travellers at home with the family. In effect, we thought up the "answers" – 'fix-its' – which plugged our client airlines, countries and hotels – and Roger's team dreamed up a treatment for the young contestants who wrote in their thousands wanting to fulfil their dreams – often wildly ambitious and set in far away places. It was a joke in our office that the Jim who fixed it was not Savile but Dunn! It wasn't quite that simple, of course.

When I had first met Sir Jimmy, his famous bleached-blonde straggly mop of hair was black and white – the left side dyed black, the right side platinum blonde. It was 1965 and I was visiting Radio Luxembourg's Mayfair studios in London during my first visit to the capital at the height of the 1960s fashion and pop music mania. I was writing a feature for my column for the Gourock Times back in Scotland and toured the studios agog, also meeting David Jacobs and the late Alan "Fluff" Freeman, then young, fresh-faced DJs eager to make it big on national radio and TV. All three were hosts of the BBC's new music show *Top of the Pops* which began the previous year. But I had an inkling that it would be the strange, cigar-chomping, former miner from Leeds, Jimmy Savile, who would succeed as a mainstream entertainer – which he did in 1975 by landing a prime TV slot with *Jim'll Fix It*.

So, watching the programme years later, it struck me that with all our travel and holiday clients, we could assist the production team in sifting through the thousands of viewers' letters and quickly suggest those which could be amusingly and easily made to work to produce good TV. I rang the programme's production office and spoke to Roger who readily agreed to meet and discuss possible ways in which we could co-operate. It was the beginning of an arrangement that worked brilliantly for us and for the show, which ran until a few years ago. Almost every week we'd be involved some-where, somehow, fixing it in a way which involved one or more of our clients.

Dreams included a big game hunt in South Africa (where the Tourist Board was now our client); a real Chinese meal in Hong Kong (I always thought this a brilliant idea from a child wanting a free trip to Hong Kong) and, the one which gave me most pleasure, a little girl's dream of spending a day as a VIP or being A Princess For A Day. We created a day in which she had her hair done by top stylist Ricci Burns, chose an outfit from Harrods (which, unlike other companies who gave all facil-ities free, charged us for the clothes), drove around in a limousine and visited Greyshott, a health farm, another of our clients by then. She ended her day as the guest of honour who opened a new hotel, one of the Holiday Inn chain and our client, of course. This ten-minute film, shown on prime time BBC One, was hailed as a classic 'fix-it' and used as an example for aspiring PRs of how they can work successfully with television.

So, no arm-twisting was needed to interest me anyway in this young TV producer who stood before us with his 'bril-liant idea'– a proposal for a video and television production division. About that time there were rumours that the BBC was changing its monopoly policy. Instead of making all programmes themselves, something called Producers' Choice would be brought in, enabling outside production companies like the one being presented to us, to offer to make programmes for them as well as the other networks. We felt we should be in there, at the beginning. What we were getting into, it turned out, was another fine mess.

A production company had already been set up that had made *Lichfield On Photography*, a video series presented by the late Patrick, Lord Lichfield, with an accompanying book of the same title. They had offered the programme to Channel 4 which was commissioning aggressively in this, its first year of operation. They hoped to interest other people in investing in the company to make more programmes on the back of the Lichfield film. The company also had an impressive line-up of committed associates. One was Lord Romsey, Norton, Lord Mountbatten's grandson, whose father, Lord Brayborne, was also a film and TV producer (he produced the Agatha Christie film *Death On The Nile*). There was a city financier who worked for an American bank, a lawyer and other investors including a restaurateur and a broadcaster, well known then to ITV viewers. We were persuaded to invest £15,000 and also provide them with a small office on the top floor at our headquarters in Grosvenor Gardens.

The Original Image team then spent the following few years writing 'treatments' for television programmes and getting them rejected by Channel 4. They did become good friends and even bought a small weekend house near us in Norfolk. Personally, we all got on well but, in business, their division didn't seem to be going anywhere.

The new video and TV production enterprise was, initially, snapped up by Arthur who wanted to spend time away from the important but somewhat 'dry' accounts department of our expanding group. For most of the early 1980s I was travelling with media groups and concentrating on our overseas clients in Europe and Asia, so it was left to him to attend the board meetings of the different TPS companies. I was delighted. Board meetings were always 'bored meetings' to me. He now had to attend Original Image meetings and report on what they weren't achieving. The team also attended MIP, the television 'market' held in Cannes. As someone who was ill at ease with theatrical people, it was especially painful for Arthur to host meetings in expensive and unfamiliar venues and assist in attempts to 'talk up' the programmes. None was ever sold, they were far too dull it was said. And the magic of Lord Lichfield's name was not working in our favour. His membership of the Royal Family (he was one of the Queen's cousins) was failing to dazzle and his style was perhaps seen as a touch old-fashioned. Original Image's first programme on Lichfield did not sell.

One series of programmes that was sold to Channel 4 – to everyone's relief – was *Daley Thompson's Body Shop*, in which the Olympic decathlete advised six celebrities on fitness. Channel 4 required us to work out a production budget for the first time and then gave us a generous sum to make the programmes. We signed our celebrities, who included Lulu, Suzi Quatro, Barry Humphries and the late actor and writer Brian Glover. The series was broadcast and well received but sadly not sold anywhere else. We did little more than cover our costs.

It was at this time that airlines were beginning to use professionally made in-flight broadcasts, giving information on safety and destinations, and I saw an opportunity here for Original Image. I approached our long-standing client Cathay Pacific and the team travelled to Hong Kong to see the airline's cabin services director. Thanks to our good relationship with Cathay and a vast amount of work, we were commissioned to produce various safety demonstrations and training programmes for cabin crew, some of which won airline industry awards.

With Original Image now making a profit at last, we decided to try to whip up interest in our services with other airlines. This was how a Nigerian tribal chief, one Chief Buki Okinawu came into our life. The name Nigerian Airways can still bring many of us – and especially Arthur – out in a cold sweat.

Quite how this rogue was introduced to us, no one can recall. Somewhere he had seen the work Original Image had produced for Cathay and he announced: "This would be good for Nigerian Airways!" We didn't know that Nigerian Airways had precisely three aircraft at the time and very little money. We soon found ourselves however, invited to the Nigerian capital, Lagos, to pitch for the business. Everybody was apprehensive but thrilled that a new client was literally on the horizon. They promptly applied for visas and booked their seats with, of course, Nigerian Airways. Arthur was going together with the managing director of Original Image who, wise man, cried off the trip for some reason or other so Arthur gritted his teeth and prepared to go solo. When he rang to confirm the flight, Nigerian Airways recommended that he switch to the now defunct British Caledonian Airways, an ominous sign but one he was very happy to comply with.

On arrival at Lagos Airport there was no sign of Buki, who had promised to meet and escort Arthur to his hotel. At customs he was briskly ordered to surrender the Nigerian currency his London bank had supplied the day before and buy new naira notes from the airport exchange office. Then he was obliged to get in a taxi and was promptly joined by other travellers – complete strangers. He was convinced he would be murdered for his new naira.

Happily, Arthur was safely deposited at the hotel where, eventually, Buki turned up in his magnificent traditional robes and took him to his house and then on to Nigerian Airways headquarters. This resembled the throne room at Buckingham Palace. There was a vast table around which dozens of people sat, clearly waiting their turn to speak to the airline boss, a man dressed in ornate uniform and called the Air Marshal who, Arthur was told, should be addressed as Your Excellency.

Eventually Arthur was able to stand and give his prepared short speech about Original Image's experience of superior in-flight film-making. His Excellency asked Buki about Arthur and finally pronounced: "This sounds like a very beautiful suggestion for Nigerian Airways. Thank you very much."

Totally mystified, Arthur flew back to London where he later learned to his amazement that Original Image had won the contract. The programmes were made and paid for – although the costs had to be generous to include the "fees" for Buki and his sidekicks. The work with this obscure airline did make the process a lot less nerve-racking when it came to successfully pitching similar ideas to British Airways for their in-flight programmes.

Thus, Original Image was able to make a little profit for a couple of years. Little did we guess what lay ahead to change that.

43

CLIENTS – WE LOVE THEM...
BUT...

TPS CONTINUED TO EXPAND AND to be special to all of us who worked there. It seemed to engender loyalty – frequently way beyond that expected in the normal course of duty. With most of the team at least.

We developed a great client list – generally agreed to be the best in the travel and leisure business by far. We had a real sense of purpose and worked ourselves and our staff very long hours. We did have some truly difficult clients, and many journalists were demanding of "special care" – to put it mildly and politely. There were some who wouldn't board a flight unless they were seated in business or first class and wouldn't stay at a hotel unless allocated a suite. But we had many fabulous clients – some of whom are friends to this day – and there were also some really great journalists who supported us in so many ways.

Some of our clients were generous with both fees and praise – we often found that the two went together – and verbal pats on the back always served to make the team work even harder for these customers. We had our share of stingy clients too – and the memory of them still lingers.

We never expected a newly set-up business or a really small client to pay us fees on a similar scale to those of some of our larger accounts but some established and successful businesses were run by people who were plain greedy and mean. And, surprise, surprise, it was these miserable people who shouted the loudest, complained the most and, despite our Herculean efforts on their behalf, were most stinting in their praise.

So, we had to try and compensate for the difficulties our staff encountered by fostering a good spirit within the company. Much of this came from a shared sense of humour and holding a "united front" against the most difficult clients and journalists – albeit in private. One day, after I found a girl in the office in tears of frustration because a client she'd been working overtime to please had fired off a string of complaints to her, I devised a stress-relieving chant for everyone in the office to use on such occasions. "Clients Are Shits!" became a TPS mantra. Some clients would expect the impossible. Often you'd deliver wide editorial coverage, national publicity and they'd still want more. Other times, you'd have been on a press visit and had only a few hours sleep over the weekend, yet they'd complain if you were not in the office to take their call at nine thirty on a Monday morning. In nearly thirty years in the business, I think I saw only five bunches of flowers sent as a "thank you" to members of our staff who'd worked exceptionally hard to achieve good results for their clients. There were probably a similarly small number of congratulatory notes and 'phone calls.

We'd always try to educate our clients, to point out that if they gave an interview to a journalist, that journalist would not have total control over the article that appeared, would not write the headline nor pick the day of publication. Those matters were up to the editors. We also pointed out that if a journalist had been present on a press visit, coverage would not appear on the following day or even necessarily during the following week – you can't control things in PR as you can in an advertising campaign. Yet still the moans and groans would come. I had complaints from one tour operator when, after his package holiday had received a full seven-minute plug on ITV's *Wish You Were Here* followed by the screening of price details and telephone booking numbers, the company hadn't been inundated with inquiries. It seemed impossible to make such clients understand that while we could get their products on screen, we could not actually force the public to buy the holidays.

In the late 1980s, at the zenith of our success, we had an outstanding team – mostly women and mostly highly attractive ones. This always brought them numerous, unwelcome, sexual advances. There was an American client who was particularly lecherous and persisted despite firm verbal and physical rejections. Later his son started to accompany the father on his UK visits and he was even worse! Nowadays, when companies have learned to fear charges of sexual harassment among staff, I suppose something could be done. But the climate was different then and my girls put up with all of this for "the good of the firm".

Client contract and fee re-negotiations could be tortuous, unpleasant and demeaning events. We always tried to be fair and establish some relationship between fees paid and work undertaken. In general, however, we almost always over-serviced accounts – particularly those where the people were considerate and treated us as professionally and generously as they could afford.

I remember three of us sitting in a basement room near one of London's mainline railway stations to negotiate a new contract with a long-standing, but unbelievably tight-fisted client. We provided a first class service on this account and their product's promotion and, to a great extent, sales were almost exclusively provided by our PR efforts. No massive advertising budgets here. We argued for a couple of hours over an increase in our fee of something like £200 per year. Goodness knows how much that cost in executive time – on both sides. We eventually had to compromise on some lesser sum. The lead negotiator on the client's side was a hard-nosed accountant who, no doubt, thought he had achieved a victory rather to the embarrassment of his more urbane partner. Is this a good way to get the best out of suppliers? I think not. But we continued to deliver our best for this client. That was the way we worked – probably not the most commercial approach but successful overall. While many of us would have liked to tell those stingy clients where to stick their retainer fees, we felt that by behaving in a gentlemanly way that we held the moral high ground.

On one occasion only did I actually snap during the re-negotiating process. Again it was a client who paid us very little, got excellent results from us and was frequently deeply unpleasant to the team. For some weeks we argued back and forth – mostly by letter – over a paltry fee increase. Finally, on one of my rare black days, I fired off my last word and resigned the account. It was the one and only time I have ever taken this action. This was a small but active account and we had to notify all our media contacts that we no longer held it, so we sent out a message citing a failure to agree terms of a new contract. Even then I didn't have the last word – the client sent out a counter notice saying the company had fired us for incompetence. Fortunately nobody believed her – she was well known for her difficult ways. It's believed that she once caused a journalist to have a heart attack by ranting and raging over the telephone to him over an article that hadn't appeared!

Dealings with foreign clients were not always all plain sailing. Our work for the American Holiday Inn hotel chain coincided with the opening of about thirty new hotels in Europe during the eighties, half of which were in Britain. In each of the cities where hotels were opening, it was our brief to attract new franchises through business media stories, dealing with local councils and teaching the new hotel managers about local promotions and how to deal with their regional media. At a time of great expansion, companies frequently change their senior executives and Holiday Inn was no exception. Thus David Woodward, the Holiday Inn managing director for Europe arrived and settled himself at Windmill House, the company's European headquarters close to London's Heathrow airport.

He was a demanding tough-talker with an aggressive management style and he was not always fair or reasonable in his dealings with us. Regularly I would find the team in tears. It seemed that although he kept renewing our contract we could do no right in his eyes. Motivation was certainly not part of his management style. I had to keep reminding myself that the Memphis-based hotel company's massive expansion probably put enormous pressures on him. Even then, he terrified the life out of me and to say he ruled the account by fear is no under-statement. If we didn't manage to get positive coverage for Holiday Inn in every edition of the weekly trade newspaper TTG, for example, our lives were not worth living. He would not accept that, as our good contacts on the newspaper pleaded, they simply could not carry yet another picture story of the arrival of yet another jet-lagged and bleary-eyed Holiday Inn executive. These were, after all, usually men who clearly did not know where in the world the UK was, let alone the rest of Europe. I was never impressed with the calibre of Holiday Inn's Memphis-based executives who would arrive in London with all guns blazing but not really make sense in a local context. They would order us all about, rewrite the rules, then disap-pear back to Elvis-land never to be heard of again.

David did support me against some of his American colleagues, however, when I maintained that when promoting Holiday Inn to the media in Europe they should use our loose chain of local PR associates in each target country. His colleagues were hostile towards any discussions not conducted in English but they eventually backed down and our European associates handled the local media work in their own language but overseen by us.

To add to my misery when working on this account, David's wife was soon appointed to head all marketing in Europe and we had to deal directly with her. She was very difficult – at least as far as I was concerned – and had impracticably long fingernails which she liked to drill on her desk as she made her points. I dreaded every meeting with her. But for the fact that the account was challenging and high profile and more importantly, we needed the money, I would have resigned.

The contract with Holiday Inn almost lost me the friendship of the immensely important Elisabeth de Stroumillo, Travel Editor of The Telegraph. She asked me to find some summer holiday work for Venetia, one of her daughters. I found suitable temporary work for her on the reception desk at the Holiday Inn in the Place de la Republique in Paris. All was well until there was a robbery at the hotel late one night and this poor English lass was among those trussed up and held at gunpoint behind the reception counter. Mercifully the police arrived and Venetia was released, unhurt. She did, however, complain to her mother about how badly she thought Holiday Inn staff were treated by their bosses. I was inclined to agree when I heard the complaints.

When I passed this on to David Woodward, however, his attitude was, "It's nothing to do with me" and "she should get back to work."

Despite all this, David Woodward called us first when he was later appointed to the challenging job of general manager at London's Grosvenor House in Park Lane. He handed us the PR account on a plate. We accepted and, I have to say, he seemed to have mellowed in the meantime.

44

MR BENIDORM

I WAS BECOMING USED TO the comfortable, indeed luxurious, life I'd carved out for myself in travel PR of first class flights, suites in hotels and chauffeurs on tap but one telephone call from Spain was to present me with a new PR challenge – certainly not at the luxury end of the market. The call was to ask us to help promote the wide-scale changes underway in Benidorm.

The massive resort on Spain's Costa Blanca had a 'fish and chips' and 'lager lout' image but was the busiest destination for UK holidaymakers. Whole streets of people would go on holiday there every year when the local factory closed and people would board their flights home only after arranging to meet friends on the beach in 12 months' time. It was – and is – cheap, cheerful and great fun. You can eat well, the booze and cigarettes are cheap and while the hotel standards then rarely notched over three-star, they represented good value – things have changed, but not much. Benidorm had one other great thing going for it: the tabloids loved it because their readers went there to sunbathe and watch Coronation Street and Eastenders in the bars each evening which, when my work for the resort first began, were flown out on video – the pre-satellite days.

I loved this Spanish resort and every minute I spent publicising it and did everything I could to succeed, including decking myself out in tartan and being photographed on the beach to gain coverage in the Scottish papers – some PRs will do anything for coverage. Inevitably some travel writers began calling me "Mr Benidorm".

Benidorm had recognised that it was slipping in its tourism "offer" to the British holidaymaker and visitor figures were falling, particularly at a time when more people were looking outside Europe, to Florida and the Far East, as long-haul flight prices came down. The object of a new PR effort, they said, was to publicise the improvements they were making to the town and the money they were investing to please existing holidaymakers from Britain, Germany, Holland and other countries and also to try to widen Benidorm's appeal.

There were a few snorts of derision from the rest of the team and some of our media contacts when I discussed the possibility of our taking on the account, but I was impressed by the improvement plans and, as time went on, was filled with admiration for what was achieved by the local council. Not only did the Benidorm authorities import vast quantities of sand every year to enhance the beaches after the summer hordes left, they also 'hoovered' those same beaches daily at dawn to keep them clean and attractive looking for the day ahead. They upgraded the promenades and street lighting and forced restaurants and hotels to carry out improvements. All in all they made the place more modern, more attractive and safe.

Benidorm had always been the resort where holidaymakers could leave their inhibitions at the airport and let their hair down. That didn't change. But now it was also a place where ordinary families with children and limited, hard-earned money, people from places like Gourock, could go for an affordable holiday in the sun without fear of getting ripped off or of clashes either with drunken yobs or aggressive local police.

We took on the account and publicised Benidorm off and on for more than 15 years. It wasn't easy at times because news editors of the British tabloids, at a loss for stories during the news-dry summer months, would try to fill empty space with photographs and copy on the "Costa Punch-up" theme. Usually they would send reporters to shadow groups of young men, buy them drinks and see what sort of rumpus could be whipped up with local Spanish people or other holidaymakers. We had to counteract those negative stories with much softer articles from travel writers about the resort's improved facilities and such things as Benidorm's 'Glamorous Granny' competitions, with stories sent to the local media in the winners' home towns in the UK. We had to explain to Benidorm's tourist officials that they had to take the good coverage with the bad – that the tabloids had their plus points even more so in the case of Benidorm. Once a week, we'd have a "yob" story and the next a very positive article in the same paper from its travel editor.

It became a challenge for us to take the most unlikely writers to the resort. "You don't know until you've tried it," I'd say down the 'phone, as I tried to persuade journalists hoping to be invited to one of our more upmarket destinations. A.A. Gill of The Sunday Times was one who accepted, a man much happier dining in a fashionable London restaurant than paddling on a Spanish beach. He gave us a very fair article on what the resort was trying to achieve. The coverage rolled in from TV, radio and newspapers – and not only the tabloids, "serious" papers like The Telegraph also produced major features on the resort. The campaign worked, visitor figures increased, British tour operators were happy and so were the town's tourist officials. We were recommended and were happy to land many other accounts on the Costas, including the Costa Del Sol region and the city of Valencia which took advantage of millions of pesetas in grants from the European Community to begin to practically rebuild the old city. Our Spanish clients were always helpful, courteous towards the team and always appreciated what we did. So we never once called them "shits".

45

THE BEAUTY PARADE

MORE THAN A DECADE AGO, I wrote a book for people working in the business entitled *Successful Public Relations*. I began by trying to define what PR is. It was, and still is hard because the work has many elements and activities. But, at a simple level, "projecting a good feeling for an organisation to its target public and turning the negative into the positive so as to contribute to sales" goes a long way to describing the job.

My own 'good feeling' for an organisation – or lack of it – often depended on the way we began business together, on the number of hoops a prospective client would ask us to jump through before they gave us the business. I'm talking about the whole procedure of The Pitch, where you present a prospective client with a strategy, a blueprint of what they might achieve, with your help, in the public arena and through media coverage.

In the early days I didn't need to know what a pitch was. Accounts came in to us because we knew people who knew other people, or we were recommended to companies by journalists. We then met the company bosses and, if they liked us and were impressed by what we did for other clients, we negotiated a fee, had a deal and got to work. This changed by the early eighties when many organisations hired a new breed of marketing director, probably with a much more professional approach and who wanted to control the public relations accounts. These were people who had studied marketing and public relations and knew more of the theory than I did but, though they'd never admit it, hadn't a clue how journalists or the media at large worked, and we did. I believe this situation still exists today. Thus it became a practice for these directors to hold a "beauty parade" of companies, to invite a collection of PR organisations, sometimes as many as ten or twelve, to compete by coming to their offices to pitch for the new account. I hated the whole process, as did most of my colleagues and competitors for the business.

Whenever news of a pitch came, a loud groan would go out from everyone on the team. Then there would be a mad rush to put together a lively document with flip charts and get a studio to produce slides and start rehearsing. The computer age has made this less of a chore, of course. The effort and expense would always depend on how much we guessed the account might be worth and whether we thought we'd get the business or not. Some organisations would give you a few weeks' warning, others would ring up a day before to say, for example, that their marketing director from the Far East was in town and would like to call in and discuss ideas. Generally we preferred this as it gave a more honest reflection of what we were like and what we could do.

These were still rather formal occasions, requiring 'best behaviour' in the office. Unfortunately my dog Tinker didn't always appreciate this. Once while I was in full flow in our boardroom during an important pitch to some foreign tourism clients, there was a loud thump on the door. Heads turned, expecting someone to walk in, but no one was to be seen. Tinker had pushed his way in on hearing my voice, sped across the room and curled up at my feet under the table, slightly alarming the prospective clients in the process.

When we had to show up at the potential client's offices with all our boxes and bundles for this "beauty parade", with rival PR people seated opposite us in the reception clutching their paraphernalia, it was often hard to stay enthusiastic. We knew that whatever happened, the clients would get a mass of ideas and documents free from six or more highly professional PR firms. How serious they were about taking up a PR account with any of the firms remained to be seen. In many cases they were just trawling for ideas without intending to pay for them. To us it felt like a game that many companies, large and small, enjoyed playing and we could all do without that.

A far better system, to my mind, would have been for a company simply to choose, say, two or three consultants and, after having done some research in the industry and in the media, give one of them the job for a trial period.

Now, while I say I hated the whole business of pitching for new business, it was vital to keep new business flowing in because clients, being fickle boys and girls, could dismiss you at any time, often without reference to a signed contract. So pitching became part of my working week. I would generally front up our presentation with the proposed account team. We had to become adept at swinging into action right away as soon as the decision to appoint was given. Our Benidorm appointment was made minutes after our presentation to the local mayor and councillors in the town hall had finished. We had not expected this. Before we knew it we were surrounded by the local radio, television and newspaper reporters of the town and the region and a massive press conference began.

So we learned very quickly what it was like to give instant press conferences.

My pitch for the PR account for the tourist promotion of Bahrain was a disaster. There was virtually no tourism then, though there were a few international hotels. But Cathay Pacific was launching a route from London to Hong Kong, stopping off in Bahrain to refuel, and I saw an opportunity for the future. I secured a meeting with the local Sheik of the ruling family and flew out with a short document, a history of our work and the reasons why we could help Bahrain's emerging tourism industry. I was duly driven to the Palace, clutching this document, together with my slide projector, a screen and a box of slides arranged in special order.

On arrival, these items were immediately taken from me and I presumed they would be examined for security purposes and returned. Meanwhile, I was ushered into a vast room where the Sheik sat with his back to the doorway through which I'd come. I sat down and the long, slow coffee-drinking and small talk ceremony began. Over his shoulder I could see down the corridor and was able to watch a flunkey lift my tray of slides and then, as if in slow motion, toss the whole lot accidentally into the air. With the slides scattered across the floor, I knew that my pitch would consist of a conversation only – which it did. A nail-biting few days in a hotel room followed as I waited to hear if the Palace was interested. Eventually, thank goodness, it was.

The easiest and most satisfying pitch we ever gave was for the South African Tourism Board account. This was just before Nelson Mandela was freed from prison in 1990 but at a time when the political climate was changing fast and his release was widely predicted. The national tourism department knew that on Mandela's release, the image of the country would change completely and they hoped it would become a fashionable place to visit. South Africa had to be ready for the world's tourism media. We were being asked to help spearhead efforts to do this groundwork in Europe. We prepared a good strategy document and arranged to meet Dale Pretorious, then marketing director of the tourist board, in Pretoria. He came into the room and before we began to show our slides said, "I want to see your proposals and discuss everything with you but you should know that I liked your advance document and we will be working together." So we relaxed but worked hard and well during a busy three-year contract for a country that fired us with great enthusiasm.

46

CRISIS – WHAT CRISIS?

CRISIS MANAGEMENT, OR DAMAGE LIMITATION, is big business in the PR world today. When we started, we dealt with all of our clients' media problems as they cropped up during the working day. We were only too glad to be considered necessary and part of their team. As the media became even more powerful and more invasive during the 1980s and then the 1990s though, every company had to be ready to react positively if they were suddenly thrust into the news in an unfavourable – or even a favourable – light. So we realised we should work at tactics to help them. And, since some of these dramas could take weeks to settle down and be forgotten, and both client and the media often had to be handled delicately, we felt justified in passing on additional charges to our clients – it's an ill wind......

Over the years we've been involved in almost every kind of crisis imaginable. These have included the early bombings by the IRA of the Europa Hotel, Belfast, which was then a Grand Metropolitan Hotel; food poisoning of holidaymakers in the Spanish resort of Salou and, as Spanish builders failed to complete hotels on schedule, we stepped in each time our client Cosmos was accused of overbooking, which was almost weekly.

Sarajevo's Holiday Inn, an up-till-then small and insignificant hotel, hit the front pages in the 1980s as the Yugoslavia conflict began. The hotel, stuffed with the world's media, was bombed and our telephones began to ring. We had days that started with a bomb scare on a Cathay Pacific aircraft, or one skidding off the runway while landing at Hong Kong (such incidents were fortunately without casualties), and days which ended with a hotel fire or a suicide jump by a guest from a top floor suite.

Newspapers and television would call us first about almost any travel-related story. If we didn't represent the company in question we knew someone who did. Our working hours officially were 9.30am to 5.30pm but, in reality, there was always someone in the office a lot earlier. That person was usually Jenny Crayford, the most talented and professional PR you could find anywhere. When you needed her she was always there. What Jenny didn't know about the way the media worked, wasn't worth knowing. The fact that her partner was Mike Toynbee, a leading business and travel trade journalist, may have had something to do with that, but her loyalty and reliability were all her own.

There were no mobile 'phones then so, in an emergency, when we couldn't make contact with someone at their office or home, we had to ring their relatives, likely pubs, restaurants, theatres, shops – you name it – and plead for searches to be made to track down the wanted individual. The first PR I heard of having a mobile 'phone was Doug Goodman, the superb in-house PR for Thomson Holidays, now running his own successful agency. He certainly needed one to handle a non-stop stream of tabloid enquiries about Britain's largest tour operator. The mobile in question was a bulky, heavy box of tricks containing a telephone. We all said it wouldn't catch on!

One crisis telephone call nearly didn't reach me. One weekend in Norfolk at our country home, the recently-purchased Guist Hall, the telephone rang. We heard nothing more for a few minutes. Suddenly Ronald, the cook, who enjoyed a drink, came skipping down the tiled floor to the dining room and knocked on the door politely. "Sir, I've tried to get rid of him but he's insisting. It's some gentleman from Cathay Pacific to say he's got a problem and needs to talk to you. I've told him you're at dinner but he won't go away".

The "bothersome" call, it turned out, was from one of our most important clients – John Olsen, head of the airline in Europe – to tell me that an engine had caught fire on a Cathay 747 travelling from Gatwick to Hong Kong. He thought I should know just in case there were press enquiries and also because Alan Whicker, the TV presenter, was on board on a visit arranged by me. "Oh, by the way", John Olsen added, "we must be paying you too much if you can afford a butler to answer your 'phone!" It took me a long time to live that one down.

Later John became chief executive of Cunard and one of his first tasks was to oversee the refurbishment of the liner QE2 in the early 1990s. In their wisdom, Cunard agreed that a BBC TV film crew could follow the multi-million pound refur-bishment of the ship and join the happy cruisers on its first voyage. There were problems, however. The refit schedule was delayed, the standard of work turned out to be so poor that cabins were not ready, the sewage system didn't function prop-erly and there was evident chaos on board. And BBC cameras were there to film every detail for nightly news bulletins of the QE2 "disaster". It was a major catastrophe for the company and went down in PR history as how not to present the relaunch of a famous liner.

Sometimes press people did sneaky things to us when, on a client's instruction, we couldn't give out more than a bland statement of facts and a "we are looking into it" response. One reporter for a tabloid gave our office number to the frustrated holidaymakers and we were then inundated with personal enquiries about an overbooked holiday flight. Most inconvenient!

The saddest crisis we ever handled was the murder of three-year-old Leonie Keating, whose body was dumped by a river in deep woods in the heart of Norfolk in 1985. Leonie had been staying with her parents at a Ladbroke Holiday Village in Great Yarmouth on the Norfolk coast. She'd been abducted, sexually assaulted and drowned. All media enquiries other than direct police and forensic details were referred to us. It was a very bleak assignment to handle, all the more so because the crime was never solved.

Companies going bust, chairmen resigning and being chased by tabloid reporters, P&O ships in danger, outbreaks of food poisoning on aircraft – these became everyday occurrences for us as the number of our clients increased and we became even more deeply involved in the travel industry.

47

BROTHELS AND SAM MISSILES

ONE EXPERIENCE WITH A POTENTIAL Russian client back in the late eighties, just before the collapse of Communism, was bizarre. It resulted from an initiative taken by my colleague Russell Stenhouse, who was approached at the annual World Travel Market by a couple of Russians. They told him, through an interpreter, that they wanted to get British tour operators to start delivering adventurous holidaymakers to Moscow with all the ground arrangements looked after from there by their operation. It would be the start of mass tourism to Russia! They claimed to have a network of hotels ready and he and I were persuaded to fly out to Moscow for a few days sightseeing and an inspection of their operation.

It was a mistake. It was November. There were four feet of snow and the taxi from the airport to the centre of Moscow took hours. I'd brought a warm coat but had to buy a Russian fur hat in Red Square to stop the shivers. Our two clients turned out to have no real business, they were simply travel agents in a tiny shop in a backstreet seeking to launch themselves in tourism.

The "hotel" we had been promised proved to be an unmarked door on a run down block in the Moscow suburbs which, when we knocked, was unlocked from the other side and a window mysteriously slid open. We entered a long corridor, followed by our two hosts who left us at the lifts and said they'd wait for us to freshen up before going out to dinner. Exiting the lift, I noticed that the corridor was lit by red light bulbs and there were rooms on each side. Only when we saw other men, many appearing furtive and unkempt, walking along, peering into the rooms where half-dressed women were waiting on beds, did we realise we were in a brothel and a very rough one at that. We were shown into a sparsely furnished two-bedroom suite with one basic bathroom. Forget your in-room toiletries. I'd have been amazed if the lavatory flushed. In unison, Russell and I looked at each other, shook our heads, said "No thank you" and swiftly made our way downstairs to reception, asking the way to the nearest five-star hotel. Our hosts were in the entrance, laughing. They presumably thought they'd done us a favour.

I might have been curious as to what goes on in brothels had I not already been to a few in Europe and Asia – in the course of duty, of course. The first was a so-called "Love Hotel" in Frankfurt city centre. I was taken there while on Holiday Inn business with a group of company executives venturing out of Memphis for a travel agents' event. They were keen to explore this "hotel" in the city's red light district and it was assumed I would tag along. The place turned out to be another large apartment block, on every floor of which a variety of sexual fantasies were offered by girls wearing different combinations of not very much clothing. Varieties of thigh-high boots, stiletto-heeled shoes, leather mini-skirts and negligees were in abundance. For the other men it was like being a child in a sweet shop and their eyes were out on stalks as they surveyed the goods available. As they made their choices and negotiated prices, I slipped away. Not my scene.

At a Cathay Pacific sales conference in Amsterdam, though, I didn't emerge unscathed. I was again asked along by the airline's sales guys, not too unwillingly, I admit. They knew me well and knew I was gay and unlikely to appreciate the finer points of their choice of club – one offering a porn film screening, live striptease show and live sex. For the first time in my life, I felt the "thrill" of an extremely well-endowed woman rubbing huge breasts on either side of my face. It was great entertainment for the client, watching me squirm…

The annual World Travel Market was an irregular source of new business for us. The Syrian stand was predictably exotic. I drank strong black coffee in tiny cups sitting in the tent on large, colourful velvet cushions, intricately embroidered, looking at pictures of camels and sand dunes. Syria was a recent casualty of a bruising war and, to all intents and purposes, a closed country. It was impossible for most people to get a visa to enter. Nevertheless, a young Syrian Minister of Tourism was in attendance at the Market and he told me that he hoped to bring top journalists to Syria so that they could extol its attractions and help establish a fledgling tourism industry for the future. I duly began to arrange press visits, obtaining airline tickets from the Syrian Embassy in London. We could then offer journalists the dubious delight of flying on Syrian Airways to Damascus to see this beautiful medieval city and to the ruins of Palmyra, the Roman city in the desert which, I was to discover, is particularly magical at sunset and sunrise.

The hotels, which resembled Holiday Inns with a few Arabian tassels here and there, were functional. But, as we drove across the desert, it was hard not to notice the lines of SAM missiles aimed at Israel. I, of course, tried my hardest to point out the spectacular sand dunes in the opposite direction. Journalists keen to come on our group visits turned out not always to be travel writers but often defence correspondents who were refused entry to Syria by any other means.

The deal was that they provided a travel piece for their weekend section as well as their war report which they researched by sneaking off for briefings at the British Embassy.

I never felt nervous on the Syrian trips except occasionally in hotels where Arab men, other guests or staff, seemed to take a shine to me and were hard to shake off. I never understood what their true intentions were but, as the tour leader, I just assumed that they were keeping an eye on me. The process of getting paid for our PR services scared the life out of me. The Syrians never wanted bills from us. The Tourism Minister would ring me in London on a crackly telephone line from Damascus and tell me when he was arriving and his preferred location for handing over the money. If it were autumn, I would wait until the World Travel Market came round, sit in the tent and patiently wait with my coffee until someone arrived with a briefcase. Then, after a signal from one of the Syrian team, I would move behind a large, hanging curtain on the tent wall and be handed an envelope containing anything between five to ten thousand pounds in cash in outstanding retainer fees.

Alternatively, the rendezvous would be at one of those small and obscure hotels in Bayswater which Arabs inhabited in great numbers in those days. Arthur would drive me there after work and wait outside in our white Jaguar, engine running. I would find myself ushered into a ground floor waiting room where a number of veiled Arab women would be seated. At one such meeting they were all uncomprehendingly watching Trevor MacDonald on *News At Ten*. After a long wait, an Arab girl with beautiful eyes came up to me and asked, "Would you like a banana?" "Yes, that would be very nice," I replied, fearing a refusal might cause offence and somehow keeping a straight face. Eventually the Tourism

317

Minister would appear from the lift with an envelope of cash for me. And I would bow out – into the waiting Jag.

48

LUXURY... AND ELIZABETH SOMEONE OR OTHER

FOR MOST OF MY YEARS as a travel PR, I lived like a prince at my clients' expense. I sold the idea of a world of five-star luxury to others while sampling it myself all over the globe, for free. And I loved it, of course. It was hard work but I never forgot exactly how privileged I was. How could I not? The poor boy from Gourock had re-invented himself almost completely, but not quite. One visit to Hong Kong, in lots of ways like so many other visits to the territory, stays in the mind.

As the aircraft began its final approach to Hong Kong, the place they call the exotic pimple on the nose of China, I could see the familiar twinkling of the lights of the famous "Fragrant Harbour". And, as always, I smiled to myself at the official name of this stretch of water, an open sewer in fact, with the worst smell ever to assault the human nose.

I was on my way to help organise part of the celebrations to mark the 25th anniversary of The Mandarin, one of the world's most grand hotels and a client. Today the word 'Oriental' has been added to its name but to those like me who adore it, it will always be simply The Mandarin, Hong Kong.

My media group had enjoyed a jolly and comfortable flight out of Gatwick Airport. How could they not in Cathay Pacific's first class? Owned by one of the great 'Hong' families of Hong Kong, the Swires, the airline had an enlightened approach to public relations, encouraged by me and partly out of self-interest. All passengers with a connection to the media travelled business class with an automatic upgrade – what a magical word that has proved to be – to first or at least first "SA", meaning space available. So, on this trip, my lot had all travelled first class. The airline gambled that this would lead to positive coverage in print and also, given that media people like to boast to each other, that they would spread the word at press receptions, over dinner tables and in offices, talking glowingly of the comfort and luxury of their trip with the airline.

From my first class seat, number 1A (I always bagged this one unless a paying customer annoyingly asked for it as it meant no one was sitting beside me), I could peer out at the sturdy columns of Hong Kong's myriad skyscrapers, the teeming mass of its traffic and a fair number of its five million inhabitants. Those who remember the approach to the old Kai Tak airport will recall the dramatic descent that was necessary. Many travellers insisted that as the aircraft banked between the tall buildings, they could see so clearly into people's homes that they could spot what food was in the chopsticks as the families ate and what programmes they were watching on television. That's an exaggeration, but not much of one. The new airport, Chek Lap Kok, designed by British architect Norman Foster, does not alas have half as interesting an approach. Such is progress.

A series of Mercedes limousines were waiting, air conditioning full on. As we left Kai Tak airport my chauffeur, stern-faced, peak-capped and in a white cotton uniform with razor sharp trouser creases, contacted the hotel reception on his car telephone to report the group's impending arrival. Even as the mere European Public Relations adviser, I was always treated as a VIP by The Mandarin. The journey to the hotel in the central business district on Hong Kong Island from the airport took about 25 minutes in those days (now it's twice as long, if you're lucky). This was long enough to catch up on local news by flipping through that morning's copy of The South China Morning Post left, as ever, ironed and awaiting my perusal, on the back window ledge. The car's linen seat covers were their usual pristine white. When we drew up outside, there was The Mandarin's duty manager on the front steps to greet me and my party. No question of our registering. A porter took our bags from the boot and escorted us to our suites. Here again The Mandarin always showed an enlightened approach to its suppliers. If a suite was available, I was always given one. I could do a better job of 'selling' the place by recommendation if I were in one of its top rooms rather than its ordinary rooms – even though an ordinary room at The Mandarin is far from ordinary.

On this visit I was allotted the Tamar Suite, probably my favourite, though I've enjoyed The Chinese, The Bauhinia, named after the national flower of China, and – joy of joy – The Mandarin Suite, the hotel's best. All are furnished with Asian antiques and artwork and look out on Hong Kong's dramatic skyline.

I closed the door but I couldn't relax. Not yet. I knew The Mandarin Arrival Ritual had only just begun. This is how it works: as soon as a guest arrives in his room or suite, word goes round. Within minutes a member of staff in a black linen suit knocks at the door to offer a choice of soaps and toiletries. Would I choose Chanel or Hermès this time? He is followed swiftly by another to demonstrate how everything in the rooms works, though I already knew as much as I needed to know. The final visitor brings Chinese herbal tea in elegant crockery, always refreshing after the 13-hour flight from London.

This ritual involved extreme tipping, of course. I smiled as I found my local money. I'd long ago calculated that a guest needed then about £15 to tip the various people who turn up on arrival. When they come to collect your luggage as you leave, The Departure Ritual has to be performed, again with a similarly punishing effect on the wallet. The room boy comes in to check that your stay has been "happy times", the bell boy arrives for your luggage and, down in the lobby, all the senior reception staff line up to wish "Bon Voyage" to the media group.

On this arrival, I would have about half an hour to wash, change and take all the regular welcome calls from Hong Kong friends and clients. This was more time than usual. I'd become expert at making telephone calls while inserting cufflinks and changing socks. The first call was always Gerrie Pitt, The Mandarin's highly-efficient in-house public relations lady – now doing sterling work at The Ritz, London – who needed to check that my suite was in order and get the brief on the group. The call ended with a promise to meet her in the lobby in fifteen minutes. So it was off with my PR 'uniform', the Jaeger suit, Bally shoes (essential for the thrusting young executive in the 1980s), discreet gold cufflinks and Piaget wrist watch, and into the bathroom.

Soon I was freshly dressed and ready for the evening's work. As I made my way to the lift and rode down to join my group in the Clipper Bar, I hoped my team back home and I had helped in a small way to maintain the glittering reputation of the hotel on this, its important anniversary. We held the public relations account for The Mandarin for most of the eighties and early nineties. That's why I was here in Hong Kong now, relaxing in a £2,000 a night suite. I had flown here on Cathay Pacific, another TPS client for over 25 years, on a ticket worth double that amount for a round trip to Hong Kong. Cathay was known by many UK journalists as 'Jim's Airline' because of the number of free tickets I could dish out in return for newspaper or magazine coverage. The effect was very good for our Hong Kong clients and they never complained. For a considerable time the men and women of the British media couldn't think about Hong Kong without going through TPS for transport and somewhere to rest their weary heads. Not only that, TPS had also represented the Hong Kong Tourist Association for over 10 years. There's a maxim in show business that you're only as good as your last review. In PR you're only as good as your client list and by then ours was blue chip.

I had visited Hong Kong at least once a month throughout the 1980s with media groups in tow and, on this occasion, my group were A-list British food writers and broadcasters. One guest was the late Robert Carrier, the chef and restaurateur, one of the men credited with changing British eating habits in the 1960s, who was to become a good friend and business partner in our group. He was also to introduce me to Morocco, a country with which he had a long love affair. Another was the author, writer and cook Glynn Christian – then well-known to breakfast television viewers – who was also to become a friend after a word in the right ear from me resulted in his being commissioned to write a weekly page in The Daily Telegraph. We also had Fay Maschler, the doyenne of London restaurant critics and a long-time star columnist of the Evening Standard, and Francis Bissell, then food editor of The Times among others.

Their collective job was to lap up the luxurious surroundings of the hotel, attend a series of banquets in its Man Wah restaurant, eating food from different regions of Hong Kong and mainland China with gold and ebony chopsticks. They would never have tasted shark's fin, bird's nest or bear's paw soup quite like this. With it they would drink the finest Cristal champagne and other wines. They would also be taken out sightseeing amidst the taipans and traders and travel on a junk, on which Robert would lose his famous large cream sombrero hat to the winds. In return, I trusted, they would each be fulsome in their praise of Hong Kong, its food, its attractions for travellers and the superior services of my other clients and express this in print at a later date.

As I padded around my suite later that evening, making notes and telephone calls to confirm arrangements, I felt pleased and excited. This was the real challenge of public relations work and it always thrilled me. It's the sharp end, out there face-to-face with the media and the clients. When it happens in an exotic location too, it's delicious. I reflected on this as I sat for a moment after a shower, warm in an expensive Mandarin towelling robe, in my huge marble-clad bathroom. What I'd never truly get used to, however often I pinched myself, was the fact that this was really me, wee Jim from Gourock on Clydeside, the same wee Jim who'd grown up in a council house with an outside lavvie and wore jumble sale clothes.

Yet here was I at 35 years of age, owning and running one of Europe's leading leisure PR companies, then employing around 40 people (and soon adding a further 20 to the payroll), whose advice was sought by some of the most important people and companies in the British travel industry, from tour operators and travel bodies to tourist boards of entire countries. And I was sitting in the world's fanciest hotel, The Mandarin, Hong Kong, which regularly played host to world leaders such as Henry Kissinger and Margaret Thatcher, most of the British Royal Family and half the stars of Hollywood.

When I eventually joined my guests downstairs in the Clipper Bar they were in the middle of a heated discussion, fuelled already by several bottles of champagne and the effects of jetlag. They barely registered my arrival. Foodies, like actors, antique experts or opera buffs get completely absorbed in their world. They were discussing Elizabeth David. "Elizabeth who?" I asked. My blankness registered immediately with the group. Silence fell around the table and one by one all those familiar faces turned to me in astonishment.

It was Robert Carrier who broke the painful silence and answered my question. "Well," he said in his thick American brogue, "she's only Britain's most celebrated cook – apart from us, that is!"

Whoops. Not a great start to the evening, Jim, I said to myself. If I'd done a spot of homework I would have known that they were talking about Britain's first and most influential food guru.

But while Elizabeth David might have been de rigeur in Chelsea, there wasn't a great deal of Mediterranean cooking done in working class Clydeside when I was growing up.

49

KNIVES OUT FROM OUR FRIENDS

IN JUNE 1988 WE WERE living in a small house in Queensdale Place, an exotic street in Holland Park where our next door neighbour was Elton John, soon to be Sir Elton, who kept two magnificent green Bentley cars there. We always knew when Elton was about to take up residence. The doors of the double garages would open a day before the big arrival for a team of flower arrangers to begin work on dozens of spectacular creations. It used to look as if Covent Garden flower market had been transported to our little cul-de sac. Finally he would arrive in a flurry of expensive cars, chauffeurs, hangers-on, luggage and clouds of expensive cologne. We saw nothing of him during his stays but he would depart in an equally flamboyant style, the only evidence that he had been there at all being a heap of dead flowers and not a small collection of empty bags from his favourite shops such as Versace, Gucci and Yves St Laurent.

We loved this little house but whenever I think about it I remember one particular sad, summer night there. If it wasn't quite the night of the long knives, it was the night of the medium-sized ones and the pain they delivered is still sharp in my mind.

It became our habit on sunny evenings after work to collect something for supper on the way home – usually fish and chips from around the corner – and take our food and a bottle of wine out on to the tiny top floor terrace which overlooked the cul-de-sac, from where we could watch the comings and goings of Elton and others.

At the end of one long day at our offices in Grosvenor Gardens, I came home first and prepared a simple supper – if I was preparing it, it was always simple. When Arthur walked in an hour or so later I knew immediately something was wrong. I could not have guessed in a hundred years what it would turn out to be. For this was, beyond doubt, the worst moment of our business life.

In all of our offices people tended to pay attention to me and notice what I was doing. Perhaps that's because I'm gregarious, chatty, noisy – pick your own term. Very few people watched Arthur because he's the opposite of me. He speaks only when he has something worth saying, a great talent, and can enter a room unnoticed and observe things others miss. Somehow he saw and heard everything of importance around the building. He says he's like Mr Cellophane, the character in the musical *Chicago*, the quiet guy who nobody thinks about. But underestimating Arthur is a dangerous thing to do.

Anyway, it had long been Arthur's habit to wander around the building after everyone had left for the day. For him, it was a way to wind down at the end of a working day spent largely in his ground floor office where most of the team's problems would end up. He often had some of his best ideas on these prowls, when the place was empty and quiet. Of course, he often glanced at things pinned on notice boards and left lying on people's desks to remind himself of what was going on and also to make sure no personal valuables were in danger of being lost or stolen. (Small robberies were not uncommon in most London office buildings, in those days before the emergence of stringent security). But much more important to him, as our financial director, were the little piles of supplier invoices, partly completed expense forms and time sheets, all of which should have been dealt with to speed up the accounting process the following day. He also spotted occasional letters of complaint from clients, which somehow people had 'forgotten' to show me, or half-completed CVs – indicative of an employee's possible resignation or at least disenchantment. There were all sorts of little clues that helped us keep on top of things and, we hoped, run the business effectively. On this particular evening he'd discovered something else, something infinitely more serious and more sinister.

Arthur needed to check something or other – he's long forgotten what exactly – and had a specific reason to visit the offices of Original Image, our video division, whose managing director was also a main board director and a firm friend. Arthur had been closely involved in most of that company's ups (and more frequent) downs. At this particular time, the television division was actually doing quite well with a number of valuable contracts – notably one with British Airways. In fact, for the first time, the company was making money.

Arthur didn't find what he was looking for because his attention was grabbed by a folder on the top of the desk. Peeking out of it were printouts of the Group accounts. Directors were entitled to see them but what was odd and immediately alarming here was that with the accounts were a series of notes and projections, elements of a new business plan. This began gradually to indicate to him that some kind of walkout by senior executives was being prepared and was at a fairly advanced stage. Spearheading the rebellion were this executive and another close friend. Directors of three of our divisions were also implicated, together with a City banker with whom we'd had some dealings. The main document was in classic business plan format including a section on "strengths and weaknesses". One of the weaknesses listed was "J & A's reaction". In a state of shock, he closed the file and rushed home to Queensdale Place.

When Arthur told me I felt physically sick. It was clear from the document that there was a conspiracy to try and engineer the mass seizure of a large part of our business and move it into some new venture. I don't think I slept that night – I was hurt, very hurt. Arthur was furious. It was not just that these directors wanted to leave who, by then – thanks to us – had considerable power in the company. It was also the fact that, as clients would generally move with the person who was handling their work, we could lose some of our largest accounts. It seemed to us, on the face of it, a monstrous betrayal by people we thought of as real friends and we could not see how we could possibly have deserved it.

How successful the planned walkout would have been was, fortunately, never to be tested. We were determined on that. It would not happen. But the real wound was the fact that two supposedly loyal, long-term friends were the leaders. We were in and out of each other's houses, weekending together, meeting for dinners during the week. We were all pals as well as business partners – or so we'd thought.

If they were so unhappy with the set-up at TPS – and it seemed that they were – the least we would have expected of them was that they broached the subject with us in a straightforward, businesslike way, expressing their feelings, not just as work colleagues but as friends. Instead we were to be presented with a "fait accompli" which would have been damaging to the company and would have put at risk the jobs of many of their colleagues working as back-up on accounts.

Clearly the issue had to be tackled head on – and quickly. We managed to arrange a meeting that evening with our lawyers. Then we prepared ourselves for the following day's confrontations, which our lawyer had confirmed as the most appropriate next step. The lawyer's only regret was that Arthur had not managed to photocopy the crucial documents. In the event, however, our colleagues proved quite capable of incriminating themselves without them.

Our first move was to go into the office early and see each of the directors in turn and ask them to tell us their side of the story. As soon as they arrived, we asked them to come into the boardroom. I said: "I think you have something to tell us." They did indeed. They told us it was all about money; that both had been advised that if they ever wanted to see real profit from their enterprises, profits that would enable them to become as wealthy as they insisted we were, they should extricate themselves as soon as possible from us. One of our so-called friends felt strongly that Arthur and I were blocking the way to the financial success she felt they merited. We told her this was nonsense and even if it had been true it would not excuse what we saw as a betrayal. But we gave her the chance to say she was sorry. She was adamant that she was not 'sorry'. We didn't argue. It was very cold. A friendship and business partnership of some 14 years was at an end. She was the pal, the woman I'd had so many laughs with, the woman many people told me, only half-jokingly, I should have married. And I probably would have wanted to marry her, but for the small snag that I was gay. Instead I'd have settled for being brother and sister with her. And we were that, almost.

Her partner in the rebellion tried to backtrack, saying that they were going to invite us to be involved in this new business they were planning to set up. Big deal! We then called a board meeting at which all the directors were present and we decided both our friends had to go. There was no other way. We would buy back their shareholdings. Arthur quickly typed two letters of dismissal, setting out our decisions and reasons. I escorted my friend out of the building. I was fighting tears. I would not speak to her again for ten years.

Arthur went to see her accomplice. His position was more complicated in that our Group was the largest shareholder in Original Image but there were a number of other directors and any decision to dismiss him was not ours alone to take. We did, however, own the building and Original Image people were there because we allowed them to be. So we had decided to ask him to leave the building immediately and to make arrangements to remove the rest of the company by the end of the month.

He left. One of the other Original Image directors insisted that "because of the undertaking we had given to other directors including Lord Lichfield and Lord Romsey", we should continue our involvement with their company, allow them to remain in the building. He urged us to allow him to arrange for the MD to resign and to forfeit his shares. Neither Arthur nor I was aware of any such "undertaking" given to anyone in respect of Original Image but we allowed ourselves to be persuaded that this was the most appropriate way out of the mess. It was a mistake. We ended up with a company with no MD, a disenchanted staff with varying degrees of loyalty to their departed boss and big contracts, including the British Airways in-flight films, which we were sure we would lose.

Exactly that happened. We were left with a sour taste, a load of worthless shares in a defunct company and a write-off of a quarter of a million pounds.

It was a very sad time. The whole affair could have been averted if the discontented friends had spoken out rather than let resentment rankle. We felt, and still feel, misused. We had rescued Original Image from certain bankruptcy, helping our friend and his famous shareholders. We had pumped money and executive time into the business. I felt personally let down. I've always said that you should expect to be knifed in the back in business. But I never expected it to happen to us when those holding the knife were our friends.

Life went on. We put the end of Original Image down to experience. We lost one small piece of PR business as a result of the dismissals but all the other clients stayed with us, accepting that "these things happen".

To many of our mutual friends, it seemed a storm in a tea cup. "Why can't you just make up?" they asked. I couldn't. The magical spell of good friends working in business had been broken and those advocating reconciliation were not business people and couldn't appreciate how deep our disappointment was.

It took over ten years for us all to start speaking again after several attempts by them for a rapprochement. As far as my pal was concerned, I picked the opening of a glamorous London hotel, One Aldwych, as the occasion to end our feud. We met around a pillar purely by chance at the reception, kissed and hesitantly made up on the night. A few days later we had lunch at Conran's Pont de la Tour restaurant near Tower Bridge. There were tears and a few recriminations but then we vowed never to argue about the matter again.

50

LOVE LETTERS FROM MR GUMMER

WE WERE STILL AT CARTER LANE when we received our first letter from a gentleman called Peter Gummer. He's now well known as Lord Chadlington but then he was already one of my heroes in the PR world. He started in a small way, rather as we did, and because he was highly focussed, he gradually built up his London-based company, Shandwick PR, through generic expansion and acquisitions. It became the world's biggest PR group with offices and associates in every major world business centre.

Peter has a reputation for being flamboyant, smooth and something of a social climber. He is not generally popular, but that's partly because he is much envied. Like most successful and wealthy men, he has his detractors. He certainly used Shandwick as a stepping stone to the peerage, on the way becoming an advisor to the Conservative Party and a personal advisor to John Major when he was Prime Minister.

His 'love letter' was prompted by the fact that TPS had been listed at number 20 in the table of the top hundred PR companies by the magazine PR Week. Times were good for us. Our reputation was at an all-time high. We had a highly professional and hard working team and our figures were good. He sent us his congratulations on entering the chart and added that if we ever felt like joining a bigger organisation and making some money, we should let him know. He was asking us to sell TPS to him. The thought of selling had never entered my head for a moment but, I was surprised to find, it *had* entered the head of Arthur, always the accountant. Similarly, while I had not the vaguest idea how much the company was worth, Arthur, who watched such deals going on and read the financial press, had a fair idea. But while we were intrigued, we replied "No thanks," but suggested he should keep in touch. We knew smooth Gummer had hooked us but we weren't complaining and we weren't biting – yet.

We were flattered. Anyone would be. It was a sign that the company we'd invested so much of ourselves in had gained approval from an expert who knew his business, and it is always satisfying to know you have something that someone else would like to buy.

In his next letter, which followed another mention of us in the PR trade media, he wrote, "We should meet." Again we did nothing except reply saying politely that we'd think about it. Think about it? Arthur had his calculator out before I'd finished the letter!

After the third letter, delivered as before to our home in Holland Park by his chauffeur – this man had style! – we agreed it was best he had a look at our offices and invited him over. He duly arrived in his car, a converted London taxicab. I showed him around discreetly and we chatted amicably. We all seemed to get on together. We were worth a great deal, he told us, but not as much as we would be if we waited, we decided. If we'd accepted his price, and taken our clients to Shandwick, he would have had a great deal. We turned him down again without too much thought, but we agreed to still keep in touch.

When a few years later we moved to Grosvenor Gardens and effectively doubled our PR business, his wooing became more fervent. We never truly understood why an office move could contribute to such a sharp increase in business. Grosvenor Gardens was certainly an expensive and smart address and, in the 1980s, companies seemed to like their PR and advertising agencies to adopt such an image. No matter, the move seemed to generate a continuous stream of new business pitches, a 'dealflow' in today's language, many of which we won. Things were looking very good.

Shandwick had satellites specialising in city, financial, events and general PR. They had no travel and leisure specialists or at least none concentrating wholly on the industry. We could bring not only our expertise and our clients, we could also function as a central PR division, helping other Shandwick PR companies throughout the world with our travel expertise. Peter Gummer was, of course, busy acquiring other London PR companies but he made us think we were top of his wish list.

Finally, four years after Peter first contacted us and after much wooing by letter and 'phone calls, he invited me to a breakfast meeting at the very grand Connaught Hotel in Mayfair. Arthur encouraged me to attend. "I won't know what I'm talking about," I said. I have never been good with balance sheets. "Just start the ball rolling, I'll pick it up," he replied. And so I accepted and made sure I arrived at precisely 8am, the agreed time for breakfast. I was still apprehensive. But I'm not going to sign anything, I kept telling myself.

I can't remember what I ate at Peter's regular breakfast table at The Connaught, but cornflakes or kippers are probably the least important thing at a 'power breakfast', certainly at a breakfast that would, like the cup of coffee with George Matthews all those years before, change my life.

I didn't sign anything. All Peter did was to 'sell' me the idea of our putting TPS into his larger worldwide group, making me nominally head of Shandwick's travel PR division and eventually giving Arthur a similarly high-profile role in the group. We would receive a tranche of money up front and some form of "earn out" over the following three years. We discussed these details over The Connaught's bacon and eggs – or whatever it was – and then I returned to mull things over with Arthur.

And what a process that was! I had not had a boss to answer to since Jimmy Simpson all those years ago in Scotland and I had to think hard about whether I wanted one now. More importantly, after nearly two decades of building our company, should we hand over the reins, surrender our independence, risk having to make compromises, perhaps deal with clients we did not like, work with people we would never have hired?

We were, however, tasting real success at last. We were making good profits. We featured regularly in the top 20 PR companies in the UK. We also had all the trappings of successful businessmen: a house in the smart part of Notting Hill with live-in help; a large weekend home in Norfolk, also with staff; the Jaguar and a chauffeur in London and a 1956 Bentley S8 in the garage in Norfolk. There was also a house in the Dordogne region of France. I could choose how much time I spent travelling with media groups – by then it was about one week a month. All in all, life was good. Why make such a radical change?

There was no single reason why we should consider selling but there were several things that were getting me down. I would spend the first hour of every Friday evening moaning that I was fed up with PR, fed up with clients who made ever more unreasonable demands and fed up with some members of staff who could also be highly demanding, often threatening to leave (possibly with a fickle client in tow) unless they were awarded a pay rise. More than this, I was getting bored with the same old routine. I was approaching 50 and probably having my mid-life identity crisis. I wanted a new challenge. We liked the thought of becoming millionaires – who wouldn't? But at what cost, we asked ourselves? We didn't, however, wait for the answer for very long.

We decided to say "yes" if we could agree the right terms with the Shandwick group. There were many subsequent meetings with bankers over several weeks. We were instructed to clean up our books, removing from the payroll and records anything that might cause embarrassment when outside accountants studied it. As it happened, we didn't have to remove private yachts, flats and cars for mistresses or lovers but we were charging our supplies of dog food to the company. 'Security' we told the bemused taxman! Hardly a scandal but we amended the records nonetheless.

All the directors of TPS had shareholdings in the company by now and we told them early in the proceedings that we were in talks with Shandwick. We offered them the chance to raise venture capital and mount an alternative management buy-out. I will never forget the disappointment I felt as I looked around the table at this sea of blank faces. Not a single person raised a hand to say "Well, let's talk about it." They weren't interested in taking over the company so the Shandwick deal went ahead.

One Friday in 1990, at what is now seen by some to have been the high point of this era of takeovers of small PR companies, we finalised the sale. Another enormous change in my life had occurred – though I hardly had time to think about it then.

We called a meeting of the more than 50 members of staff at five in the afternoon. We told them that Shandwick had taken over TPS but nothing effectively would change for them.

They looked stunned and worried. I did my best to calm them. They would retain their jobs, salaries and benefits, continue to work with the same clients and contacts in the same offices, I explained. I stressed that I would be around for at least three more years and, to the outside world, nothing would change. I said I believed it was our biggest challenge. Shandwick had bought us, I said, for our expertise, service, reputation and, of course, our clients and I doubted that they would want to tamper much with our operation. I stressed the advantages of working for an international PR group, which were considerable.

They seemed then to relax. No one resigned. Only one of the directors, a woman who was half of a marketing partnership we had recently bought, grabbed her enormous cheque, her share of the sale, and waved a happy goodbye as she walked out of the door. I couldn't help smiling. All in a PR's work for a day!

All the clients were delighted for us. Most saw the business sense of joining a larger PR outfit. One said he knew there would always come a time "when we would want to cash in our chips."

And it was with chips that we ended the deal and began our years of having 'real' money in the bank. To celebrate our new found and hard-earned wealth, Arthur and I took ourselves off to our favourite local restaurant, Geales of Notting Hill Gate, for fish 'n chips and a chilled bottle of Chablis.

51

THE END AND THE BEGINNING

WE STAYED WORKING REASONABLY HAPPILY with the Shandwick organisation for a further seven years until one day when I spotted an advertisement for an ancient finca in Majorca ...for sale.